Nickel On The Grass

Nickel On The Grass

Reflections of a U.S. Air Force Pilot

Colonel Phil "Hands" Handley

iUniverse, Inc.
New York Lincoln Shanghai

Nickel On The Grass
Reflections of a U.S. Air Force Pilot

iUniverse books may be ordered through booksellers or by contacting:

iUniverse
2021 Pine Lake Road, Suite 100
Lincoln, NE 68512
www.iuniverse.com
1-800-Authors (1-800-288-4677)

ISBN-13: 978-0-595-39735-8 (pbk)
ISBN-13: 978-0-595-67740-5 (cloth)
ISBN-13: 978-0-595-84141-7 (ebk)
ISBN-10: 0-595-39735-2 (pbk)
ISBN-10: 0-595-67740-1 (cloth)
ISBN-10: 0-595-84141-4 (ebk)

Printed in the United States of America

For my beautiful and loving wife, Solvejg. For our children, Phil and Andrea. For the many gallant officers, NCOs and airmen with whom it was my privilege to serve our country. For my dear friend and fallen comrade in arms, Captain Jack "Karst" Smallwood.

Contents

Table of Figures

Acknowledgements

I would like to thank all those who helped me bring this book together, and after many years to finally "get it done." In particular, I would like to acknowledge the contributions of: Colonel Russ Everts who provided pictures he personally took of landmarks on the Ho Chi Minh Trail, as well as his first-hand account of the unsuccessful SAR to rescue my squadron commander and his weapons system officer. I thank Captain Don Boulet for the riveting account of his shoot down and rescue. I thank Colonel T.C. Skancky for his detailed account of the mysterious and bazaar events which transpired following the mid-air collision north of Nellis AFB, Nevada in early 1981. Finally, I thank all those who provided suggestions, details, encouragement and proof reading.

Preface

This is a series of articles which draw on my personal experiences, recollections, and reflections of a 7,000 hour flying career spanning 26 years as a pilot in the United States Air Force. My goal is to provide the reader a balanced and realistic appreciation of what it was like to "fly the line" for all but a few months of those 26 years, during peacetime training, and in war.

(Author)

Figure 1—Author in F-15A above snow covered Bitburg Air Base, Germany

It has been said that "fighter pilot" is an attitude, not an AFSC (Air Force Specialty Code). I couldn't agree more and will go one step further. It is my considered observation and opinion that not all of those who fly a fighter aircraft are fighter pilots, and indeed there are multitudes flying cargo, bomber, rotary-wing and utility aircraft, who are unconditionally qualified and deserving of the title. Indeed, the typical "fighter pilot" does not fit the widely-portrayed, stereotypical image. Although each has gone through rigorous screening and demanding training, intentionally designed to eliminate all but the "best of the best", those who eventually earn their wings come in all sizes, races, degrees of intelligence, bravery and patriotism.

Each of these stories is based on happenings and events of which I have direct knowledge. Many are written in the first person. In the vast majority of cases actual names, dates, and places have been used. However, in some instances the naming of individuals, living or dead, could be disparaging and possibly bring undeserved distress to their friends and families. To avert this eventuality I have intentionally made a limited number of alterations of names and dates. Despite this the stories themselves remain authentic, as they are firmly rooted in actual events. I realize many readers will be unfamiliar with the acronyms, jargon, and slang typically associated with the tactical fighter mission. Indeed, such examples of these are prolific within these stories. However, I feel it would dilute the content and distract from the tone and pace of the stories should I attempt to reword or directly explain all unique and unfamiliar terms "on the spot." Instead, I have, for the most part, chosen to include such expressions within a Glossary of Terms.

Since my retirement from the Air Force in 1984, I have been asked on numerous occasions, "Do you miss it?" My reply has consistently been, "Every day that I'm alive." Try as you may, it is not possible to explain to someone who has never been there what it is like to hold 50,000 pounds of thrust in your left hand, fly a tight formation with a trusted leader in weather so thick you can't see anything but the green navigation light on a right wing tip, mere feet from your eyes, then suddenly break into the incredibly bright sunlight of a pristine blue sky and in your peripheral vision watch the top of the dense cloud bank from which you have just emerged fade rapidly beneath you like a big, white, feather bed. One cannot begin to explain the self-satisfaction which accrues from the heartfelt thanks and embrace of a wingman whose life you have just saved, the élan of a truly, tight-knit, combat squadron, or the sheer thrill of successfully defying terrible odds.

I will always consider myself one of the luckiest men alive because God gave me the body, talent, and opportunity to experience incredible things for over a quarter century, which others have only dreamed about in their wildest fantasies. I hope the reader will enjoy these stories as much as I have in their recall.

Phil "Hands" Handley

Colonel, USAF (Ret.)

About The Author

Colonel Phil Handley earned his commission and wings through the Aviation Cadet program in 1959. He was a distinguished graduate from pilot training, fighter upgrade training and instructor pilots school. He "flew the line" for all but eleven months of a twenty-six year career, during which he accumulated over 7,000 flying hours in aircraft vintages F-86 Sabre through F-15 Eagle, including an early career stint in the C-130A Hercules. He flew 275 combat missions during two tours in Southeast Asia in the F-4D and F-4E. During his career he commanded the 22nd Tactical Fighter Squadron, was Chief of USAFE Standardization and Evaluation, was the 1st Tactical Fighter Wing Deputy Commander for

(USAF File Photograph)
Figure 2—Colonel Phil "Hands" Handley
United States Air Force (Retired)

Operations, and Commanding Officer of the 405th Tactical Training Wing. He is a graduate of Air Command and Staff College, the Industrial College of the Armed Forces, and the U.S. Army War College. Colonel Handley is a member of The Red River Valley Fighter Pilot's Association (River Rats), and a MiG Killer credited with the highest speed air-to-air gun kill in the history of aviation. On the occasion of his retirement in 1984, his awards included 21 Air Medals, 3 Distinguished Flying Crosses, and the Silver Star. Colonel Handley and his wife Solvejg live in Midland, Texas.

The Rising Sun

- 1959 -

Prologue

As an aviation cadet in 1958, I took my primary flight training in T-34s and T-28s at Spence Air Base, which is located near the community of Moultrie, Georgia.[1] The flying school itself was a civilian contract operation called The Hawthorne School of Aviation which was owned by the famous world aerobatics champion "Bevo" Howard. During a business trip in 1992 to Robins AFB, Georgia, I couldn't resist the temptation to take the Moultrie exit off I-75 and see what remained of the place where I had learned to fly.

Upon finding the old base I discovered it had been turned into an industrial park with all of the former cadet facilities torn down. However I could still see the tower standing in its original location and noted that Maule Aircraft was running a manufacturing facility near the ramp. Proceeding to the ramp, I found with the exception of an old hangar now used by Maule, everything seemed to have been razed. However as I rounded the bend in the ramp leading to the old parking apron where the T-28s had operated, I was delighted to see one

(USAF File Photograph)
Figure 3—North American T-28A Trojan

---

[1] The aviation cadet program was originated at the outset of World War II, closed down after the war, then reactivated again in 1947 and continued until 1962. Unlike the current Specialized Undergraduate Pilot Training (SUPT) course in which a college degree is prerequisite, the aviation cadet program required only sixty college credit hours for academic qualification. The program itself consisted of three distinct phases: Preflight (at Lackland AFB, Texas), Primary Flight Training, and Basic Flight Training. There were several Primary and Basic training bases located throughout the states.

flight shack still standing…and that it was the one from which my flight (Tiger Flight) had operated many years earlier. It obviously had been deserted for a long time, with the last evidence of its use being a Civil Air Patrol squadron some 10-15 years earlier. Lingering inside the old circa 1940's building for a long while, I nostalgically recalled the origins of a military flying career that began for me near the spot where I then stood.

My Undergraduate Pilot Training (UPT) class was designated 60-B.[2] It was unique in that a small group of hand-picked World War II (WWII) Japanese pilots accompanied my class through the entire UPT program, with some of them also going on to the fighter lead-in courses which many of us attended upon earning our wings. The stated mission of these Japanese pilots was to gain experience of the running of USAF military flying schools, since upon return to Japan they would constitute the initial cadre of instructors for the emerging post-war Japanese Self Defense Force. One of those Japanese fighter pilots is the subject of the following story.

Story

My first impression of a certain Japanese major (whom I shall call Hatsuyo) was that this guy was absolutely too young to have been in the second wave of the attack on Pearl Harbor, much less to have accumulated over 2,000 combat hours in a Zeke, the Japanese Navy's version of the famous Zero fighter. Actually he was in his late thirties, but like most Orientals simply did not show his age. In addition, he smiled all of the time and never said "zilch." Since many of our civilian instructors were Georgia "good ole boys" who had themselves flown fighters in the Pacific Theater during WWII, it quickly became obvious that at least with them, old wartime hatreds died hard, for their open prejudice toward the likes of Major Hatsuyo was open and shameless.

---

[2] Since the military operated on a fiscal year, the designation "60-B" meant that this class was the second one scheduled to graduate in the 1960 fiscal year, or actually on 1 September 1959.

I got the idea there might be something special about this guy Hatsuyo when a fellow cadet related a story about something he had seen while awaiting his turn to fly the old Link "Blue Canoe"[4] instrument trainer. These simulator lessons were about one hour in duration and required the student fly a particular series of precision instrument maneuvers that took him around a 360 degree course. There was a scribe on a circular scroll adjacent

(Author)

Figure 4—Mitsubishi A6M Zero-Sen (Zeke)[3]

to the simulator that traced the path of the simulated flight, and if by some miracle the student happened to nail every airspeed, altitude, vertical velocity, turn rate, et al., at the end of the lesson the scribe would close the trace at its point of origin. No one ever came remotely close.

However on this particular day as the previous student's hour was almost up, my friend noted the trace was coming tantalizingly close to its origin point, and to his amazement actually intersected it just as the session ended. Sure enough, out stepped Major Hatsuyo smiling as usual and saying nothing beyond perfunctory salutations. And so as our six-month training period at primary flying school came to an end, despite all the obstacles placed in his path, Hatsuyo had scored the highest check ride scores ever recorded on his transition, instrument, and aerobatics flight checks. We then proceeded off to basic flight school where we eagerly

---

[3] Of the more than 10,400 Mitsubishi Zeros produced by Japan during WW-II, this is the sole remaining flyable model. It is located at the Commemorative Air Force (CAF) Headquarters in Midland, Texas.

[4] The Link Trainer was called the "Blue Canoe" because it was painted blue with yellow trim and was equipped with control surfaces on its little wings and tail that actually moved in harmony with stick and rudder inputs. Additionally its fuselage and wings were adorned with insignia giving it a real personality of its own. I suppose the word "canoe" got into its nickname simply because it rhymed with "blue" and sounded cute.

looked forward to checkout in the "slightly sonic" Lockheed T-33A T-Bird at basic flight training school.[5]

The defining moment of Hatsuyo's talents became readily apparent during the formation phase of our upgrade training. Formation flying is a learned hand/eye reflex skill. The longer you do it the easier it gets, but when you first begin it is definitely not your strongest suit. To fly good formation you need to simply look at your leader's aircraft and make very small stick and throttle movements to maintain the desired sight picture. At the same time you need to keep the aerodynamic pressure trimmed off the stick unless you happen to be endowed with sixteen inch biceps. However since most new guys are so pumped with adrenaline they squeeze the stick grip hard enough to make the buttons pop out, they couldn't feel any stick pressure if they wanted to.

Hatsuyo had soloed on his first formation ride and while the other two cadets of the four-ship T-bird formation "bobbed and weaved" their way through the early missions with a white-knuckled instructor pilot in the back seat, he effortlessly flew formation as if he were welded to the leader's wing. It was during one of these missions that Hatsuyo, as number two on the leader's left wing, found himself at the apex of a "lazy eight maneuver" looking up through the formation straight into the sun.[6]

(Author)

Figure 5—Aviation Cadet Phil Handley on wing of Lockheed T-33A T-Bird at Reese AFB, Texas

---

[5] The T-33A T-Bird was the training version of the Air Force's first operational jet fighter, the P-80 Shooting Star. Although by today's standards it was slow and woefully underpowered, it was a marvel in its day and served the Air Force well for many years.

[6] The lazy eight and chandelle were simple but demanding maneuvers for the student pilot since the attitude, airspeed, "G," and trim of the aircraft changed constantly throughout their execution.

As he reached up and lowered his helmet visor, other members of the shaky formation gasped when they saw the dust cover protecting the visor from scratches was still attached. With all of the self-confidence in the world, Hatsuyo calmly released the stick and throttle and with both hands casually untied the retaining strings on the visor cover, letting it drop into his lap. By the accounts of those in the formation, throughout the entire drill, which took about five seconds, Hatsuyo's aircraft seemingly never moved an inch out of formation position. I can assure you, had any other student wingman in the formation released the stick at that moment, some spectacular high-G maneuvering would have ensued.[7]

By the time my class graduated from UPT, Major Hatsuyo's reputation had preceded him to F-86 upgrade training. Now I will tell you outright, few collective categories of individuals are more cocky and arrogant than the instructor pilot cadre found at a fighter-school house. I don't say that sarcastically for I used to be one and later in my career had the pleasure of commanding hundreds of them. Accordingly, it is not difficult to imagine the skepticism of these instructors concerning the supposedly amazing flying abilities of this aging Japanese warrior. Their attitude could generally be summed up as, "He might have been good in a Zero, but he doesn't know a damn thing about supersonic swept-wing fighters. We are going to teach him a thing or two."

---

[7] This brings to mind an incident involving a fellow classmate at UPT. At some point in the two-ship formation training mission, as my classmate was struggling along on the leader's wing, he thought the instructor had "shaken the stick," which signaled he wanted to take control. So when he released the stick, the aircraft went immediately into a high-G, nose-up climb because of its deplorable state of trim. Thinking they had experienced full nose-up runaway trim, the instructor shouted "RUNAWAY TRIM" and grabbed the stick in an attempt to push the nose of the aircraft down. Eager to help, my classmate got immediately on the stick and upon feeling the strong forward pressure began to pull for all he was worth in the opposite direction. The situation came to light to everyone on the air when the IP announced over "guard channel" they were in big trouble in that it was taking both of them on the stick just to hold the aircraft in controlled flight. When another instructor in the area logically asked in which direction the trim had runaway, directly opposite answers came from my classmate and the instructor. When it was suggested by their flight leader that both of them carefully take their hands off the stick to determine which way the trim had actually run away, the ole T-Bird breathed a sigh of relief and flew perfectly level.

Throughout our upgrade training I lived in the same BOQ (Bachelor Officers Quarters) as Hatsuyo and spent many hours drinking beer with him in his room while trying, with limited success, to pry war stories from him. He was a quiet and dignified man who said little of his past, but when he did speak it was well worth

(USAF File Photograph)

Figure 6—Grumman F6F Hellcat

the wait. I recall on one occasion I had asked him which one of the U.S. fighters he believed was the toughest adversary? Without hesitation he replied it was the F6F Hellcat. Exploiting this unexpected candor, I launched into a discussion about why I thought the F4U Corsair or P-38 Lightning might have been better. He listened attentively, nodding and smiling politely throughout the duration of my simplistic monologue. So when I finally wound down and asked him why he specifically thought the Hellcat was the best, he simply reached up and parted his jet black hair to reveal a long scar than ran along the left side of his head and said, "This was made by a 50 caliber bullet from a Hellcat. The F6F shot me down three times." That explanation seemed good enough for me to go "cold mike" and hopefully preclude further display of my naivety.

Although such revelations of his experiences during WWII were extremely limited, they were a veritable avalanche compared to any dialogue about his current F-86 checkout experience. Had it not been for one particular instructor pilot, who in an advanced state of inebriation at our graduation banquet finally "getting it off his chest", I would never have learned of the following episode.

An IP, with whom I had flown very little during the course, began by saying that since I seemed to have spent a good deal of time with Hatsuyo, he assumed we were probably pretty good friends. I told him I would like to think so. He then asked me point blank if Hatsuyo had ever told me about what had happened on his second ride in the F-86. When I replied that Hatsuyo had never told me a damn thing about any of his rides, much less his second one, the IP simply shook his head and said, "Well, I'm going to tell someone tonight what happened and it might as well be you."

Now on the second ride in the Sabre the students would go out into one of the transition areas and practice aerobatics and stalls to get a better feel for the airplane, and then return to the traffic pattern for some touch-and-go landings. Traditionally the IPs looked forward to those missions since it gave them a chance to disassociate themselves from the wearisome students and to form up into "IP only", four-ship flights for the purpose of "terrorizing the countryside" while doing a little dog-fighting on their own. One such flight led by the IP with whom I was talking, viewed this mission as the perfect chance to "put a little humble" on this guy Hatsuyo. Their plan was simplicity itself. Since they knew exactly where he was going to be, they decided that they would show up in his area and essentially beat the hell out of him for a while before turning to the more serious task of honing their already impeccable BFM skills against one another. Specifically, their plan involved entering the area up-sun and well above the unsuspecting Hatsuyo so that they could begin the festivities by rolling-in on him just as they would on a towed gunnery banner, sequentially "strafing him like a truck."

Quoting the IP as I remember it now, the following is the essence of what he told me on that evening more than forty-seven years ago:

"I took the flight over to a discrete frequency we had briefed so we could talk freely among ourselves without anyone listening in. As we arrived in Hatsuyo's assigned area, sure enough there he was, a good 10,000 feet below us doing a series of stalls. We were perfectly positioned with the sun directly behind us and I was certain he hadn't seen us. In fact I almost felt a little "sheepish" because it was such a shameless setup. The rest of the flight took very little spacing as we peeled-off from a left echelon and started "down the chute." As I reversed left into a "curve of pursuit" Hatsuyo had just fallen nose-low out of a simulated traffic pattern stall and I noted that his left wing dropped slightly into me. For a moment I thought that perhaps he had seen us, but then rationalized that it was only sloppy aileron control. However when his gear came up, his nose stayed down, and his left bank began to increase, I thought 'ah ha,' the great Jap ace does see me. Now I won't feel bad at all about gunning his brains out. I was still feeling good about the pass until I noted that Hatsuyo's tightening turn was really starting to "jam me" and I was having to bury my nose more than I would have liked to stay in his plane of motion. Added to that I was really going fast by now and had to yank the throttle clear back to idle to control my overtake. It was only after I had begun to pull my nose up to track him I realized too late his nose was up, and mine was buried. I thought about breaking off to reposition but the rest of the flight was right behind me and that would have been embarrassing.

So I pressed on in, convinced I could still get a good high-G deflection shot on film before having to quarter-roll and zoom. With Hatsuyo now really starting to crank into me and the range rapidly decreasing, I knew I had to take my shot within the next few seconds. By now my high-G turn at idle power had bled more airspeed than I had counted on and the plane was turning very hard in the mild buffet.[8] With my pipper now tracking less than an aircraft length behind him I knew it was now or never to pull lead on this pass. However as I increased back pressure to bring the pipper up, the aircraft went instantly through the heavy buffet into wing rock. It was almost like Hatsuyo was sitting in the cockpit with me because at the instant I felt the stick shudder in my hand, he snapped immediately into a nose high reversal to the right, and with his speed brakes fully extended rolled over the top of me, disappearing into my deep six.

At this point I had but one thought in mind. Even if I had to tear the wings off this jet, I would not let this Jap track me. So for the next half minute or so I slammed the aircraft all over the sky, which had the immediate effect of scattering the rest of my flight like a covey of quail. What ensued was a gaggle of four wildly gyrating Sabres; all looking exactly alike as we reversed wildly around in a series of random high-G maneuvers without a clue as to who was who. When I was certain no human could have followed me through the wild gyrations I had just executed I eased off my turn and happened to look in my mirror."

At this point the IP said directly to me, "Did you ever see that movie The Hunters?" "Yeah", I replied. "Do you remember the scene where the guy was dog fighting with Robert Mitchum and when he looked in his mirror the intake on Mitchum's jet looked as big as a barn door?" "Yeah." "Well that's exactly what I saw. I was so surprised I just rolled out and sat there straight and level with Hatsuyo sitting not more than fifty feet behind me. I just stared at him in the mirror for what seemed like an eternity, when he suddenly pulled up hard into a steep climb and did a single aileron roll. Then his speed brake came out, his gear and flaps came down, and he started doing traffic pattern stalls."

---

[8] Although the F-86 had a 35 degree swept wing it flew a lot like a straight wing aircraft in that you could use the ailerons to roll the aircraft at high angle-of-attack without causing it to depart in the opposite direction, as was precisely the case with the F-100, F-4, et al. At high AOA in those jets you had to keep the ailerons centered and use the rudder to roll the aircraft or they would often violently depart controlled flight, which caused a huge accident problem for the fighter command until most of the pilots learned to fly them at high AOA. In contrast the F-86 really "talked to you" through the vibration transmitted via the stick and airframe. As the lift produced by the wings increased, the frequency of the transmitted vibration progressed from mild buzz, to light then heavy buffet, to wing rock and finally to complete wing stall. Consequently you needed to stay below the last two stages of the process if your were in the least interested in turning performance.

The IP told me that after gathering up his flight and landing, they went straight into a flight debriefing room, closed the door, and swore everyone to secrecy. Apparently throughout the five plus months which had passed since the occurrence, Hatsuyo had never said one word about the incident to anyone, which didn't surprise me at all.

I am convinced had it not been for the IP's advanced state of inebriation, compounded by a lingering sense of guilt which simply would not go away I would never have known either.

"Herc" the Great

- 1960 -

When in 1959 I graduated from F-86 upgrade training and was unceremoniously assigned directly to Evreux-Fauville Air Base, France as a C-130A co-pilot, I was ready to cut my heart out. Years later and far wiser, I realize how misguided my perceptions were at that time. Memories of the C-130 mission, the people, and the aircraft itself are indelibly etched in my mind's eye. It was my distinct privilege and honor to fly this classic bird, which will surely go into the history books as the greatest prop-driven cargo aircraft of all time. The following paragraphs chronicle my personal experiences with the C-130A Hercules from my initial imprudent disappointment to a final, and ever-lasting, admiration for this truly magnificent flying machine.

Three other officers with whom I had attended F-86 training had also been given the ominous choice between assignment to a SAC (Strategic Air Command) B-47 or the C-130 at Evreux-Fauville Air Base, France. Among ourselves we tried to look objectively at these seemingly dismal options. The case for the B-47 was that at least its mission was to drop bombs on an enemy. In contrast, the C-130 was commonly called a "trash hauler"

(Author)

Figure 7—Tactical Air Command Lockheed C-130A Hercules

with a primary mission of transporting combatants and their supplies to prosecute the mission at hand. The only advantage any of us could see in favor of the seemingly non-glamorous C-130 assignment was that Evreux-Fauville Air Base was only 70 miles west of Paris, France. Hell, this was a no-brainer, so we resigned ourselves to the cruel injustice that the flying talents of four of the world's greatest fighter jocks would be squandered, and unanimously sprung for the sabbatical to far-away France.

At McGuire AFB in New Jersey, we all boarded an Air Force C-118 transport plane which would fly us to Paris, France. After one aborted takeoff roll due to some sort of engine malfunction, we set sail for the city with the Eiffel Tower at a mind-numbing true airspeed of just over 200 miles per hour. To make the trip even less enjoyable, the passenger seats all faced rearward as a safety enhancement feature in case the plane crashed. After what seemed an eternity we landed in Paris, then boarded a train for the trip westward across the French countryside to the Normandy village of Evreux-Fauville. From there a waiting Air Force blue bus transported us the final five miles to the base for in-processing.

Of the twenty or so new pilots in our group, about half were married with their families scheduled to join them several weeks later. In the interim, everyone would be residing in the BOQ (Batchelor Officers Quarters) as their orientation and aircraft checkout training proceeded. Three of the four of us who had come from the F-86 school were single. This included Ernie Hasselbrink, Steve Larson and me, while the fourth, Don Dupree was married with children and a bit more conservative than us. I was assigned to the 40th TCS (Troop Carrier Squadron), while Ernie and Steve went to the 39th TCS, and Don to the 41st TCS.

Early on a Monday morning Captain Roger Leach from the 40th TCS popped in at the BOQ to welcome me to the squadron and set up my checkout in the aircraft. He was a friendly guy with whom I talked candidly about what I thought of my assignment to the C-130. As it turned out, he had himself come to Evreux just over a year earlier from an F-100 squadron. He told me he understood how I felt, but was certain I would come to like the big bird once I was checked out since "it flew like a four-engine fighter." I held my tongue but mentally stored that assertion as just so much BS.

Upon entering the main briefing room at the 40th Squadron I noted a .50 caliber machine gun in one corner, as well as what appeared to be an old VHF aircraft radio. It turned out that the souvenirs had been salvaged earlier from the remains of a B-24 named "Lady Be Good" which had become lost, run out of fuel, and crash-landed in the Libyan Desert south of Tripoli in 1943. Its disappearance had been a mystery until the incredibly well preserved aircraft was discovered by British oil prospectors overflying the area in November, 1958. To assist in the subsequent exploration and recovery operation, several of the 40th TCS C-130s had been dispatched to the scene, landed on the desert floor, and on one of the missions returned to Evreux with the waist gun and radio I now observed.

Over the next few weeks we completed the academics and simulator phases of our upgrade training, and then began our checkout program in the aircraft itself. My first impression of the C-130's flight characteristics were that it certainly was not a jet fighter and was loud as hell in the cockpit. However, it did handle quite well and the 15,000 shaft horsepower transmitted through the four Aero Products constant-speed, three-blade props was instantly available and produced surprising acceleration on takeoff roll and at low speeds. I wasn't totally convinced this big, lumbering giant was indeed a "four-engine fighter", but the assertion no longer seemed ridiculous. Our flight training was completed expeditiously and after a final check ride, we were full-fledged C-130 copilots just in time for the great Congo Airlift of 1960.

That summer of 1960 was, in my books, one of the most interesting of my flying career because of the situation in Africa. When the Belgians withdrew from their for-mer colony, the Belgian Congo, the riots and genocide that ensued triggered a United Nations emer-gency relief mission which required a massive airlift to the besieged region. This effort was largely shouldered by the C-130s from the three squadrons of the

(USAF File Photograph)

Figure 8—Douglass C-124 Globemaster II

322nd Air Division at Evreux, and the trusty, old work- horse of MATS (Military Air Transport Service), the huge, piston engine driven C-124. The plane was affectionately called "Old Shaky" by those who flew her, or sometimes more aptly referred to as "two million rivets flying in loose formation." Those who ever watched it taxi around on the ramp were treated to a performance called "Sahib and the Elephant." Sahib was the flight engineer protruding waist high from a porthole on top of the aircraft to get an unobstructed view of the aircraft's clear-ance from obstacles and pass information to the pilot. Old Shaky was of course the elephant as its brakes produced a penetrating screech that sounded eerily like the trumpet call of a bull elephant.

As a copilot I was crewed with some of the more experienced aircraft command-ers in the squadron as we flew day and night throughout almost every country in Sub-Saharan Africa. Over the course of the hundreds of flying hours I logged in the right seat during that summer, there were too many noteworthy and exciting events to relate. As soon as we flew south of Tripoli, Libya radio communication, and particularly communication with the command post back at Evreux became near impossible. This meant, more often than not, aircraft commanders "rode to the sound of gunfire" while proceeding to any destination requiring emergency evacuation of refugees, the delivery of critical supplies, or the transport of United Nations troops to hot spots such as Leopoldville in the Congo.

The navigators used a sextant which protruded from the top of the fuselage. We picked our way through the highest thunderstorms I ever saw, many with tops above 65,000 feet. At night, with the cockpit's white thunderstorm lights at full illumination, a zillion dancing fingers of static electricity in the form of St. Elmo's fire[9] would attach itself to every square inch of the big bird's aluminum skin, and the props of the four engines looked like spinning wheels of fire.

The quality of logistic support varied widely; one of the aircraft commanders actually filled the aircraft fuel tanks using his American Express credit card and claimed it as an expense on his per diem voucher. On some occasions when no billeting facilities were available and we were flat-ass out of crew rest, we would literally sleep inside or under the wing of the aircraft, after heating C-Rations with Sterno or over an open fire.

It was during one of these "sleep under the stars" events that a particularly memorable event took place, as related to me by the aircraft commander. On this occasion, the navigator was an old major named Ernie who was near retirement. He had earlier been a B-36 navigator for many years in SAC (Strategic Air Command), and was now on his final tour before retirement. He had truly "been around" and was well liked and respected by all who knew him. The loadmaster of the crew was a huge airman named Smith, who was one the strongest men I ever saw. At any rate, after the C-ration meal under the stars, someone on the crew remarked how quickly the temperature was dropping from the searing heat of the day. This prompted the good major, who was a master story teller and great kidder, to launch into a story that went something like this:

"Ah yes, the desert is truly beautiful at night, but often deadly. Have you noticed how many of the native population you see in the market places have only one eye? Or there are huge scars on their cheeks where chunks of flesh are gone? Well, that's the result of nights in the desert just like this. Because it is indeed cold, much of the nomadic population that sleep in the desert wrap themselves in a blanket with only their faces exposed. It is under this setting that roaming packs of hyena-like predators, know as "face eaters" attack with a single ripping bite using their razor- sharp fangs on the exposed face before disappearing once again into the darkness."

---

[9] St. Elmo's Fire is a beautiful, eerie form of static electricity that often appears in stormy weather around church spires, sailing masts, and airplane wings. During thunderstorms, the air between the clouds and the ground becomes electrically charged, resulting in a "flow discharge"—the same phenomenon used in fluorescent tubes.

Apparently no one gave it another thought after laughing-off the tall tale and went to bed. At some time after midnight everyone was suddenly awakened by the reports of Airman Smith's .38 caliber service revolver blasting into the darkness as he ran in a wide arc around the aircraft shouting, "It's the damn face eaters, it's the damn face eaters." Apparently Ernie's story was realistic enough to create for Smith a "nightmare from hell" convincing him that imminent attack from the mystical creatures was at hand.

A memorable demonstration of Smith's incredible strength occurred about two years later in Athens, Greece when several of the Division's C-130s were deployed there for an exercise of some sort. A rather large group of us had congregated at one of the local bars for a few drinks. I had noticed there was some sort of activity going on across the crowded room at one of the tables, amidst intermittent shouting and cheering. About this time the assistant operations officer of the 40th, Captain Bill Goodwin approached my table and said, "Lt. Handley, come take a look at this." Arriving at the scene of the activity I saw there were multiple arm-wrestling matches going on with lots of money changing hands.

(Author)

Figure 9—The infamous "Chateau" in Acquigny, France

The "king of the hill" who was winning every match was a rather unimpressive looking Greek whom one would not expect to prevail in such a contest. However after watching him beat a couple of much larger and more muscular challengers, the reason became apparent. This guy would hook his right leg around the table leg nearest him, and then somehow throw his right arm out-of-joint at the shoulder to form a mechanical lock that prevented stronger men from forcing his arm to the table in traditional style. Goodwin told me that a bunch of our group were certain that I could beat this guy and we could make some money in the process. I told him that I thought I probably could beat him, but that I knew someone in the squadron whom we could be damn certain would win. With the help of several of the enlisted men, we fanned out to the surrounding bars and soon recovered Airman Smith.

When I briefed Smith on the plan he was apprehensive, especially after seeing the size of the pot of money now on the table, and kept saying, "Lt. Handley, I'm just not sure. I'm just not sure. I've never done this before." I reassured him and told him how the Greek's "trick" worked. Just before they faced off at the table I told Smith, "Now the instant the signal is given, I want you to use every ounce of your strength to drive his fist clean through that table top." When Smith put the elbow of his huge right arm on the table, the Greek actually smirked as he once again went through his pre-match routine that had apparently never failed him. When the start signal was given by the tap of a beer bottle on the table, three things instantly occurred: There was a dull thud as the Greeks fist hit the table top, followed immediately by the table crashing to the floor when lifted up on one side by the hooked right leg, and a piercing scream from the "Greek with the trick" as his right arm snapped like a toothpick. After paying for another round of beer, we gave half of the winnings to our highly deserving loadmaster.

It didn't take long to realize there were better ways to spend one's time back at Evreux than living in the BOQ. Having spent considerable time rubbing elbows with the other new pilots who arrived during the same time period, good friendships had been forged, particularly among those of us who were bachelors. So it wasn't surprising, after arriving back at home station following one of the extended Africa trips, I got news that one of our group had located a house for rent in the village of Acquigny, which lay some 15 miles north of Evreux. Seven of us agreed to rent the place, which we vainly named "The Chateau" and moved in some time during the month of July in 1960. In addition to Ernie Hasselbrink, Steve Larson and myself, there was Bill Rossetti, Roy Palmer, Tom Sparr, and Charlie Beauchamp. All of us were Lieutenants except Steve Larson, who had been an Air Force navigator in a previous life and was now a rich captain.

The Chateau itself was old, big, walled, and wonderfully suited for the priorities of a bunch of young, single pilots, and we immediately set about to customize it with our belongings. Sadly, these were strikingly similar.

We had seven sports cars and seven hi-fi systems. Beyond that, we basically had nothing more than clothes and "must have" items such as monkey skin rugs and native, construction-paper art each of us had picked up during trips to the Congo. However, we all loved to eat, drink, and party. It didn't take long before our bar was better stocked than the officers club at the base, and our refrigerator and freezer loaded with the best steaks available from the base commissary. With the exchange rate of our US Dollar to the French franc at four-to-one, all of this high living ended up costing us $70.00 each, per month. In no time at the entire place was the talk of the base, as augmented by gossip within the officers wives' club, as the lavish parties occurring on weekends quickly made it "the place to go."

As the stories about The Chateau became increasingly exaggerated its activities became a subject of interest of the Division Commander, who directed the Base

Commander to "find out what was going on out there" and report back to him. We had just issued invitations to about 100 of our closest friends for a Saturday night Christmas Party when our intelligence network informed us the Base Commander would be "on a mission" and would crash the party. The Base Commander seemed to be a nice old guy who was ready for retirement. Having seen him at the officers club on the base, we were aware he enjoyed a drink and told endless stories about his flying exploits in a low, monotone voice through lips that scarcely moved, creating a feeling the information he shared was "confidential." Knowing this, our plan was to never leave him alone, with all of us taking turns listening to his stories, while at the same time making certain his glass was fully charged.

When he navigated his Chrysler New Yorker, the size of a small yacht, inside the walls of The Chateau, we all faked surprised delight that he had graced us with his presence. The rotation began. Sometime well into the evening Bill Rossetti and I were on shift and stood on each side of the good colonel at the bar, with our backs to the three piece band belting out a loud tune. As with most parties where drinking occurs, tempers can sometimes flare as the evening wears on and I immediately recognized the sound of a fist making contact followed by a thud to the floor directly behind us. Rossetti instantly reacted and sprang backward from the bar like a gazelle to shove the aggressor away. By the time the Base Commander had halted his story, sat his drink on the bar and turned, Rossetti had already helped the fallen victim from the floor and was dusting him off while laughing and jovially quipping something about a nasty fall. The good colonel took all of this in for several seconds and before picking up his glass and continuing his interrupted story, he looked at me with the slightest trace of a smile and said in his low, monotone voice, "Rossetti fighting."

By 2:00 AM the only remaining guest was the base commander. We were all tired and truly glad as we accompanied him to his car to say goodnight. Unfortunately after he got in and started the motor and heater, he rolled down the window and continued to talk with us for another fifteen minutes as we all froze in the cold winter air. He told us in confidential tones, he had actually come to the party at the request of the Division Commander to check things out. He added, although he had observed Rossetti in an altercation, he didn't consider it a serious infraction and we had nothing to worry about.

The next morning we learned the good colonel had apparently been too sleepy to drive back to the base, as his New Yorker was found about two miles down the road, 100 yards into a big green meadow, totally undamaged, gently resting with its front bumper against a large tree with motor idling. Asleep on the front seat was the "secret agent" of the previous evening.

Sports cars were a big deal among residents of The Chateau as evidenced by the parking lot outside the side door. We all went to rallies, gymkhanas, time trials, and frequently made high-speed trips to Paris, which were dangerous to say the least. One of the orientation briefings we received upon our arrival at Evreux was conducted at the base theater where all of the month's recent arrivals were seated. The briefer asked everyone to look around at those seated about them and then said: "Three out of every four of you will be involved in a major automobile accident during your tour here." This was an "attention getter" to say the least and proved to be a totally valid statistic. Evreux-Fauville Air Base had the worst accident record of any U.S. Military installation in the world because of the weather, the driving habits of the local population, and the fact that it lay squarely on the three-lane highway that connected Paris to the beaches at Deauville on the Normandy Coast.

Built by forced French labor when the Germans occupied France during WWII, it was still the best highway in France. It was pitifully inadequate by American highway standards, and its three-lane concept had to be the worst idea for highway safety ever concocted. The middle lane was commonly referred to as the "suicide lane" as there were no set rules for its use and it became a constant game of bluff as oncoming cars weaved in

(Author)

Figure 10—Typical Citroen CV-2 "Cigarette Roller" casualty of the three-lane road to Pairs

and out to avoid head-on collisions. To make matters even more dangerous, there were tremendous differentials between the speeds of the thousands of cars competing for position. At the bottom end of the speed food chain was the Citroen CV-2, a silly looking and flimsy little car made of corrugated metal. It was nicknamed the "cigarette roller" as it bore a strong resemblance. It was probably capable of doing 55 MPH when going down hill with a tail wind.

At the other end of the spectrum were Ferraris, Maseratis and Aston Martins capable of speeds well above 150 MPH. In the middle were droves of the amazing Citroen DS which looked like a half-melted bowl of Jell-O, but cruised along at speeds over 100 MPH. I also recall reading a report stating that by 2:00 PM an alarming percentage of the French were driving with a blood alcohol content which would classify them as legally drunk.

In an effort to encourage safety and warn of the genuine danger of driving on French highways, the Air Police went so far as to display the mangled hulks of cars that had been smashed during the preceding week. So it was in this environment our group's mix of cars "took their chances" on the sorties to Paris. I drove an A.C. Bristol (the forerunner to the A.C Cobra), Tom Sparr an Austin Healy 3000, Ernie Hasselbrink an MGA Twin-Cam, Steve Larson an Austin Healy Speedwell Sprite, Bill Rossetti a Porsche, and Charlie Beauchamp, a Sunbeam Alpine (of all things). Roy Palmer was the only one of the bunch that did not initially own a sports car as he continued to procrastinate over a choice while driving a Peugeot 503 sedan until finally purchasing an Alfa Romeo.

To understand how Beauchamp could possibly make a considered decision to purchase a "rat gray" colored Sunbeam Alpine and then spend the next six months trying to justify its existence in the presence of authentic sports cars requires a closer look at the man himself.

Charlie hailed from Alabama and held a degree in aeronautical engineering. Prior to entering the Air Force, he had worked for Boeing Aircraft. Back in the States, Charlie Beauchamp had pronounced his last name "Beech'-um", but it didn't take long for him to become totally enthralled with the international flavor of France and began to introduce himself as Charles Beauchamp (pronounced "Bow-Shomp"). Although we kidded him endlessly about this transformation, he wore the name as a badge of honor and told us a literal translation of his name referred to "a beautiful meadow." As suggested by Roy Palmer, we started calling him "Fertile Fields", and as time went on, "The Country Count", names to which he will respond to this day.

At any rate, Charlie was exceedingly smart, as was proved when he was inducted into Mensa International, a society for people whose IQ is in the top 2% of the world's population. This was aptly demonstrated when he decided to take advantage of the French language classes that were offered during evenings at the base. While the rest of us learned just enough French to ask directions to the bathroom, Charlie learned to speak and write both conversational and technical French in a surprisingly short time.

While the rest of us bought the proven sports cars which graced the pages of Road & Track Magazine, Charlie conducted his own research and decided that the newly introduced Sunbeam Alpine represented the wave of the future in sport car design, and besides that, it had rollup windows! Despite the fact that it was under-powered and under-steered terribly, he continued to support his decision in the face of the continuous ribbing we administered. Charlie went to Paris at every available opportunity and always seemed to return with a wilder story of his driving experiences. In what was without doubt the most dramatic of these stories, he related a tale of how, while carving a perfect line through a high-speed curve at the edge of a small village, he suddenly lost traction, spun 180-degrees, and found himself proceeding down the main street of the village backwards. He said he used the rearview mirror to navigate the length of the village, but over-controlled slightly just as he neared the far end and once again spun 180-degrees before arresting the spin, down-shifting into 3rd gear, and accelerating on toward Paris. We all had a good laugh at this latest assertion.

In an attempt to foster favorable relations with our French neighbors, we had several French guests over to "The Chateau" for a Sunday afternoon of drinks and hors d'oeuvres. While viewing the fireplace mantel that held the numerous racing trophies we had collected, one of the guests who spoke excellent English inquired, "May I please ask which of you is the fantastic driver of the gray Sunbeam?" We were stunned when he related in detail the exact scenario Beauchamp had claimed and concluded by saying, "It was the most incredible driving exhibition any of us had ever seen."

As our first year of Chateau living was coming to a conclusion, one by one the original seven were steadily replaced as we departed the ranks of bachelorhood. I was the first to go after falling in love with a gorgeous Dutch girl named Solvejg, who has forever since been my roommate. I was closely followed by Steve Larson, and then others, until only the legends of "The Chateau" remained among those who were assigned to Evreux Air Base at that time, and the older residents of the French village of Acquigny.

As I continued to pile up flying hours in the C-130, I became increasingly comfortable with its flight characteristics and was soon upgraded as a first lieutenant to aircraft commander with my own dedicated crew. My co-pilot and close friend was 1st Lieutenant Bob Scible until he was also upgraded to aircraft commander status, and at the navigator's table was 1st Lieutenant Dan O'Leary, who had replaced me at "The Chateau." Through "luck of the draw" two NCOs (Non-Commissioned Officers), Sgt. Bill "Dave" Davis and Airman Dean Bradley flew the vast majority of my missions seated behind in the flight engineer's chair. Both of them knew the C-130 inside-out and could fix anything that broke, day or night, in any weather conditions. Airman Bradley was also the sharpest dressed enlisted man on the base. He went so far as to always carry extra sets of heavily-starched fatigues on our trips allowing him to change clothes after performing any work which would render his uniform anything less than spotless.

It was during this period I really came to admire what this big bird could do. Part of its mission capability was the "tactical pattern", which replicated the 360-degree overhead pattern flown by fighters. I particularly enjoyed landing out of this pattern when possible and with practice could consistently touch down "on the numbers" in less than one minute after the break. Other tactical maneuvers in its arsenal included the assault takeoff and landing, both designed for operations from short, unprepared strips. When these maneuvers were performed "by the book" they were impressive. When they were embellished through various techniques and light gross weights, they were downright spectacular. Although not authorized, rolls in the C-130 were easily performed as long as the nose was well up before beginning the maneuver.

The aircraft's positive 2G load limit was easily sustained in the dense air below about 16,000 feet by the four powerful T-56 Allison engines. When combined with an incredibly low corner velocity (the speed at which the aircraft is capable of making its quickest, tightest turn), its turn radius was surprisingly small as compared with that of a much faster, but more heavily wing-loaded fighter aircraft. As comparison, the corner velocity of an F-4 pulling over 7.3Gs is approximately 420 knots. I was convinced that, were I ever attacked by an enemy fighter my best course of action would be to get as low as possible to deny the attacking fighter vertical maneuvering room, then use the aircraft's superior turning radius to continually "overshoot" him.

My chance to test the theory came during one of the numerous trips we made from Evreux to Athens, Greece. While cruising with only light cargo aboard down an airway over the Mediterranean Sea southwest of the "Boot of Italy" an Italian F-86 jock apparently decided it would be good practice and fun to make mock firing passes at a "sitting duck." After watching a couple of his "curves of pursuit" from my left cockpit window, I asked and received clearance from Roma Control for a block altitude from 15,000 to 22,000 feet. As the Italian fighter pilot rolled-in off the perch high and above me to the left, I began a descent at full throttle to gain indicated airspeed. By the time the Sabre reached mid-point down the slide and reversed his turn to a curve of pursuit, I was well below his altitude with my nose slightly up and beginning to "jam" him with an increasing left turn.

In a vain attempt to stay on the inside of my turn, the Italian extended his speed brakes and pulled his power to idle, at which time I pulled hard into him and then up about 30 degrees as he badly overshot and flushed to the outside of the turn. I continued my right roll over the top and for a brief, shining moment sat squarely at his six o-clock before he accelerated quickly away. As I climbed back up to 22,000 feet the Italian repositioned a mile or so to our left, then slowly slid into formation off our left wing. After removing his mask, he flashed a big smile, gave us a "thumbs up" signal and did a split-s maneuver down and away.

Another memorable deployment occurred in late 1962 during the Sino-Indian war, a short border conflict between India and the People's Republic of China. The 40th TCS was alerted for deployment on Thanksgiving Day and was the first to arrive in New Delhi, India, where we were given the royal treatment by the Indian government. However as the weeks passed, we were moved from our plush billets at the Ashoka Hotel to a hotel of considerably lesser stature named The Jampath, which we referred to as the "Jampacked." Ultimately, we were once again shuffled to some run-down government contract quarters that were even worse, which we nicknamed "The Cootie House." However, it really didn't matter that much as we flew most of the time and only used the hotel as a place to grab a meal and crash before the next day's long sortie.

The sorties we flew involved the airlift and airdrop of troops and cargo into the conflict area along the Himalayan border. They were long, repetitious, and interesting. If nothing else, the daily flights over the Himalayan Mountains were well worth the price of admission as they made the French Alps look like foot hills. Flying the overpowered C-130 through these massive mountains was not challenging. However it took some imagination to appreciate the airmanship of those who "flew the hump" in all kinds of weather through the valleys beneath us, some twenty years earlier during WWII in piston driven C-46 and C-47 aircraft.

One of the more challenging missions was the airlift of men and material to Leh, at that time (and still) one of the highest airfields in the world. The installation was being fortified by the Indians since was positioned near one of the few logical invasion routes from Chinese Tibet. The airfield lay on the floor of the Indus River, and was approximately 11,500 feet in elevation. Surrounding the field were mountains that topped 23,000 feet. The runway itself was about 3,900 feet long, constructed of PSP (pierced steel planking), and had an upward slope of about eleven degrees from the end nearest the river.

Near the end of the runway some sort of extension pad had been added which was about six inches higher than the original runway. The lip that existed at the leading edge of this area had to be avoided on landing roll-out. This fact was brought to light when one of the C-130s in 39th TCS landed with a 25 knot tailwind and hit the extension hard enough to knock the nose gear into the cargo compartment.

Since the field had no control tower, operations in and out were conducted strictly under VFR (visual flight rules) conditions with the individual aircraft commanders coordinating among themselves to avoid conflicting traffic. After descending turns into the valley, we always made our approaches from the river end onto the upslope runway, and then took off in the opposite direction, down slope. The landings required a fair degree of skill and only the most experienced aircraft commanders were authorized for the mission. The air was thin enough that we would leave one of the engines running to assure enough air pressure to re-start the remaining engines for departure.

The Tibetan natives from the nearby village were obviously fascinated by all the activity and daily stood by some mud huts next to the runway to watch. On one of our trips we were carrying an Indian major who had spent a lot of time at Leh. After we had shut down three of the engines and the loadmaster began unloading some jeeps we were carrying, he pointed out a group of the natives standing next to an eld-erly man, whom he said was one of the local chieftains.

(Author)

Figure 11—Author at Leh Airfield, Tibet
Note the C-130's #4 engine is not shut down to insure sufficient pneumatic air pressure for start of the remaining three engines in the thin Himalayan Mountain air.

Apparently the chieftain had been telling the wide-eyed children watching the jeeps emerge from the rear cargo ramp they were "being born" and would one day grow up to be big silver airplanes.

No trip to India would be complete without some tourism, which of course included a visit to the famous Taj Mahal at nearby Agra as well as trips into down-town New Delhi to prowl through the market places where a wide array of beau-tiful, brass artwork could be bought at fantastic prices. I would bet there was not one man on any crew who did not return to Evreux with at least one brass tray. When we wanted to go downtown on shopping trips or to get a good meal, we were relegated to the use of local taxi cabs as we had no contract vehicles. This was probably a darn good thing since the streets were jammed, the Indians like the Brits drove on the wrong side of the road, and the rules for driving were based in large part on a game of bluff.

We had noted that most Delhi cab drivers had one thing in common. As soon as they engaged the clutch and began to move, they also began to honk the horn at every moving object in sight. Since there were no set fares for any particular destination, one simply haggled with the driver until an agreed price was reached. On one occasion after Bob Scible, Dan O'Leary and I had negotiated a price for return to the hotel, we told the cab driver we would pay him double the fare if he could make the trip without honking his horn. He quickly agreed. Although often tempted, he managed to restrain his instincts as other vehicles maneuvered around and about him with their horns blaring. We were literally within sight of the hotel when another cab cut him off so blatantly it simply became too much to bear. His right hand hovered for at least three seconds above the horn ring as he weighed the options of a double fare versus ultimate humiliation, before repeatedly smashing the horn button down with total resolve.

One of the missions, often repeated, involved a lengthy, all day, round trip to a distant airfield whose name I can no longer recall. At any rate there were multiple C-130s on the ground at once, which afforded the opportunity for us to make single-ship "short-field takeoffs" as the remaining crews sat beside the runway and critiqued the performances. The subsequent flight back to New Deli was often flown in two, three, or four ship formations. On one of these occasions I decided to see how high we could climb before beginning descent into the airport at New Delhi, where Indian Air Force (IAF) Folland Gnat fighters would often scramble to intercept us. By the time we hit the Delhi FIR (Flight Information Region) the altimeter read 39,800 feet as the big bird hung on the props. Despite their high rate of climb and service ceiling, the IAF fighters which came out to intercept us could not reach our altitude before we began our descent, leaving the IAF pilots totally amazed that the contrail above was being laid by none other that a visiting USAF C-130.

During the period 1956 to 1960, there had been a C-130 demonstration team known as "The Four Horsemen" who flew four-ship, formation maneuvers at air shows throughout the States and Europe, often "stealing the show." One of the basic formations they flew was the classic "diamond", which we decided to replicate during the long, boring trips back to New Delhi. Kent Davidson was the leader, Al Swanson flew left wing, Bob Scible right wing, and I was in the slot. We became very proficient at this totally unauthorized formation and had great fun with it on numerous missions. This lasted until we received permission from New Delhi Tower to make a low-altitude formation pass over the field which we did with a steep pull up and roll off to the left as we took spacing for landing. It was a big hit among all of the Indian Air Force personnel and other observers on the ramp, but struck a sour note with our commanding officer who was ready to start proceedings against us until the American Ambassador requested a repeat performance. Despite the Ambassador's request, no more of the four-ship diamonds appeared over Delhi, but we all kept our jobs.

During this time period, President John F. Kennedy had selected John Kenneth Galbrath as the United States Ambassador to India. To show appreciation for the

USAF support efforts, of which we were the largest contributor, the Ambassador had arranged a large garden party at his quarters. It was a high-class affair with numerous dignitaries among the guests who enjoyed the music, food and drink in the cool evening air on the grounds behind his embassy home. All U.S. Embassies are guarded by a cadre of U.S. Marines, and about four of them, who were obviously off-duty, were also enjoying the free-flowing beer at a table of their own. Among our group was a contemporary officer and pilot, 1/Lt. Joe Criswell, who in addition to being an outstanding pilot was a brilliant historian, funnier than a crutch, a hustler, and a man who could chug-a-lug beer faster than any human on earth. A lot of people have perfected the technique of opening up their throat and simply pouring the contents of a glass down the open gullet. Chriswell had taken the art one step further in that he had somehow learned to literally suck out the contents of a glass in a fraction of the time required by gravity assist alone.

Well into the evening Bob Scible alerted several of us to the activities of the Marine Guard table where an apparently "wasted" Joe Criswell sat with the group and repeatedly lost bet after bet on beer chug contests to the gleeful Marines. As we watched from a distance, knowing full well what was about to happen, Joe told the group he just couldn't drink any more and would have to leave. The Marines, eager to pick up a few more bucks, slapped him on the back pleaded for him to have just one more contest. In a slow and slurred "ah shucks" southern drawl, Joe told them he just couldn't do it unless it was for a really big pot. Since all of them had beaten him and their "champion" had beaten him badly, they were more than delighted to accommodate him. After Joe fumbled around and emptied the contents of his billfold, the Marines quickly covered the bet with a big stack of bills. The glasses were then charged and the go signal given by a slap on the table. The Marine's glass had barely touched his lips when Criswell's empty hit the table. As Joe swiped the stack of bills into his left hand he rose immediately from his chair and said in a deep and totally coherent voice, "Thank you gentlemen" while turning to walk away.

The 40th TCS was again on rotation duty when the operation in New Delhi wound down in April of 1963 and the aircraft were loaded for the long, non-stop flight back to Evreux. The best seats in the plane were of course in the cockpit where one could at least see outside, thus having something to do. In contrast, the cargo compartment was noisy, crowded, and totally boring. Since there was a large contingent of higher ranking, staff officers assigned to the 322nd Division and 317th Wing who had shown up in the final days of the deployment, to purchase their brass trays and other goodies, all the seats up front were quickly taken.

Under normal conditions, the 290 knot cruise speed of the C-130A would complete the trip in just over 12 hours. Unfortunately there was a strong and persistent, westerly headwind making the enroute time much longer. As the 15th hour passed, one of the loadmasters on the headset in the back approached me and said I was wanted up front. As I climbed the steps up into the cockpit I asked the navigator what was up. "We're low on fuel and the winds at Evreux are off the charts" was his reply. The colonel who had been flying was equally candid and asked me if I thought I could land the aircraft in the existing winds, which turned out to be a direct ninety-degree cross at 35 knots, gusting to 42 knots. I told him I could and took the left seat.

Other than the strong winds, the late afternoon weather at Evreux was fine and I choose to put the 90-degree crosswind to my left so I could see the clearance between my left wing tip and the ground as we approached touchdown. With near instant differential thrust from the big turbo-prop engines, the C-130 has tremendous capability for landing in extreme crosswinds such as the ones at hand. The technique involves landing in a forward slip with the upwind wing down and the nose aligned with the center line by opposite rudder and differential thrust. This basically involves keeping the power up on the two engines on the upwind wing, with a corresponding reduction of power on the two engines on the downwind wing to facilitate the necessary yaw to slew the nose into alignment.

Once the throttles are correctly set, very little rudder is required to track the aircraft straight down final approach. Touchdown is made on the upwind main gears, after which skillful manipulation of the throttles into differential reverse thrust will continue to track the aircraft down the runway centerline as the nose is lowered and the aircraft slows to taxi speed. The colonel whose place I took had chosen to stand behind me and hold on to the left seat during the landing. As we cleared the runway he lifted the left earpiece of my head set and said, "That didn't look so hard." Since it really wasn't, I simply smiled and replied, "Thank you, Sir."

For a fleeting period of months in late 1963, I thought I had a real opportunity to gain reentry into jet aircraft as an RF-84F unit was being formed at Chaumont Air Base, France. There were limited slots available but through endorsements and letters of recommendation, I managed to make the list of only three "in-country" selectees who were not current in fighters. My heart sank when my present billet as a C-130 instructor pilot was declared a vital resource by USAFE Headquarters and the assignment was denied.

Since the President of France, Charles DeGaulle was making life for American forces in France miserable as well as kicking SHAPE (Supreme Headquarters Allied Powers Europe) Headquarters out of Paris, the entire American operation at Evreux Air Base was slated for closure. Consequently, the 317th Troop Carrier Wing was scheduled for transfer to Lockbourne AFB in Columbus, Ohio in the spring of 1964. By now I had concluded that it would be my destiny to fly the C-130 for the rest of my natural life, and rationalized that things could be a lot worse.

Back at Lockbourne, Kent Davidson and I had become two of the wing's standard-ization/evaluation flight examiners, and were given responsibility for the C-130 portion of the air show for the Wing's Armed Forces Day Open House scheduled for the 4th of July, 1965. Our only guidance was that our demonstration should include a short-field takeoff and landing, and to "keep it short and sweet" since we would be performing just prior to the climactic air show performed by the USAF Thunderbirds Demonstration Team in their F-100s. We understood the instructions and developed a plan to showcase the extraordinary maneuverability and performance envelope of the "Herc", all in a short time, and within close view of the spectators. It went like this:

Kent would takeoff without fanfare about fifteen minutes prior to our performance and climb into an upwind holding pattern about five miles out from the departure runway. At the appointed time, I would perform the maximum performance take-off, recover with a 180 degree turn to the downwind leg where I would extend the gear and flaps while slowing to minimum controllable airspeed and descending to 500 feet above the ground on a short final approach. Simultaneously the loadmaster would open the troop jump doors on both sides and extend the cargo ramp. As this was occurring, Kent would have begun a dive from his high holding pattern so as to pass directly beneath my slow flight path at maximum redline airspeed just prior to show center, then do a 2G pull-up to the vertical and "ride it up" until running out of airspeed. After Kent passed beneath me and the loadmaster had closed the troop jump doors and aft ramp, I would retard the throttles to idle and dive steeply at the runway, rounding out in time to touchdown in front of the reviewing stands and stop. The entire scenario would take less than four minutes and make way for the highly anticipated demonstration by the Thunderbirds.

In preparation for the show, SMSgt. Duke Vermeer and MSgt. Bob Porter (stan/eval flight engineer and loadmaster from our shop) unloaded all the chains, straps, and everything they could get their hands on to lighten the plane. They estimated that they had both aircraft's gross weights down to around 69,000 pounds and then put on only about 8,000 pounds of fuel. In the aircraft I flew, Capt. Maury Galey was in the co-pilot's seat, MSgt. Buddy Hesser in the flight engineer's chair, and TSgt. Hobart Lilly in the cargo compartment as the load-master. This was by no means "our first rodeo" as some of us had been doing modified, maximum, performance takeoffs all over the world for well over four years, but never in an aircraft as light as the one in which we now sat. As noted earlier, the standard, maximum performance takeoff is performed with half-flaps and rotation as soon as the prescribed speed is obtained, producing a very short takeoff roll, followed by a slow but moderate climb angle. The technique we would employ differed significantly.

All of the bleed-air valves from the four Allison engines would be closed to increase available shaft horsepower. The takeoff would be performed with zero flaps to reduce drag. The aircraft would be accelerated on the runway to approximately 150 knots indicated airspeed before beginning a rotation just slow enough to avoid dragging the tail, followed by a smooth, steady pull to a vertical climb. Once the horizon is no longer visible from the cockpit windows, the only way to know when your angle of climb achieves pure vertical is to look at the J-8 attitude indicator on the co-pilots panel. When it reaches its 87.5-degree gyroscopic gimbals limit, it will flip over, at which time…you're going straight up.

Kent had taken off as planned, with SMSgt. Vermeer in the flight engineer's seat and MSgt. Porter as the loadmaster. We started engines shortly after their uneventful takeoff and taxied to a holding position short of the active runway, where an unexpected delay occurred when "The Flying Farmer's" comical routine in a Piper Cub took far longer than expected. This didn't impact our fuel status, but Kent was forced to shut down the #1 and #4 engines in-flight to conserve their minimum fuel load. When we were finally cleared by the tower for takeoff, we closed the bleed air valves, held the brakes, let all four engines stabilize at maximum power, and released the brakes. The ultra light weight of the big bird was immediately apparent as it accelerated faster than I had ever felt. Passing 150 knots indicated in a remarkably short distance, I smoothly rotated and Maury

(John Barnas)

Figure 12—Rotation to vertical climb from takeoff at Lockbourne AFB, Ohio on July 4, 1965[10]

---

[10] Of the thousands of spectators with cameras at the Armed Forces Day Airshow at Lockbourne AFB on July 4, 1965, this distant, grainy, non-telephoto lens shot is the only known photograph of the takeoff. I am most grateful to Doug Marshall for sending it to me. The text of his email to which the JPEG file was attached contains an explaniation that is strikingly similar to that given by numerous other individuals as to "why they didn't get the shot."

"I was there, watching on the flightline as you stood the C-130A on its' props. I recall there was a good headwind and I had my camera ready to shoot the picture. I was so shocked, I thought the Herc was going over on its back!! I didn't get the shot but my friend, John Barnas got it. I have a copy of it in my collection."
Doug Marshall—317th Veterans Group

retracted the gear as soon as the weight came off the wheels. I continued to pull until the J-8 on Maury's instrument panel tumbled as planned, then relaxed back pressure on the stick. We were able to sustain the vertical climb for much longer than normal because of our light weight, while the strong 30+ knot headwind moved our flight path backwards toward the takeoff end of the runway. I began the roll-off and recovery to the left, with strong left aileron, left rudder, and forward stick as the airspeed decayed rapidly through about 100 knots, giving the appearance of the aircraft pirouetting around its longitudinal axis. As the nose dropped, the collective thrust of the four Allison engines once again exceeded the weight of the bird as it literally hung on the props in level flight about 900 feet above the runway on a close, short downwind leg.

After extending the gear and full flaps, TSgt. Lilly opened the cargo ramp and troop jump doors as planned. We slid around the base turn and stabilized in level flight at 500 feet AGL just short of the VIP reviewing stands, which were immediately adjacent to the active runway. Now at an indicated airspeed of 61 knots, which gave us an effective ground speed of approximately 26 knots, Kent's timing was perfect as he passed directly beneath us at a ground speed of 370 knots before pulling into his vertical climb. He rapidly traded airspeed for altitude before pushing over in slow flight at airspeed of about 90 knots at approximately 6,500 feet.[11] As soon as Kent had passed underneath us, I initiated the final element of our demo, an assault landing. With the troop and cargo doors now secured and the parking brake set to exploit the anti-skid braking which would occur as quickly as the WOW (weight-on-wheels) switch on the main gear closed, I retarded the power to flight idle, dove steeply at the runway, flared at the last moment and went into full reverse thrust on all four engines just before touchdown. As the wheels touched the runway, the nose came down and immediately back up as we instantly stopped. I do know the precise length of our landing roll, but was told by several of the flight engineers who were adjacent to the point of touchdown, that the airplane appeared to stop in about two aircraft lengths. As we turned right, ninety degrees to exit the runway at mid-field, we "took a bow" by simultaneously adding power and hitting the brakes, making the nose gear strut alternately compress and extend, causing the big bird's black nose to move dramatically up and down. We shut down the number one and four engines as we

---

[11] In conversations with Kent Davidson, now a retired USAF MajGen., neither of us can explain how his vertical climb somehow escaped the wing commander's wrath to which I was treated. Our only rationalization is that the "wing king's" attention was focused upon my assault landing vs. Kent's simultaneous and spectacular two-mile vertical climb directly above the reviewing stands.

became the largest, heaviest aircraft to land and take off unassisted from a carrier.

Vietnam. That
perfectly an air-
e future. Other
, some in ways
was warpaint.
toms had been
t if the C-130s
hands and go
ctly the airlifts

The Herk is also the largest and heaviest airplane ever to land and take off, unassisted—no arresting wire or catapult—from an aircraft carrier. In 1963 the Navy briefly considered using C-130s to replace its twin-engine Grumman COD (carrier onboard delivery) C-1s, which had limited range and payload, so they gave carrier pilot Lieutenant James Flatley a quick four-engine checkout and had him do 29 touch-and-goes and another 21 full-stop landings and takeoffs from USS *Forrestal*. Ultimately, the Navy decided that with a C-130 taking up space on a carrier's deck, not much else could move until the Herk either departed or, in an emergency, was pushed over the side. The minimal clearance between the C-130's right wingtip and the carrier's island was also a bit too sporty for routine operations.

exited the runway and proceeded right on the parallel taxiway back to our parking spot. Along the way, hundreds of the spectators were wildly cheering and waving with some actually throwing hats into the air.

I had no sooner shut down the engines when SSgt. Richard Caruthers, the NCO (non-commissioned officer) in charge of ramp operations scrambled up the crew ladder into the cockpit to inform me that the wing commander's instructions to him were: "Don't let anyone on the aircraft or off the aircraft until I get there!" This was quickly followed by a message that I was to report to the Wing Commander's office immediately. The jocular mood of only moments before instantly evaporated as I sensed that absolutely nothing good was likely to come from a private meeting with the "wing king." With the Thunderbirds now taking off for their show, I proceeded to my car and drove straight to the wing commander's office in the headquarters building where I found him standing behind his desk with the look of a man capable of murder.

He didn't bother to return my snappy salute as I stood at rigid attention, but launched into an angry tirade as he railed at me for at least five minutes. Having said nothing beyond "yes sir" and "no sir" during the entire "conversation" he finally wound down and looked silently at me for a long time before saying, "Captain Handley that was the greatest damn air show I ever saw. I actually peed in my pants. Now I'm going to tell you one thing. If I ever hear of you doing that damn fool stunt again, I am going to personally drum you out of this man's air force. Do you understand me?" After I had replied "yes sir", he again paused and added, "What the hell are you tying to prove? What is it that you want?" Since this was my first opportunity to deviate from my preceding two-word answers, I answered, "Sir, I'd really like to get back into fighters." He didn't hesitate a second before replying, "Well I'm going to damn well help you do precisely that, now get the hell out of my office." I saluted, did an about face and walked out the door with a tremendous sense of relief, realizing I had just dodged a career-ending bullet.

The wing commander was a man of his word and before the end of the year I received notification I was being reassigned as an instructor pilot to Williams Air Force Base in Phoenix, Arizona. This closed the book on my association with the great C-130 until some eight years later when it was my privilege to escort its gunship version while flying an F-4D from Ubon RTAFB, Thailand.

Frozen Stick at 30,000 Feet

- 1967 -

In 1967 I was assigned to the flight test section at Williams AFB, Arizona, where four other pilots and myself conducted functional check flights (FCF) on the T-37s, T-38s, and F-5s assigned to the wing. FCFs were typically required after maintenance flight control rigs, periodic inspections, or special problems identified for a specific aircraft. This was a great flying job which typically entailed around twenty-five sorties per week. This is the story of one particular FCF I performed in a T-38 "White Rocket" after it emerged from a routine 100-hour periodic inspection. In my opinion this short flight proved to be my closest brush with the "Grim Reaper" during my flying career.

The FCF flight profile for the T-38 called for an afterburner climb from takeoff to 43,000 feet, followed by a supersonic run with a 180 degree turn reversal back toward Williams AFB. At the conclusion of the turn reversal, we would routinely do a "junk check" to collect unwanted items hidden within the confines of the cockpit as the result of previous flight or ground maintenance actions. Such foreign objects included pencils, nuts, bolts, coins, paper clips, etc., any of which could potentially end up in the wrong place during in-flight maneuvers and cause trouble due to mechanical blockage.

(USAF File Photograph)

Figure 13—Northrop T-38A Talon (White Rocket)

To perform the maneuver you needed to apply just enough negative G to "float" such objects upward to the canopy above your head, where they would rest until positive G was reapplied. My practice was to initiate the maneuver with the nose up about 20 degrees and after rolling inverted, shake the aircraft through several cycles of negative to positive G to positively dislodge the unwanted objects from their resting places. Following this I would run in enough forward (nose-down) trim to sustain just a fraction more than zero G while I picked up the junk from the canopy above my head with both hands, unzipped the left upper pocket of my flight suit (which I had emped before the flight), stuff the junk inside the pocket and rezip it before rolling back upright with positive G. Having done hundreds of these checks, it was a totally routine but effective maneuver which had produced a surprising volume of the unwanted cockpit foreign objects.

On this day everything was totally routine as I re-zipped my flight suit pocket and applied left aileron and aft-stick to roll upright. As the aircraft approached the upright position and I attempted to move the stick back to the right to arrest the approximate 120 degree-per-second rate of roll, I simply could not move the stick back to the right and the aircraft continued to roll left under positive G, with the nose precipitously dropping with each inverted attitude. As I grabbed the stick with both hands and pulled as hard as I could to move it back to the right, I looked directly at both of the aircraft's hydraulic system pressure gages which were rock solid at the full system pressure of 3,000 pounds per square inch. The stick absolutely would not budge and the aircraft was really beginning to "wind-up" as the nose dropped further toward the vertical with each turn. I yanked the throttles to idle and extended the speed brakes in an attempt to slow the rate of acceleration, but with the high starting mach number near 25,000 feet, the airspeed was already transonic and increasing. As I continued to yank at the stick with both hands with all of my adrenaline-augmented strength, I realized I only had seconds in which to get this problem under control, or pull the ejection handles as the aircraft passed through 10,000 feet. I also knew that ejecting at my near supersonic airspeed was a terrible "least worst choice" as the slipstream would probably break me apart like a rag doll.

As I passed about 20,000 feet I rationalized that since the hydraulic pressure was obviously not the culprit, something had to be mechanically blocking the flight controls, and it probably had something to do with the negative Gs I had applied during the junk check. Since the stick would move freely in the pitch axis, I started pumping it back and forth to alternate between positive and negative G, and after several cycles the stick suddenly broke free. I immediately stopped the roll in a wings-level upright attitude and applied about 6Gs to pull the nose back up to the horizon as I passed through approximately 8,000 feet.

After declaring an emergency, I set course directly for Williams AFB where I flew a straight-in approach. Anyone observing my flight path back to "Willy" must have thought they were observing the most uncoordinated pilot they had ever seen. Not anxious to repeat the preceding scenario, I made certain I didn't move the stick from the neutral aileron position, choosing instead to skid the aircraft around with rudder to final approach alignment and a perfectly normal landing.

Once parked on the ramp, I ran the ailerons back and forth through many cycles without a problem. After explaining what had happened to the maintenance personnel, all agreed this emergency had to be the result of some sort of mechanical blockage. The aircraft was towed over to the NDI[12] hangar where the portions of the wing housing the aileron encasement boxes would be examined. Although this particular bird had undergone NDI inspections on a routine basis over its service life, it had failed to detect a 3/8"x 4" bolt which had apparently been left inside the aileron containment box when it had been opened for some sort of maintenance actions over two years earlier. The bolt had been rattling around within ever since.

On this particular day one of "Murphy's Laws" finally prevailed when I transitioned from negative to positive G just as the left aileron was up for my left-hand roll. One of the maintenance NCOs put it into perspective by saying this was the equivalent of a single quarter in a piggy bank with a slot no bigger than the quarter itself. Given enough repetitions of flipping the piggy bank from upright to inverted, the quarter would eventually standup and precisely align itself with the slot in the bank and fall through. The bolt was removed and the aircraft returned to service without any further problems. Although I held the bolt in my hand, I regret I didn't have the foresight to keep it as a souvenir and reminder of that day.

Precisely how my final actions of shaking the aircraft with alternating positive and negative G dislodged it is not clear to me, but I'm darn glad it worked, as my options would otherwise have been dubious at best.

---

[12] NDI: Non-Destructive Inspection much like an x-ray machine for metal equipment.

Killer Vertigo

- 1969 -

Every pilot, and particularly military pilots are well aware of the causes and effects of vertigo. Man's normal method of orientation is based upon what our eyes tell us, coupled with the inertial movement of fluids in the semi-circular canals of the middle ear and the gravity-induced pressure sensations applied to the seat of our pants. However of these three factors, the eyes always "hold the trump card" and override the other sensations in almost all instances. By nature, an airplane that is free to move three dimensionally provides the ideal crucible for vertigo. Therefore, from the outset it is pounded into a pilot's head that once the visual sensory channel is lost or restricted, one simply cannot trust any source of attitude reference beyond that of the aircraft's onboard instruments. This fact has been clearly demonstrated to one and all and no sane pilot would dispute its validity. The bottom line is that once clear reference to a visual horizon is lost, "get on the gages" and remain there until you can clearly see where you are going.

There are various types of vertigo, some of which are more dramatic than others. There is "the leans" whereby you feel you are flying in a banked attitude, despite the fact the attitude indicator tells you wings are level. It is not uncommon to observe a pilot physically leaning left or right in the cockpit as he diligently flys instruments. Or, there is the disconcerting feeling that you are not simply "banked" a little, but in fact turning in the opposite direction as indicated by your instruments. Then there is the sensation you are climbing, when in fact you are either in a straight-and-level attitude or descending…and hundreds of other variations on the theme.

Probably one of the most disorientating variations of vertigo is the "coriolis effect" variant which can produce the sensation of tumbling, which is induced by sudden upward movement of the head while rolling the aircraft in a perpendicular axis. The practical application of this being, if you drop something in the cockpit and reach over to pick it up, do so with caution as you could easily encounter this totally disorienting effect and it will take more than a few seconds to "re-cage" the eye balls to the point you can once again read the instrument panel.

Over the years I lost several friends who apparently "bought the farm" as a result of vertigo. I am convinced that for the most part none of them died "tensed up", as they probably never realized what was happening. It isn't just clouds or darkness which can cause loss of visual orientation. One of the worst and most insidious environments occurs when practicing air-combat maneuvering (dog fighting) over water, on a hazy day when the horizon is not clear. Since the pilots of the fighters engaged in the dog fight are looking almost entirely at the opponent while maneuvering for position, it is very easy to lose all orientation and dive into the ocean while thinking all the while you are pulling straight up. I have personally observed a very highly experienced pilot do precisely that, while transmitting mutual support information over the radio to his wingman.

While flying F-4Cs at Davis Montham AFB, Arizona in 1969, I was a senior pilot[13] with over 3,500 hours of flying time who had experienced what I thought was every variation of the dreaded vertigo thousands of times. I considered it a matter of discipline that once a vertigo situation was recognized, I would simply "get on the gages" and scrupulously maintain the desired attitude and flight parameters until things returned to normal. What happened to me at the conclusion of a routine air-to-ground gunnery mission to the range was, for me, a one-time experience for which I was totally unprepared.

I was flying the number four position in a "fingertip formation[14]" returning from the gunnery range to our home base at Davis Montham AFB on a pretty VFR[15]

---

[13] Air Force officers who are pilots are referred to as "rated officers." The three types of silver wings worn by Air Force pilots are pilot, senior pilot, and command pilot. The wings initially awarded upon successful graduation from pilot training are the pilot wings, which are often referred to as "slick wings" because of their absence of a star and/or wreath above the center shield. When pilots have been rated for seven years and logged a minimum of 1,500 hours of flying time, they earn senior pilot wings which are identified by a star affixed above the insignia's shield. Upon accumulation of fifteen years rated service and a minimum of 3,000 hours of flight time, command pilots wings are awarded and can be identified by the addition of a wreath (sometimes referred to as a toilet seat) around the star.

[14] Fiingertip formation: A four-ship formation with aircraft positioning that resembles the four extended fingers of the hand. The lead aircraft is the middle finger, #2 is the index finger, #3 is the ring finger, and #4 is the little finger.

[15] Visual Flight Rules: A "see and be seen" situation, whereby the pilot is responsible for seeing and avoiding other traffic without assistance from ground based radar or other Air Traffic Control agencies.

day with only scattered clouds at approximately 10,000 feet. As we approached the scattered deck, the flight leader rocked his wings, signaling his three wingmen to close-it-up to close formation during the brief period we would be transiting the clouds. Flying as the outside aircraft on the right side of the formation, I slid onto the right wing of my element leader, the number three aircraft, and "put the "light on the star" to hold position until we broke into the clear within no more than 15-20 seconds.

I absolutely could not believe what I saw when we broke out of the bottom of the cloud layer. I instantly recognized that somehow, the flight leader had rolled us inverted while within the clouds, and there before my unbelieving eyes was our four-ship formation of F-4s in an inverted attitude. I looked immediately at my attitude indicator on the panel which indicated we were in fact in a wings-level attitude with the nose down about ten degrees, but I couldn't believe it as in my mind's eye I clearly saw sky below and ground above the formation.

As I was doing this I exclaimed to my WSO[16] in the rear cockpit, "What's our attitude." "Wings-level and nose down" came his instant reply. Once again I looked directly at the instruments I had trusted implicitly for thousands of hours and mentally confirmed what he was saying. Despite this, I simply could not forsake what my 20:10 eyes were telling me when looking at the sky and earth, and remained totally convinced I was the only one of the eight individuals in our formation who realized we were indeed inverted and about to "split-s"[17] into four smoking holes in the Arizona desert.

"No we're not, we're inverted" I shouted as I grimly maintained formation position. "You're vertigo, Phil, you're vertigo! We are almost straight and level!" he said. Looking once again at the instrument panel the gages confirmed he was dead right. Despite this I simply could not overcome a fear of death I knew would occur within moments unless we rolled to an "upright position" to pull up. Looking directly at the attitude indicator which clearly belied my perception, I put both my hands on the stick to resist the temptation to roll 180 degrees and live to fly another day.

Despite everything I could do, and with my backseater now screaming at me and trying to hold the stick steady, my good right arm rolled the aircraft to what I

---

16 WSO: Weapon systems officer (Also know as the GIB, or Guy In Back)

17 Split-S: An aerobatic maneuver where by the aircraft is rolled inverted and pulled vertically through 180 degrees of turn, thus reversing the initial course.

"knew" was an upright attitude and began a high-G pull, which in reality was a split-s maneuver directly toward the ground. Unable to overpower me on the stick, the backseater screamed at me, "Phil, you've got to let go or I'm going to "punch us out." Every fiber in my body told me he was dead wrong as I released the stick and observed his 180 degree roll which I was certain would fly us into the ground. Only after our nose was well up and I had looked repeatedly at the horizon, the formation above us, and the attitude indicator, did my normal spatial equilibrium slowly return to normal.

In the remaining 3,500 hours of my military flying career, I never again experienced this phenomenon, and I can only thank God that on this single occasion I had the good fortune to be flying in a two-seat fighter with a WSO who saved my life. There is not a doubt in my mind I would have continued my dive into the Arizona desert and died totally convinced that I was the only man in the formation who realized the formation was inverted.

It is only a matter of speculation as to how many pilots have "bought the farm" under similar circumstance. However, it stands to reason that mine was not a singular, isolated incident and more than a few of the fatalities of pilots who unexplainably dove into the ground on a clear day were victim to "killer vertigo."

The Survival Schools

- 1970 -

Prologue

I wrote the following chapter of this book on the afternoon of 9 May 2004. During dinner that evening my satellite television dish was not working and I was forced to watch antenna-received network programming. By chance I was tuned to CBS, which following the news aired the GRAND, FINAL, CLIMACTIC program of a "reality series show" called "Survivors." After grasping the essence of the show, I realized this was a staged and transcribed TV production where the goal of the fifteen or so participants was, through deception and false alliance, to "vote out" their fellow contestants one-by-one until the final "survivor" left standing was awarded a one million dollar prize. It struck me as a cruel irony that the grand prize for the thousands of airmen attending the real survival schools of which I had just written, was to return home alive, while the average daily compensation for pilots who flew combat missions into the most heavily defended areas in the history of aerial warfare was $40.46.[18]

Story

Pilots destined for the Vietnam War attended three distinctly different survival schools before their deployment. First in line was the Global Survival School located at Fairchild AFB near Spokane, Washington. Next was the Water Survival School at Homestead AFB in Miami, Florida. And finally, while enroute to Southeast Asia, the Jungle Survival School, commonly called "Snake

---

[18] Based on monthly pay for a USAF Captain: Base pay $801.60, food $47.88, quarters $105.00, flight pay $165.00, family separation $30.00, hazardous duty $65.00, for a total monthly compensation of $1,214.48.

School", at Clark Air Force Base in the Philippines. The following chronicles my experience in these three, distinctly different schools.

The stated mission of any of the survival schools is of course to indoctrinate and prepare the students for the combat environment into which they are about to enter. As the name would imply, the Global Survival School at Fairchild AFB (which was the longest in duration) attempted to cover the basics of survival in a 14 day period. I believe my opinion of the school was typical of most of its attendees who regarded it as "least favorite" of the three schools. In fairness, if I were trying to design the curriculum, I probably would not have done better considering the diverse backgrounds of those in attendance.

If you were a farm boy who played sports, spent a lot of time hunting, fishing and tramping around in the woods, you were much better prepared for the Fairchild experience than those who had grown up in the city and possessed limited native intelligence of nature. Regardless, since all of us would be going into much the same combat environment, we were exposed to some pretty basic stuff. Included in the training syllabus were exercises demonstrating that if you were out of shape you couldn't keep up; if you didn't eat you got really hungry; and if you were stuffed into a three cubic foot box, you would get cramps, etc.

Since Fairchild AFB is located in the northwest United States, the best time to attend the school was in summer since the experience was even more miserable when slogging around in knee-deep snow during winter. I was fortunate to be scheduled for the month of June and the weather was actually very nice. When I arrived at the school I ran into a young lieutenant, Andy Ivan, whom I had known earlier at Williams AFB, Arizona when he was going through pilot school. He had just completed WSO training in the F-4C and was now enroute to DaNang Air Base in South Vietnam as a backseater. He was an interesting "hair on fire" first lieutenant that one could not help but like. At one time he had been an outstanding football quarterback and told me it was he who taught Joe Thiesman (the future Hall of Fame NFL quarterback) to throw a football when Joe was in high school.

The first few days of the course were spent in the classroom being shown indoctrination films and receiving a great deal of material through lectures. Things got more intense when we were "captured" one evening and interned into "the compound." For the next several days we were interrogated, starved, and abused in a manner designed to prepare us for such an environment were we captured by the North Vietnamese. It was a miserable experience, but in reality a "cake walk" compared to the real thing as endured by our POWs during the war, as we were never actually tortured by the cadre playing the roles of the prison guards and interrogators.

Following the "compound experience", came the field trip to the woods. It began early one morning with a relatively long forced march to a particularly dense section of the woods surrounding the base. It was during this march when those members of the class who were physically out of shape were exhausted to their limits, with some unable to continue without the help of their buddies. We were not allowed to take any food or water with us beyond that normally found in the survival kit available after bailout. At the end of the hike were several pickup trucks bearing parachutes which were issued to each of us for the ensuing training.

For the next few days we remained as a group and were taught basic "E & E" (Escape and Evasion) techniques under the supervision of the school's training cadre. During this instruction phase we caught fish in the local streams, ate fruits and nuts we picked, cooked anything we caught or killed on a campfire, and slept in tents fabricated from the parachute we had been issued. A good deal of the E&E instruction centered upon day and night navigation using only a map and compass. After several days we were paired up and given individual destinations, to which each two-man team was expected to navigate while avoiding detection by the aggressors present in the area.

I was teamed with Lt. Ivan as we began our trek just before sundown. Everything seemed to be going quite well as we navigated through much of the night to get as far away from the base camp as possible before concealing ourselves for some sleep. The next day was very hot and travel through the dense underbrush extremely difficult. Around noon Andy was not feeling well and began to throw up at regular intervals, accompanied by a serious case of dysentery. It was amazing to observe just how quickly dehydration set in, sapping the strength of this well- conditioned athlete, rendering him almost helpless. He quickly consumed all of his own water as well as mine and I knew it was imperative we find a stream to replenish our water supply or things would get a lot worse, really fast. By now he was too weak to walk on his own, so I supported him with his arm around my neck as we pressed on. When he finally collapsed to the ground he was literally too weak to raise his head as he told me to leave him and seek help. When he passed out only moments later, I was truly fearful he was about to die.

From my survival map I could see there was supposed to be a clearing less than one-half mile from our present location. Knowing I had to get Andy and myself to that location if we were going to have any chance of being spotted, I picked him up in a "fireman's carry" and with great difficulty and many rest stops made my way to the small clearing. Upon arrival at the clearing, which was about 100 yards in diameter, I laid Andy in a shady spot, noting he was pale and his breathing seemed short and shallow. Gathering sticks and dry brush, I built a fire in the middle of the clearing, and continued to feed it until it was producing a large cloud of smoke which I hoped would be easily spotted. In less than fifteen minutes I heard the "womp, womp" of an approaching helicopter which turned out to be a USAF helicopter from the base.

Among its crew was a medic to whom I quickly explained the situation as others loaded Andy onto a stretcher and into the chopper, which immediately departed enroute to the base hospital at Fairchild. Thankfully the medic had handed me two canteens of water before he boarded the chopper, and I was able to continue to the end point of the navigation route without further incident. I was not to see Andy again until the course was completed later in the week.

Finally, the graduation exercise entailed our capture by enemy forces and internment in a base camp, which would eventually be "overrun" facilitating our escape and evasion back through very dense woods to a specific "*SAFE*", (Selected Area For Evasion). We were told it was a pass/fail situation requiring that we successfully reach the designated SAFE without detection and capture, or we would have to repeat the course. This was of course BS, but after ten or so days of being starved and deprived of sleep, no one was anxious to test the validity of the story.

The cadre running the internment base camp were a particularly cocky bunch who ate, drank, and slept very well, while regarding themselves as really tough hombres. They were generally despised by those who were subject to their whims. So by the time "the great escape" began, most of us had made up our minds that after completing this course and getting cleaned up, we were going to go to one of the local bars serving great food in hopes of running into one of these hot shots under different rules-of-engagement.

When the claxon sounded early one morning signaling our escape from the base camp, we all made a dash for it and individually began to navigate back to the designated SAFE point, which could be reached by late afternoon. Unlike the canned navigation exercise where the students were paired up, those who fled the base camp mostly proceeded alone. By noon, I had made what I considered very good progress while taking all precautions against capture by avoiding open areas and sticking to the dense undercover of the brush-covered woods. About this time I found myself on the crest of a small rise in the terrain with an approximate three foot drop along the route I was traveling. Noting there appeared to be nothing but soft-looking undergrowth below, I jumped from my perch into a large bush and got the surprise of my life as I landed squarely on the back of a large, black bear concealed therein. I don't know who was more startled, but the instant adrenalin rush I received allowed me to literally sprint away from the scene through ground cover which had previously limited my movements to a crawl. At any rate, the bear did not pursue me and I was far more cautious as to where I jumped thereafter.

It was probably not by accident the designated SAFE destination lay adjacent to a dirt road just beyond a large green meadow no more than a couple hundred yards across, but more than a mile in length. From the approach side of the meadow one could see the welcome-looking, blue Air Force bus that stood on the dirt road. Crossing the open meadow to "freedom" would only take a matter of minutes, while continuing to employ the best method of concealment meant circumnavigation along the parameter of the meadow, probably taking at least another hour. There was no doubt in my mind that blatantly entering the open field would bring an immediate response from an aggressor who no doubt had the place staked out.

I was not the first to arrive at the leading edge of the meadow, and already there were at least a half-dozen other tired and pissed-off trainees contemplating the same decision. One of these was a very large Air Force captain who had been a defensive lineman when he played college football. Without comment, he got up and began to jog toward the waiting bus on the far side of the meadow. Almost immediately a burst of blank-ammunition automatic weapons fire rang out from the edge of the clearing as an aggressor sprang from his hiding place and began shouting, "Halt!" The captain never broke the cadence of his slow, methodical jog across the field as the aggressor fired another burst and continued to shout at him. Now swearing and dropping his gun, the aggressor took off on fresh legs like a cheetah in pursuit of a gazelle, tackling the lumbering lineman near the center of the field and crashing to the ground.

Springing immediately to his feet, the aggressor stood over the fallen captain shouting profanity at him and declaring he was lucky he wasn't dead, as well as something about getting to do all of this again. Slowly but surely the lineman removed one shoulder strap of his backpack, then the other and rose from the ground. The aggressor was really beginning to get wound up as a crashing right hand landed squarely on his jaw, lifting him off his feet as he flew backwards landing flat on his back, totally unconscious. Along the line of trees where the rest of us were concealed, there rose a spontaneous clapping of hands and shouts of "bravo." As our hero slowly replaced his backpack and continued to methodically jog, he was joined by the rest of us timid but grateful souls as we made our way directly to the waiting bus.

The next morning I went to the base hospital to check on Andy Ivan and was allowed to visit with him. He was weak and had only recently been taken off the intravenous feeding tubes that had been attached immediately upon his arrival. I spoke with one of the doctors who had treated him and was told that he was indeed near death when admitted. Andy expressed his profound gratitude for my efforts and really hoped he would not have to repeat the whole miserable experience again. When I departed Fairchild the next day no decision had been made, but I learned a week or so later that following his release from hospital he was indeed rescheduled for the course.

He completed the course without incident the second time around and proceeded to DaNang Air Base, South Vietnam where he served a one year tour as a WSO. Volunteering for a second tour, he underwent upgrade training to the front seat of the F-4 and returned to Udorn RTAFB, Thailand, where tragically, he and his WSO disappeared without a trace while on a daylight mission to the Barrel Roll combat sector of Laos.

As compared to the Global Survival School at Fairchild, the Water Survival School at Homestead AFB, Florida was an enjoyable vacation. We were billeted in the visiting officers quarters (VOQ) and ate most of our meals at the Officers Open Mess. Classes consisted of swimming pool drills teaching techniques for getting clear of the parachute after a water landing, and of course the "upside down ejection seat" plunge to the bottom of the pool. Finally, we were pulled aloft by a motorboat and parasailed out into the bay, where we cut loose and dropped into the ocean to board our raft. After several hours of fishing, catching some really strange looking fish, we vectored-in a rescue helicopter with our survival radio, popped the locator smoke flare, jumped from the raft and mounted the harness which was lowered to us, then hoisted up to the door of the hovering chopper.

The third and final school was the Jungle Survival School (commonly referred to as "Snake School") which all of us attended while enroute across the Pacific Ocean to our assignments in SEA. Since we knew we would be spending a considerable amount of time in the jungle, we were apprehensive that this would turn out to be another food deprivation exercise. However, we were assured during our first classroom briefing this would not be the case. We were told no one would be hungry or thirsty nor deprived of rest. It was stressed that the sole purpose was to teach us to survive in a jungle environment basically identical to that found in Vietnam and Laos.

After a few days in the classroom where the information presented was current, relevant, and often classified Top Secret, we proceeded to the field for exposure to the real jungle with its two-hundred foot, triple-canopy trees. Our instructors were absolutely top notch and augmented by, perhaps the greatest jungle experts in the world, the diminutive Philippino Negrito. Using little more than blow pipes which propelled poison tipped darts as weapons, and

(Author)

Figure 14—Philippino Negrito Natives preparing dinner for "Snake School" students

their unrivaled expertise in jungle guerilla tactics, they had been the scourge of the occupying Japanese forces in WWII. Although they spoke little English, they understood what our instructors wanted them to demonstrate for us. As we left the Air Force bus to begin our hike into the jungle we were told once again that anyone carrying food in their flight suit pockets should get rid of it immediately, not because of retribution by the instructor cadre, but rather the risk it posed in attracting rats as big as house cats while you slept. We all heeded the advice.

Upon arrival at our base camp we set about making one-man tents from parachutes and gathering leaves and other soft materials for a makeshift mattress. After some demonstrations of the Negrito's amazing accuracy and range with the blow pipe, our instructor announced that Matumba, the Negrito who accompanied our group, would demonstrate how one should hide in the jungle. On the instructor's signal, Matumba stepped quickly into the thick jungle and disappeared from our view. He had no sooner gone when our instructor told us we could all now look for him, and that he could be found within 10 yards from the spot where we all stood.

Now with twenty-five guys searching a circular area of only 700 square feet, you would assume no human could escape detection. After about five minutes of fruitless searching our GI instructor called out for Matumba to give us a hint. Immediately there was a soft "hoot" from an area behind us, to which we all proceeded immediately. When once again we could not spot him, the instructor told him to give another hint, which produced the same "hoot", this time from a clump of bushes immediately before us. As we folded back it branches, we could finally see the white eyes and teeth of Matumba grinning up at us. We were told again that on the final night in the field all of us would be given a chance to hide from Matumba and his buddies, with the added latitude of hiding anywhere on the Philippine Islands vs. the 10 yard radius afforded Matumba.

Following this our instructor announced Matumba and his buddies would prepare our evening meal, using only food stuffs gathered within the now totally familiar 10-yard radius of our location. On cue, the grinning Matumba whipped out a long machete and began to harvest the materials for the meal he would prepare. In less than a half hour he had assembled a pile of food stuffs which he had hacked out of vines and trees, and built a cooking fire without use of matches. To create pressure cookers for the wild rice he had gathered, he chopped up some sections of bamboo which he filled with fresh water he had drained from certain plants, poured in the rice, plugged the ends, and suspended them over the cooking fire. He was equally adept at preparation of several other kinds of meat-like foods which he had extracted from the various trees and plants. In no time he served the entire group a full, five-course meal on plant-leaf plates resembling big elephant-ears. After a delicious desert and tea we were not only amazed, but very pleasantly stuffed.

As darkness fell we all retired to our individual tents which were not grouped or adjacent to each other, but erected at separate locations near the base camp. I got into my tent just as the last rays of light seeped through the triple-canopy jungle and after tying up the tent's entry flap, fell almost immediately asleep. Something woke me several hours later and I noted the luminous dial of my Rolex indicated it was just past 2:00 AM. Very quickly I became painfully aware of heavy breathing and movement within the leaves and underbrush just outside my tent. Images of a prowling tiger came immediately to mind and I didn't move a muscle until several minutes later when all was quite once more.

I carefully undid the tent flap to peek out and was totally unprepared for the sight I saw. There was no tiger or other dangerous animal, but the floor of the jungle looked like a scene from a night-vision scope, as it was littered with what appeared to be small, glowing rocks casting an eerie, green color. Reaching out, I recovered one of the glowing objects which turned out to be a chunk of tree bark. I later learned this bark was typically laced with phosphates that glowed in the dark. I never found for certain the source of the animal sounds that woke me, but the best speculation suggested a pack of stray dogs forging for food.

As advertised, the final of the school consisted of a "hide and seek" exercise in which the (hiding) students were given a two-hour head start on the (seeking) Negrito instructors, with the latitude that we could hide in any location of our choice. As an added incentive for our capture, we were all issued a special chit to be surrendered to any Negrito that located us. In return the Negritos could exchange the chit for a bag of rice. Having seen the Negritos work, I figured there would be very few of us who could manage to evade capture before morning, when the exercise was scheduled to end. I theorized my best chance lay in getting as far away as I could from the point of origin in the two hour grace period, before concealing myself totally out of sight and well off any beaten paths.

So late in the afternoon of the final day when the signal was given to start the exercise, I took off just as I had planned and after a couple of hours had made my way deep into the jungle before darkness began to fall. Finding what I thought would be a perfect hiding spot, I crawled under one of the zillion fallen trees littering the jungle floor, making certain I did not leave tell-tale tracks or other clues in the process. I figured even if a pursuing Negrito could travel at twice the speed it took me to get to my destination, and if he knew precisely where to look for me, it would be at least two hours before he was even in my vicinity. Boy was I wrong!

Shortly after the sun had disappeared and it was so dark I could not see my hand before my face, I heard rapidly approaching footsteps and saw the beam of a flashlight headed directly toward me. Only moments later I was looking at the smiling face and extended open hand of my captor as he collected my chit.

We had been briefed that in the event of our capture, we should all rendezvous at a pre-designated location, build a fire, cook a meal, and wait for pickup the next morning. I was heartened to see a roaring fire as I approached the base camp and realized more than half of my fellow students had fallen to the same fate as me. As the rest of the class trickled in, everyone's story was basically the same, with the similar end result of pursuing Negritos having come directly to their well-chosen hiding places as if they had rotating beacons atop. It turns out that because of our diet and culture, we emit a unique smell that is easily detected by the native Negrito. They could literally smell us, so unless we had been armed with some sort of "Star Wars type cloaking device", we didn't have a chance to hold onto that rice-bag chit. This concluded our survival training and the next day I departed Clark Air Base aboard a C-130B for my home of the next twelve months, Ubon RTAFB, Thailand, where I prayed I would not have to use the survival skill I had recently acquired.

The Great Dietz

- 1970 -

Prologue

I was, and still am a fair racquetball player. It's a great sport for almost anyone because unlike tennis, you don't have to be very good to enjoy yourself. The geometry of the court provides an "automatic ball return machine", the weather doesn't matter, and if you try at all you'll get a great aerobic workout. Additionally the sport is "open-ended" to the extent the better you get, the more difficult the competition, and in the end, only practice, stamina, and hand-eye reflex will propel you into the upper brackets of tournament play.

Most racquetball players of my age started as handball players. I was playing handball at the University of Texas in the early 1950's when the first "racquet-ballers" showed up at Gregory Gym and began to bat the ball around using sawed off tennis racquets with friction-taped handles. I can't remember whether or not they were playing with the ball we use today or the harder and livelier handball. At any rate we handball players looked down our noses at them and generally considered their game a "sissy sport" for girls.

Today handball players are becoming increasingly rare. I don't know why so many of them switched to racquetball, but for me the decision was easy because it was based on pain. If you are a decent handball player and can hit the ball hard, your hands become "tough as a boot" with regular play. However if you don't play often (because you aren't a college boy anymore and actually have a real job), when you hit the ball hard you will put very painful "stone bruises" on your hands. Hence in 1966 I traded my handball gloves for a racquet and have never even thought of switching back.

This is a story about how racquetball led to my first encounter at Ubon RTAFB, Thailand with Larry Dietzen, an extraordinary officer and athlete, and the all too brief friendship which followed.

Story

As a captain in 1968 I was assigned to the flight test section at Williams AFB, Arizona ("Willy"), where myself and three other pilots flew "functional flight tests" on the T-37s, T-38s and F-5s assigned to the base. Our mission was to "test hop" the aircraft after they had come out of a periodic inspection, or had undergone some major maintenance procedure such as an engine change, flight control rig, etc. It was a darn good job since the functional flight test profile typically took only twenty-five minutes to complete, leaving another one-half hour to prowl around in the designated flight test area over the Superstition Mountains east of Phoenix, where numerous ad hoc "dog fights" occurred. In a typical week I would get approximately 15-20 such sorties. It was in this capacity I learned more about the practical application of basic fighter maneuvering (*BFM*) than any of the other formal courses I ever attended. This was because I regularly flew with and against two really great and crusty old fighter pilots, Major Gene Smith and Captain Bill "Moose" Moseley. Both of them had truly "been there, done that", and collectively they taught me well.

While stationed at Williams in the fall of 1968 I was playing in the finals of one of the base's noontime racquetball leagues, when I got nailed at the beginning of the second game by a very well hit ball which struck me on the left side of my neck, just below the base of my skull. It "rang my bell" a little, but I didn't think too much about it as one gets hit quite a bit in the sport. Although I had handily won the first game, I narrowly lost the second, and was totally "blown out" in the third. I was disgusted with myself for letting the championship slip away as I knew I should easily have beaten my opponent.

After showering I went back to work where I was scheduled to fly an F-5A on a routine test-hop. While waiting to take the runway for departure on Runway 30L, I found myself with the disquieting feeling that something just wasn't right. As I looked at the instrument panel, I covered my right eye and everything looked fine. However when I moved my hand over to cover my left eye, to my horror I realized the right half of the vision in my right eye was totally gone. I blinked, rubbed, and repeated the procedure several times with identical results before aborting and taxiing back to the ramp. I didn't know what was wrong but suspected it had something to do with the 100+ mile per hour racquetball hit to the back of my head.

Of one thing, I was certain. If I mentioned my present condition to anyone, let alone a flight surgeon, my military flying career would come to an instant conclusion. So I simply went back to the little flight test shack, lay down on a couch and closed my eyes in hopes all of this would go away. When anyone asked what I was doing, I simply said I wasn't feeling well…probably something I ate, and they paid little further attention to me. Periodically throughout the rest of the afternoon when I would open my eyes to look around, my right eye seemed to be looking through water in a swimming pool. At other times, the right hemisphere was simply black. I went home at 1700, had a stiff drink, ate supper, said a prayer and went to bed.

When I woke the next morning I realized two things. I still couldn't see correctly, and a sharp pain ran from my neck up to the vicinity of my right eye. Throughout the day the pain continued while the vision in my right eye alternated between "the swimming pool and black-hole effects." For the next nine months, no amount of aspirin, Ben Gay, or massaging would alleviate the pain, and my last thoughts before falling asleep each night and my first thoughts the following morning focused on the throbbing on the right side of my head. I was literally worried sick.

I never confided this to anyone except my wife and continued to fly my share of the flight test sorties on a daily basis. I apparently still had enough vision in my right eye to provide the required depth perception everyone seems to think is so vital for a pilot, as my flying proficiency seemed unaffected. What was affected however was my disposition and attitude. As the months dragged by I became increasingly irritable, got into some unnecessary bar fights, drank too much, and was rapidly becoming a royal "pain in the ass."

Fortunately I was rescued from this "slippery slope" by my best friend of many years. One day after work I was standing in the kitchen pontificating about some inane subject I no longer remember, while Solvejg was cooking dinner. Right out of the blue she interrupted me and said, "Now listen Phil, this trouble with your eye has gone on too long. You are becoming a bear to live with, you're no fun, and you're going to see a doctor right now, and that's all there is to it." I immediately launched into my rationale that "letting the cat out of the bag" by talking with any doctor would scuttle my career, when she cut me off saying, "Nonsense, we're going to see a civilian doctor in Phoenix. I don't care what it costs. He's not going to tell anyone. Don't argue, because I've already made an appointment and we're going, period." If I'd learned anything over the past nine years of living with this gorgeous, 110 pound gal, it was that she was twice as tough as I was, invariably right, and when her mind was made up, it was time for me to shut-up. I did.

After explaining the situation to the neurosurgeon in Phoenix, stressing the utter importance of confidentiality, which I sensed he found rather sophomoric and silly, he examined me and reported, "There is really nothing mysterious about what has happened here. Since you are an engineer and a pilot, think of it this way. There are two wire-bundles that run up your spine. The left bundle controls the motor reflexes on the right half of your face, and the right one controls the other. When the ball hit the base of your skull, it had enough energy to throw the nerve endings in the left side bundle into trauma, putting some little lesions on them and impairing the vision to your right eye. The muscles around the spot where you were hit are still 'as tight as a fiddle string' and you aren't getting the blood circulation required to allow them to repair themselves. I'm going to give you a shot to relax those muscles right now and a prescription for some smooth muscle relaxer pills to get some blood circulation where it is needed. What you need to do is go home and quit worrying about this because it isn't a big deal. You are going to be just fine."

Upon hearing this I felt as if a 200 pound weight had been removed from my shoulders. He gave me the shot and sent me on my way. He did however ask just before I left, "You don't still play that silly game do you?" I told him of course I did, to which he replied, "Well don't get hit there again because the next time it just might be a big deal." We went home and I got the best night's sleep I'd had for almost a year.

The next morning, I only had a slight headache and the frequencies of the "swimming pool and black hole" effects were markedly decreased. To my delight this trend continued and I was soon enjoying normal vision with no headaches at all. Since I now regarded this brilliant Phoenix doctor as a genius, I decided I damn well better heed his final advice about not getting hit on the same spot again. Having zero desire to give up racquetball, the obvious solution seemed to be some form of protection against ball strikes, and "voila", there it was, hanging in plain sight from the handlebars of my trusty Vespa, motor scooter which daily transported me back and forth along the flight line.

The test pilots were the only ones at "Willy" allowed to ride these little scooters because some enterprising soul that preceded us had successfully argued that since test pilots flew so many sorties in a single day, they couldn't afford the delays encountered when riding the regular flight- line trolley. This of course was pure BS as the normal trolley would have sufficed, but "why should we look a gift horse in the mouth?" I don't know how old these scooters were, but they had been around for a very long time and been passed from pilot to pilot over the years. I paid the guy I replaced fifty bucks for the one I was riding. It ran terribly and I had to tinker with it constantly to keep it going.

It had come with a helmet which must have been the original prototype used by Barney Oldfield at the turn of the century. It looked like a truncated egg with black, leather ear flaps, but it satisfied the Air Police requirement for head protection while riding a motorized bike. I had spray painted it an international orange color rendering it even more obnoxious. However since it seemed to be the obvious solution to the "don't get hit there again" mandate, I began to wear it every time I played racquetball.

By early spring of 1970 I had checked out in the F-4C at Davis Monthan AFB, Arizona, preceded to the global survival school at Fairchild AFB, Washington, followed by the water survival school at Homestead AFB, Florida, and finally the jungle survival school at Clark AFB in the Philippines.

My end assignment was to be an F-4D flight commander in the 25th Tactical Fighter Squadron at Ubon RTAFB, Thailand. I arrived at Ubon aboard a C-130 "Clong"[19] from Tan Son Nhut late on Monday morning, 13 April 1970. The squadron duty NCO picked me up in the squadron van and we drove directly to the squadron building to sign in. I left my duffle bag and B-4 bag in the van and walked inside where the squadron "duty hogan"[20] was going about his business, and a tall major with dark, curly hair was leaning against the duty counter sternly eyeing me. "Are you Handley?" he said in a loud voice. "Yeah, I'm Major Handley" I replied. "You were the base racquetball champion at Williams and Davis Monthan weren't you?" "I won my share" I replied. "Do you have your racquet with you?" "Yes" I said, to which he replied, "I can beat you twenty-one, zip.[21] Be at the gym at 1300." With that, he turned on his heel and walked out of the room.

This definitely was not the welcome I had anticipated and I asked the duty hogan, "Who is that ass-hole?" "That's The Great Dietz" he replied in an almost nonchalant manner. "And who the hell is The Great Dietz?" I asked. "Well" he replied, "Larry Dietzen is a squadron WSO[22] who flys mostly with the squadron

---

[19] The actual name for the C-130 was of course Hercules, but everyone in the war zone called it "The Clong," which meant river in Thailand. I suppose the rationale was that since the river moved things, so did the C-130. At any rate, the name stuck throughout the war.

[20] The squadron duty officer was typically called the "duty hogan" or "duty rube" His basic responsibility was to answer the phones and post a back-lighted plexiglas scheduling board which was used in every squadron with a flying operation.

[21] Originally, racquetball was played to 21 points vs. the 15 points currently used.

[22] WSO is an acronym standing for Weapon Systems Officer. These officers in the F-4 were also called "backseaters," and "GIB's", another acronym standing for Guy In Back.

commander. He was also an All-American football player and coached at the Air Force Academy. He's the current Air Force racquetball champion, and before he arrived here on this tour, he played in some big national tournament beating every pro there." That sounded pretty impressive to me but in my best "don't act intimidated manner" I said, "Huh! Nobody can beat me twenty-one, zip. Where do I sign in?"

After getting my gear into my room at the D-Flight wing of the barracks, I pulled out my trusty gym bag and made my way to the base gym where I found Dietz already in the court warming up. Although he had looked impressive enough earlier in his "green bag" flight suit, seeing him in a tank-top and shorts, I did a double-take. He was all of six foot, two inches, weighed 210 pounds without an ounce of fat, and resembled a Greek God. Hell, his muscles had muscles! Additionally, as I watched him warm up it became obvious he was, beyond a doubt, the most coordinated and graceful big man I had ever seen on a court.

For the first time it painfully dawned upon me this guy probably could beat me twenty-one, zip. We exchanged few words as we finished our little warm-up routine and "lagged for the serve." He won and moved to the service box to start the game. "Just a minute" I said, as I opened the little entrance door to the court and reached into my gym bag for my orange helmet. Seeing this as he stood in the service box bouncing the ball, Dietz remarked with a baffled look on his face, "What in hell is that?" "Never mind what it is." I snapped back, "Just serve the damn ball."

Like most of the great players, Dietz normally served a high lob which skirted along the left wall to a right-hander's backhand, then dropped almost dead into the back left corner of the court where it was impossible to do anything with it other than "dig it out" with a defensive return. He was however also capable of hitting the ball in excess of 125 miles-per-hour, even with the old "steam-powered" wooden racquets we were using. I suppose he thought he would further intimidate me with a drive serve and uncorked one to the left corner. In one of the rare shots he missed, it came around and set up low and perfect off the back wall for a forehand drive, which I took. I hit that first ball Dietz ever served to me as hard as I was capable of hitting a forehand, which, totally by chance, hit Dietz squarely in the back of the head as though shot from a rifle.

Fortunately, it struck high enough on his head it did no damage other than "ringing his bell." He didn't go down, but did stumble forward holding the spot where the ball had hit with his left hand. As he turned around he had the incredulous look of a man who simply could not believe what he was seeing. There stood a guy in the back of the court wearing this ridiculous looking motorcycle helmet, who on the very first shot of the game had nearly taken his head off with the ball. I don't know whether I was more worried about the possible physical injury the shot could have caused or the daunting possibility Dietz might simply kill me, but I rushed forward to see if he was OK. After apologizing and offering an explanation as to why I wore that preposterous helmet, we continued with three games in which he systematically "took me apart." With the luck of "crack shots" I managed to score two points in the first game and one point in the second. In the third game, Dietz beat me twenty-one, zip.

It didn't take long to realize the little "welcome to Ubon" act Dietz had pulled on my arrival was just that, and vintage Dietz. It was no coincidence he was the squadron commander's choice as a WSO, as he was quite competent in the back seat of an F-4. Off duty, he was a hell of a lot of fun to be around, and a man you would like to have watching your back on a "dark and dreary night." It was totally appropriate he was known as "The Great Dietz" for he clearly seemed to be the reincarnation of F. Scott Fitzgerald's fictional character of the 1920's, "The Great Gatsby." We played quite a bit of racquetball during the next few months, which was much more instructive and fun for me than Dietz. I was less than half way through my one year tour when his came to an end and he was reassigned to the 33rd Tactical Fighter Wing at Eglin AFB, Florida. As luck would have it, I was also assigned to the 33rd Wing later in April of 1971.

However, not too long after Dietz had rotated back to Eglin, we learned through the command post that bad fortune had befallen him during his annual flight physical. Lumps in his armpits proved to be malignant. Cancer in his lymph glands had apparently spread throughout his entire body, and he was flown to Wilford Hall Medical Center in San Antonio, Texas for immediate surgery and treatment. This news hit all of us hard, but there was consensus among all who knew him that if anyone could beat the grim reaper, it would certainly be Dietz. Subsequently we learned that the surgery entailed dozens of small incisions over the extremities of his body. We were also told the day following his surgery, everyone at the hospital was astounded to find Dietz in the hospital parking lot playing volleyball with some of the hospital staff. Those of us at Ubon who knew him well were not at all surprised, and many a glass at the officer's club bar was raised in toast to his health.

Despite his indomitable attitude and the superlative efforts of the Air Force's best at Wilford Hall, he had to go back for another round of surgery. Since he had naturally been removed from flying status following the original diagnosis, he performed "additional duties" at the discretion of the wing commander. So upon his return to Eglin after the second round of surgery, he talked the commander into letting him take on the responsibility of coaching the Air Force women's volley-ball team. As one might expect, he led them to the inter-service championship in the ensuing months.

It had been about seven months since I had last seen Dietz when I reported to Eglin in late April of 1971. Shortly thereafter while checking out the base gym I heard the same loud voice which had greeted me a year earlier at the duty desk of the 25th Squadron at Ubon, shouting across the length of the gym, "Handley! Court One!" I turned to look and there he stood. I couldn't believe how much weight he had lost, or the number of scars he had all over his once flawless body.

Nevertheless he retained that same cocky smile and his handshake was as firm as ever. "Get your butt dressed", he said, "I'll be waiting for you in the court." As I put on my gear in the locker room I pondered how I should play this. Would it cause great pain if I accidentally hit one of those cuts with a ball? Would he have no strength or energy to play aggressively? Should I hold back or do my best to take him out? I knew Dietz would feel insulted if he perceived that I wasn't going all out, so I decided right then and there I would hold nothing back. What a joke! He easily crushed me 21-6.

In the ensuing months at Eglin, he continued to act as the wing commander's special assistant and was a frequent visitor at the 58th Fighter Squadron where I was one of the four flight commanders. He didn't seem to be getting any better, but on the other hand he didn't seem to be getting any worse either. Throughout it all he never uttered a single word of complaint and consistently made everyone who came in contact with him feel better. In April of 1972 the North Vietnamese launched a major offensive against the South and our squadron, along with many others throughout the States, was quickly deployed in response. The 58th Squadron was deployed to Udorn RTAFB, Thailand under the operational control of the 432nd Tactical Reconnaissance Wing, where the 555th and 13th Tactical Fighter Squadrons were already permanently assigned. Our mission was to be that of air superiority.[23]

We had not been in place for more than a few months when the Eglin command post duty officer passed a message to our squadron through the Udorn message center. Larry Dietzen was gone. It seems no one had detected any change in him whatsoever. Anytime he was asked how he was doing he would unfailingly reply

---

[23] Air Superiority is one of the primary roles of aerospace power and includes all missions whose objectives are designed to gain and maintain control of the air. In a nutshell, this meant that we would be flying air-to-air MiG CAP in North Vietnam.

he was doing "just great." However, on the previous Saturday evening, Dietz had taken his wife and kids out to dinner at one of the fine seafood restaurants in Ft. Walton Beach area. After returning to their quarters on the base about 2100, he apparently helped put the kids to bed, gave them a kiss, and told his wife he was not feeling well and was going to run over to the hospital for a little while. Giving her a big hug and kiss, he assured her he would be along shortly and she should go to bed.

Quite by chance one of the guys from the squadron who had not deployed to Udorn was walking down the hall of the hospital when he encountered Dietz sitting in a chair in the hall outside the emergency room, waiting his turn. When he asked him, "How's it going Dietz?" he didn't get the response everyone was so accustomed to hearing. Dietz apparently said, "Not worth a shit babe." The squadron guy told him he hoped he would be feeling better soon and went on his way, but this time it simply was not to be. The command post message stated Major Larry Dietzen had passed away quietly, shortly after his admission to hospital that evening.

There was not a dry eye among the deployed members of the 58th Tactical Fighter Squadron on that beautiful spring day in 1972 at Udorn RTAFB, Thailand. But then, they didn't call him "The Great Dietz" for nothing.

"Hoppy the Pilot"

- 1970 -

Prologue

In 1970 I was the D-Flight Commander of the 25th Tactical Fighter Squadron in the 8th Tactical Fighter Wing (The Wolf Pack), stationed at Ubon RTAFB, Thailand. In addition to the wing's four F-4D equipped fighter squadrons, a squadron of C-130A "Spectre" Gunships was also stationed at Ubon. In the annals of USAF procurement, one shining success has to be the acquisition of the Lockheed C-130 Hercules which was first fielded in 1954. Today, many variants and upgrades later, it is still being produced, and in addition to those flown by American military forces, they are also a mainstay in the air forces of 24 other nations. It will almost certainly exceed the service record of the famous C-47 "Gooney Bird", which first appeared in 1934 and was dubbed "The Douglas Racer" when it established the coast-to-coast intercontinental speed record.

This is a story about the remarkable modification of the Hercules which transformed it into one of the most deadly airborne killing machines ever to operate in a combat environment. In particular, it focuses on the "behind the scenes" story of the upgrade of the Spectre's main gun from twin 40mm cannons to the 105 mm howitzer which has been in constant use since early 1972.

The story was personally related to me by a Spectre pilot whom I escorted on numerous night missions during my first tour at Ubon. It was during that period on 14 January 1971, he was the aircraft commander of Spectre 04, an AC-130A which destroyed 58 trucks and damaged 7 more on a three hour mission, setting a record that still stands today. I was his escort that night, flying F-4D 67-797 (call sign Killer 01). Subsequently he was the first pilot to fire the 105mm howitzer from the AC-130, which is the basis of this story. Above all, he was an unabashed showoff and a totally unforgettable character that flew the C-130 as well as any pilot who ever laid hands on its controls. Proud to call him my friend, he was Francis D. Riopel, the infamous "Hoppy the Pilot."

Story

Throughout the Vietnam War, the Ho Chi Minh Trail was an intricate network of roads, trails, passes, fords, and tunnels providing the conduit through which thousands of tons of supplies, transported by human foot and truck convey, daily made their way south from North Vietnam. Predictably, considerable efforts were expended by the tactical fighter units stationed in South Vietnam, Thailand, and afloat on carriers in The Gulf of Tonkin to

(Russ Everts)

Figure 15—Ban Phan Nop choke point on the Ho Chi Minh Trail with numerous bomb craters visible

interdict these supply routes, especially those in Laos. Although many of the "choke points" of these roads and trails in mountain passes appeared to be an "interdictor's dream", daily destruction of them by iron bombs did little to stem the flow of war supplies through this vital logistics pipeline. Almost before the echoes of departing jet engines faded following a successful "road cut" sortie, hundreds of shovel, pick and hoe wielding North Vietnamese troops, augmented by earth moving equipment would literally swarm over the bomb cratered area to repair it more quickly than could be imagined. Often, as documented by post-strike, reconnaissance aircraft, truck traffic would once again be leaving fresh tire tracks in the hastily repaired area even before the interdicting fighters had recovered at their home base.

Interdicting the Ho Chi Minh Trail was of course a 24-hour operation, with fighters and bombers dumping tons upon tons of iron bombs. During daylight hours, the trucks making their way south on the trail were far too vulnerable to visual attack, and were therefore normally concealed until darkness fell. Consequently, most of the interdiction effort during daylight hours consisted of road cuts at key choke points, and the destruction of hidden AAA (anti-air-

(USAF File Photograph)

Figure 16—O-2 Skymaster

craft artillery) gun emplacements by fighter aircraft. These targets were sought out, identified, and marked with "willie pete" (white phosphorous) rockets by both fast and slow FAC (Forward Air Controller) aircraft, for the multiple flights of bomb laden Air Force, Navy, and Marine fighters which daily attacked the targets.

At the outset of the war the vast majority of FACs were of the "slow moving" variety, flying propeller driven aircraft such as the O-1 Birddog and the O-2 Skymaster. The professionals who flew these aircraft held a specific AFSC that indicated the specialized training they had received. Flying low and slow, they performed magnificently. As the war progressed, many of their units converted to the larger and faster OV-10 Bronco. However at the same time, the enemy air defenses on the Ho Chi Minh trail

(USAF File Photograph)
Figure 17—OV-10 Bronco

increased dramatically and an environment was created in which their low performance aircraft faced almost insurmountable odds for survival. In an operation nicknamed "Combat Sabre" a select group of F-100 pilots, flying the F-100F Super Sabre out of Phu Cat Air Base, South Vietnam and using the call sign "Misty", became the first "Fast FACs" of the war. Unlike their counterparts in the "slow movers", they had received no specialized FAC training and pretty much relied upon their extensive experience in armed reconnaissance to develop the specialized tactics which allowed them operate in the most hostile air defense environment ever seen. To their

(USAF File Photograph)
Figure 18—F-100F as used by the Misty FACs operating from Phu Cat Air Base, South Vietnam

credit the program which they developed was highly successful and quickly led to the establishment of the F-4 Fast FAC mission, which was eventually incorporated at all of the major F-4 wings throughout Southeast Asia. There were Wolf FACs from Ubon...Tiger FACs from Korat...Stormy FACs from DaNang...Laredo

FACs from Udorn. By no means did the Fast FAC program supplant or over-shadow their slow moving counterparts who continued to control the vast major-ity of fighter missions in the theater. Call signs such as "Raven", "Covey", "Nail", and dozens of others will forever be "fresh in recall" of all who operated under their control. Both the fast and slow FACs proved to be absolutely invaluable assets to the tactical employment of fighters, as well as providing critical command and control functions in both normal and SAR (Search and Rescue) operations.

As night fell, hundreds of North Vietnamese supply-laden trucks would emerge from their concealment to continue a perilous journey southward under the pro-tection of thousands of AAA (anti-aircraft artillery) guns in the concealed emplacements lining the trail. This is when the show really began, and was the environment in which the AC-130 Spectre earned its enviable reputation.

The idea of using the C-130 as a gunship platform was a logical extension of the earlier aircraft platforms successfully used in the Vietnam War. First, there was the AC-47 nicknamed "Puff the Magic Dragon", employing several 6-barrell, 7.62mm gatling guns which proved quite effective against troops in the open in relatively low-threat areas. Next came the AC-119 Stinger which upgraded the 7.62mm gatling guns to 20mm, thereby providing additional hitting power capable of destroying trucks and light armored vehicles. Although both of these forerunners to the Spectre did yeoman work, they were limited in their application because of the absence of sophisticated targeting sensors and a computerized fire control system.

The AC-130 Spectre addressed both of these shortfalls with the addition of mul-tiple target acquisition devices and a state-of-the-art, computer-based, fire-con-trol system producing spectacular accuracy as compared to the previous manually-aimed shots. Predictably, evolution of the AC-130's weaponry steadily progressed to larger and more lethal, large-bore guns.

This realization of increased firepower for the highly successful AC-130 was cham-pioned by the "brain trust" scientists and engineers from DARPA (Defense Advanced Research Projects Agency) and Wright Patterson AFB, Ohio. In early 1972, an R&D (Research and Development) team from these organiza-tions appeared at Hurlburt Field in Florida to test their latest theory. As told to me by "Hop" Riopel in his unmistakable Boston accent, here's what happened:

(Ken Shanke)

Figure 19—AC-130A Spectre on ramp at Ubon RTAFB, Thailand

"The R&D guys who arrived at Hurlburt Field were what you would probably expect, a bunch of civilians and non-rated officers, somewhat naïve concerning flying operations, but brilliant in their specific areas of expertise. These guys were hired to "push the envelope", which in this case was to make the AC-130 as lethal as possible. Their theory was that if the 40mm projectiles were good, the 105mm projectile would be decidedly better, provided firing it from the left troop door of the AC-130 didn't blow the rear end off the airplane (a concern that was not lost on the crew that would first test the weapon). Armed with their slide rules and handheld computers, the R&D team members had seemingly worked out the smallest detail to the ninth-degree.

Numerous briefings were conducted by the R&D team outlining the merits of the 105mm cannon, which would be the M102, a modified version of the Army field artillery M1A1 howitzer. Additionally they provided theoretical data suggesting the employment of this considerably larger weapon would not overstress the airframe of the rugged Hercules. Despite these assurances, apprehension hung like a cloud over Hop's crew as they prepared to test fire the weapon for the first time. The initial test firing was to be a tightly-controlled affair.

Augmenting the normal crew would be several members of the R&D team including MSgt. Sanders, a senior NCO on loan from the United States Army Field Artillery Branch. Sergeant Sanders was reputed to possess unrivaled expertise on the employment of the 105mm howitzer. He was a big, black, "by the book" NCO (non commissioned officer) who spoke in declarative sentences that were typically prefixed and suffixed with the word, "Sir." Hoppy took an immediate liking to this no-nonsense soldier and deemed that MSgt. Sanders would be the member of the R&D team in the rear of the aircraft with whom he would speak on the aircraft's intercom as necessary.

On the day of the first scheduled test flight, Hoppy lifted the AC-130 from the runway at Hurlburt and proceeded directly to the range where the first shot from the door-mounted cannon would be fired. Swinging into a left-hand orbit at about 7,500 feet and completing all the required checklists, he could not help but feel apprehensive as he keyed the mike button of the intercom and told his gun crew in the back of the aircraft to "lock and load." After several seconds he heard the familiar voice of Sergeant Sanders on the intercom, "Sir." "Yes, Sergeant Sanders", he

(Mike Thompson)
Figure 20—Spectre's twin 20mm gatling guns each with 100 rounds per second rate of fire

replied. "Sir, this piece is designed to shoot up, not down." "Well, that's OK, but from this airplane we're going to shoot it pointing down", he replied. "Sir, when we loaded the round, it fell out. This won't work, Sir."

Incredibly, the finest minds of the R&D team, who had thought of every detail concerning the employment of this field artillery piece from an aircraft, had overlooked the obvious fact that unless the shell casing was "crimped", the force of gravity would allow it to slide out the front of the downward tilted barrel. So, the first 105mm shell exiting the left troop drop door of the AC-130 simply fell harmlessly to the ground, powered only be the laws of gravity. "Oh for God's sake, button that thing up and let's go home", Hoppy said.

Several days later, the R&D team had laid in a supply of freshly "crimped" 105mm shells and a second trial run was scheduled. Everything went precisely as it had on the first mission up to the point where the order was given to "lock and load" the main gun. This time the shell didn't simply fall out of the barrel, and after lining up the target with the aiming recital, Hoppy transmitted to all on the intercom, "Well, let's see if this damn thing is going to blow the tail off." With that, he depressed and held down the firing button on the control yoke and waited for the fire-control computer to achieve a targeting solution which would send a fire signal to the gun.

He didn't have long to wait as the aircraft reverberated with the loudest report he had ever heard from the rear of the aircraft. "My God!" he exclaimed as he keyed the intercom, "Is everyone OK back there?" Within seconds he heard a voice he immediately recognized. "Sir?" "Yes Sergeant Sanders, what the hell happened back there? Is everyone OK?" "Sir, in the field artillery that was what we call 'a boomer'." "What on earth does that mean?" Hoppy replied. "Sir, that happens when the powder in the shell explodes all at once instead of a steady burn. It is a one-in-a-million thing you probably won't ever hear again." "God, I would hope not, and we sure as hell aren't going to hear it again today!" he replied. "Secure that damn thing right now!"

After returning to Hurlburt, the R&D team huddled to consider why this "one-in-a-million" situation had occurred. After a few days of intense investigation and research during which they considered temperature inversions, rarified air, and a hundred other hypotheses, they concluded that this simply had to be a "Murphy's Law" occurrence. After a lot of effort, they finally succeeded in convincing a skeptical Hoppy Riopel that his crew should repeat the experiment. After reluctant agreement, the test bed AC-130 once again arrived in orbit around the range target and Hoppy depressed the firing button. BOOM was the immediate result as this "one-in-a-million" situation recurred for the second time in a row. "That's it, this is madness!" Hoppy bellowed. "We'll never fire that damn thing again!"

Now the R&D scientists and engineers were really up against it as they reexamined every possible theory as to why these explosions were occurring. Despite their best efforts, they simply could do no better that conclude once again there was absolutely no logical reason for these two occurrences, and it would probably never happen again. For days their arguments "fell on deaf ears" as concerned Hoppy and his crew. Finally they argued, since the veritable Hercules had already proven twice that although the report from the exploding powder train was disconcerting, it was not destructive to the flying qualities of the aircraft, and pleaded for one last try. Against his better judgment Hoppy reluctantly agreed they would give it one last shot, but stipulated in no uncertain terms if another "boomer" occurred, they could look elsewhere for another crew to conduct these "dumb-ass experiments."

So once again the AC-130 entered a left orbit around the range target in preparation for the third and final test firing. Hoppy braced himself for what he felt certain would occur when he depressed and held the firing button on the left yoke. To his surprise, what followed was not the explosion of the two previous trials, but a relatively mild report as the big gun fired, followed almost immediately by a large explosion at the center of the target as the 105mm projectile scored a direct hit. The second, third, fourth and fifth shots were identical, to the delight of the R&D team and every member of Hoppy's crew. Modifications were immediately begun on all AC-130 aircraft and the gun was first fired in combat on the evening of 1 March 1972.

As of this writing, I don't know if there have been any other "boomer" incidents in the AC-130, but as of the summer of 1980 when Hop told me this story, after thousands upon thousands of 105mm shells had been fired by AC-130s; there had never been another "boomer" incident. Try to imagine the unbelievable odds of this happening.

The accuracy of the 105mm gun in the AC-130 is simply stunning. Hop told me he and his crew would bet incoming students to Hurlburt "free martinis for the duration of their training course" that his crew could put the first round of 105mm inside a 55 gallon drum. They never lost.

Hoppy is gone now, but his reputation will live on within the C-130 community for years to come. You can validate this assertion by simply mentioning the name "Hoppy the Pilot" to the next old C-130 driver you run across, and then watch the smiles that inevitably appear. He was truly "one of a kind."

Hot Wings at Ubon Ratchathani

- 1971 -

I never believed in flying the base turn and final approach airspeeds as specified in the performance section of the Aircraft Dash-1, particularly under VFR flight conditions where the runway was clearly visible. I guess I was always one of those who "added a few knots for the wife and kids" as I had a deep and abiding conviction that excessive airspeed was easy to shed, while manufacturing energy in an aircraft operating under conditions of excessive drag or insufficient power could be infinitely more difficult. My contention was rooted in a belief that

(Author)

Figure 21—8th Tac Fighter Wing "Wolf Pack" F-4D on ramp at Ubon RTAFB, Thailand

the only time it was critically important that the aircraft be "on speed" in the landing pattern was as it crossed the runway overrun "in the groove." I had the opportunity to validate this belief during an emergency landing in the wee hours of the morning at Ubon RTAFB, Thailand in early 1971.

As my first combat tour in the 25th Tactical Fighter Squadron of the 8th Tactical Fighter Wing at Ubon RTAFB, Thailand was nearing completion, I had been flying strictly night combat missions for several months and had come to enjoy the duty very much. First of all, the environment was excellent, as it was relatively cool at night as compared to the hot and humid daylight hours. The officers club was not crowded when you returned from a mission and hit the bar, and you could finish your breakfast and head for your bunk by the time the day flyers were starting their day.

These night missions mainly entailed armed escort of the AC-130 Spectre Gunships which nightly roamed the Ho Chi Minh trails in the Steel Tiger and Barrel Roll combat sectors of Laos. These were typically long missions involving two to three air-refuelings between periods of time spent escorting the AC-130. As one escort F-4 would reach "bingo fuel" and depart for the tanker, a freshly refueled F-4 would immediately take its place, and the cycle would continue until the Spectre ran out of ammunition or targets and returned to Ubon.

After flying for extended periods at night, you reach a point where you don't seem to notice it is dark outside, and your dive bomb proficiency is at least that of daytime operation. Another huge benefit is you can see (and easily avoid) the aimed AAA directed at you by the NVA gunners along the trail, as they consistently used tracer ammunition to improve their aim. This produced an absolutely spectacular light show over hot areas on the trail such as Ban Tchepone as thousands of rounds of 23mm, 37mm, and 57mm would arch upward in a pattern resembling an inverted waterfall.

Evading AAA, which is visible, in a fast moving jet such as the F-4 is relatively easy under the right conditions. I don't know why the NVA gunners never fig-

(Russ Everts)

Figure 22—"Guns Valley" near "The Caves at Sam Neua." Located on the Laotian side of the border with North Vietnam in the Plain de Jars. At the time this picture was taken, there were eight AAA emplacements hidden within the valley, each containing four 37mm guns.

ured out that firing so much tracer ammunition was a really dumb idea, but I'm thankful they didn't. Not only did the tracers rounds, which ignited shortly after leaving the gun's barrel, instantly limit the gunner's night vision, but also allowed us to avoid being hit. At the same time, we could visually reverse the path of the tracers to their point of origin on the ground, then dive bomb the gun pit from which the fire emanated with fuse-extended 500 pound MK-82 iron bombs, CBU-24, or finned napalm canisters.[24] All of this worked in favor of the fighters because of our speed and maneuverability, as long as you didn't fly too close to the barrels of the AAA pieces.

---

[24] The MK-82 is a 500 lb. iron bomb. CBU-24 is a canister of munitions containing numerous 'baseball sized" sub-munitions that spread out in a circular pattern after the canister was blown open by an air burst fuse. Finned napalm, as opposed to un-finned napalm was contained in a canister with fins so that it could be dive-bombed into the target at high angles. In contrast un-finned napalm canisters had no fins and had to be delivered at low altitude and low or level release angles.

The greatest killer of tactical aircraft in a war zone is anti-aircraft artillery (AAA), not missiles or opposing fighters. Also, there is the almost magical altitude of 4,000 above ground level, below which your chances of being hit by AAA increase dramatically.[25] The lower you fly below 4,000 the greater your chances of being hit. Near the ground, there is an altitude zone know as "the area of real-time tracking" where being hit is almost a certainty at any speed.

To visualize this, picture yourself standing on the 50 yard line of a football field with your buddy standing on the goal line holding a high pressure fire hose trying to hit you with the water stream. You can easily avoid his stream by simply moving around and exploiting the period of time required for the water coming from the nozzle to travel the 50 yards to your location. Now imagine what would happen if you moved in to the 15 yard line. Your friend with the hose could simply slew his stream of water onto you even if you were faster than Deon Sanders. The bullet stream from Quad ZSU-23, a Russian made 4-barreled 23mm AAA weapon literally looks like a fire hose when it shoots, and even the most inept gunner can slew that stream of 23mm bullets onto a closely approaching fighter, provided he has enough time to react.

While speed and maneuverability of the F-4 in this AAA environment made it difficult to hit, the same could not be said of the lumbering AC-130 which was cranking along about 7,500 feet above the ground at all of 140 knots. This represented a truly lucrative target for the AAA gunners who made it the object of their affections at least 75% of the time, with the remaining 25% of their shots taken at the dive-bombing escorts at the bottom of a dive bomb pass when their altitude was at the lowest point. So the main purpose of the F-4 escorts was to intimidate the gunners by immediately dropping ordnance on their heads after they fired at the Spectre and disclosed their location. This didn't entirely work and the AC-130 spent a lot of time dodging the AAA that came its way. Naturally, the favorite location from which to fire at the gunship was from its rear hemisphere after its orbit had passed the gun pit.

To effectively spot the approaching AAA and relay appropriate information to the pilot, the Spectre flew with two scanners in the aft of the aircraft. One, called the

---

[25] F-4 Fast FACs such as Wolf FACs from Ubon, Stormy FACs from DaNang, Tiger FACs from Korat, Laredo FACs from Udorn routinely operated squarely within the heart of the AAA envelop, suffering loss rates averaging approximately 25%. The original Misty FACs, flying the single-engine F-100F experienced a loss rate of 34%.

"right scanner", a gunner, was positioned on the right side of the aircraft and looked out of a small window to spot AAA above and to the right of the aircraft from the 1 o-clock to 6 o-clock positions. The other, called the "I.O." (illuminator operator), tethered by a harness and cable hung over the bottom half of the aircraft's open aft ramp to spot incoming AAA from all clock positions. When either scanner spotted upcoming AAA, they would alert the pilot to the type, location, and

(USAF File Photograph)
Figure 23—Spectre I.O. scanner in observation position on the AC-130's open, aft cargo ramp

accuracy of the threat. On some occasions, the evasive action taken by the Spectre pilot would actually dislodge the "I.O." spotter from the aft ramp, resulting in his flailing around in the slipstream behind the aircraft until his buddies hauled him back inside to continue his most stimulating job.

So on a moonless night in January of 1971, my GIB[26] and I conducted a preflight inspection at the revetment housing the F-4D which we would fly on our Spectre escort mission that evening. As usual, the bird was fully loaded and at maximum gross weight. Under its wings on the outboard pylons were two 370 gallon fuel tanks, while both of the triple ejector racks (TERs)[27] on the inboard armament pylons of each wing secured three 500 pound fuse-extended MK-82 bombs. On the centerline armament pylon hung a multiple ejector rack (MER)[28] with six CBU-24 canisters. The F-4's ability to carry such a bomb and

---

[26] GIB: Guy In Back

[27] TER: Triple Ejector Rack. A rack that hung on the under wing armament pylons and held three bombs or other munitions, such as CBU.

[28] MER: Multiple Ejector Rack. Same function as a TER except that it held six bombs and was typically found on the fuselage centerline.

fuel load of over eight tons is testimony to what a brute it really was, and why it was fondly nicknamed "The McDonnell Rhinoceros."[29]

It was approximately 0200 hours as I advanced both throttles of the General Electric J-79 engines into 4th stage afterburner and two 40-foot cones of fire shot from the fully open exhaust nozzles of the F-4 to begin the takeoff roll on Ubon's Runway 23. I had just come out of afterburner at 300 knots during my left turn after takeoff when the master caution light illuminated, accompanied by numerous intermittently flashing lights on the malfunction telelight panel, but with one of the small indicator lights glowing bright and steady. It was the BLC malfunction light.

---

[29] It has been said: "The F-4 represents a triumph of thrust over aerodynamics." Perhaps so, but its aerodynamics were certainly good enough to permit it to fly with significant portions of its horizontal stabilators missing. Since the horizontal tail surface of the F-4 is designed with 23 degree anhedral (droop), the outer foot or so of the tips on both sides are close enough to the exhaust nozzles to dictate that their composition be of heat resistant titanium. In 1971, while stationed at Eglin AFB, Florida, I had led a four ship air-to-air training mission. Apparently at some point in the mission, I passed through the jet wash of one of the other aircraft while pulling heavy Gs and both of the outer tips of the stabilators snapped off. I never noticed any perceptible change in the way the aircraft handled and after a normal overhead pattern and landing was taxing back to the parking ramp. My wingman, who was now taxing immediately behind me suddenly came up on the UHF ground control frequency and said in a whisper, "Tango One, this is Tango Two, come up squadron common." So naturally I whispered back, "roger", and switched over to the 58th TFS common frequency (as did every other human who happened to be listening to this bizarre exchange on Eglin ground control frequency). After checking my wingman in on squadron common, he exclaimed, "Lead, part of your tail is missing!" "What!" was my immediate reply (now in a loud voice), to which he explained that the outer ends of the stabilator on both sides appeared to be gone. Try as we may, neither Jack Smallwood, in the pit, nor I could twist around and look far enough aft to see for ourselves. So, thanks to our "secret radio communication technique", every supervisor with a UHF radio equipped truck was there to meet us as we parked. Sure enough, the outer tips had indeed snapped away perfectly clean, which made the bird look even funnier with the shortened tail. To preclude future occurrences, the tails of the entire F-4 fleet were modified with rectangular metal scab patches on both the upper and lower surfaces where the titanium tips join the aluminum portions of the stabilator. The next time you look at an F-4's tail, you'll clearly see them.

BLC, or Boundary Layer Control, is a system installed on the hard wing F-4 designed to smooth the flow of air over the wings at high angles-of-attack when the leading and trailing flaps are extended, and effectively lower the stall speed of the wing under those conditions. The air blown over the wing is extremely hot as it is ported from the high-pressure turbine sections of the General Electric J-79 engines through titanium plumbing to the leading edge of the wing where it is blown through special nozzles back across the wing's upper surface.

A dreaded situation occurs if for any reason this titanium plumbing breaks loose, allowing the super-heated, high-pressure air to enter the cavity of the wing, where it would quickly melt wiring, hydraulic lines, and eventually reach the fuel stored in the F-4's wet wing. Beyond the illumination of the BLC Warning Light on the tele-light panel, the emergency procedure section of the Dash-1 points out that this critical situation will most likely be accompanied by extraneous and intermittent illumination of other system lights as the hot air melts and shorts out the electrical wiring within the wing. The only corrective action available to the pilot is to reduce power, extend the flaps (to port at least some of the air over the wings instead of into the wing cavity), and get the bird on the ground as quickly as possible. This is truly "the emergency from hell." Under normal circumstances, I would have chosen to hit the Emergency Jettison button to immediately jettison all external stores, but my left turn out of traffic had placed me squarely over the city of Ubon, where the exploding ordnance and fuel tanks would have wreaked havoc.

Hitting the fuel dump selector valve as I declared an emergency on Ubon Tower frequency, I pulled the power to idle to slow to gear and flap speed as I began a hard 270 degree right-hand turn back toward the runway from which I departed less than one minute earlier. I intended to land downwind as quickly as possible. As the airspeed decreased rapidly through 250 knots, I extended the gear, followed immediately by extension of the flaps. Because of the aircraft's heavy weight and the drag of the gear and flaps, I had to immediately apply power to sustain airspeed, which I chose to hold at approximately 240 knots.

Everything appeared to be OK as I slid around the corner during the last 20 degrees of the turn to final when the flaps suddenly retracted as the BLC air apparently burned through some of the wiring to the flap selector valve, shorting it out, and sending a flap retract signal to the hydraulic actuator. As the flaps retracted, the F-4 transitioned suddenly from a fast angle-of-attack indication on the twin AOA indicators mounted at eye level on the forward canopy, to a flashing high AOA indication accompanied by a piercing 1000 HZ tone with shaking rudder pedals indicating an impending stall. Without hesitation I hit 4th stage afterburner on both engines to remedy the situation, then reduced the power as I rolled out of my bank on very short final approach and extended the arresting hook in preparation for engaging the approach end barrier on Runway 05.

Without flaps, the stalling speed of an F-4 at maximum gross weight is amazingly high, which translated to my crossing the threshold of the runway at near military power "on the pedal shaker" which indicated impending stall, at 195 knots. As I touched down I jerked the throttles to idle, deployed the drag chute, and waited for the familiar tug, then rapid deceleration resulting from the tail hook engaging the arresting cable. I felt absolutely nothing as the approach end barrier cable snapped like a thread under the kinetic energy momentum of the McDonnell Rhinoceros. I stood on the brake pedals, knowing it would do no good until the anti-skid sensors in the wheels sensed that the speed had decreased to the point where the tires would not skid, producing immediate blowouts.

As we crossed the M-21 barrier at mid-field I felt a slight tug as it also snapped, but shortly thereafter, began to feel the pulsating response of the brakes as the tires gained braking action. Thankfully, the aircraft's speed had decreased sufficiently to allow the departure end barrier to do its work, and we came to a stop before reaching the overrun. When I felt the deceleration, I stop-cocked both throttles as both the GIB and I raised our canopies to began an emergency egress. That process entailed the unlashing of ourselves from the leg harnesses, seatbelt, seat pan, and shoulder harnesses, hoisting ourselves over the left canopy rail, hanging, and finally dropping to the runway.

As we ran from the aircraft, the fire trucks were just catching up and the fire chief ran up to me to determine the nature of the emergency, as the F-4, now sitting silently on the runway showed no apparent ill-effects or damage. "Put some foam on it!" I shouted as he approached, "It could blow up!" Before he could react, one of the firemen had approached the aircraft and upon laying his hand on the left wing, howled with pain as his skin was seared away by the wing's hot surface. Foam was then applied in short order, and nothing further happened.

In my reflections of this incident, I am absolutely convinced had I not been flying at an airspeed far, far above that recommended by the Dash-1, the aircraft would have stalled and crashed in the base turn as the flaps retracted. To this day, except on check rides where some flight examiner is grading me on how well I can maintain airspeeds calculated by an engineer, I continue to give myself an airspeed margin, until arriving above the overrun, in the groove, and on speed.

The Big Easy Flyby

- 1972 -

Prologue

As the Vietnam War entered its eighth year in 1972, the "missing man formation" had become a familiar sight during the half-time activities of many nationally-televised football games. At the close of the National Football League (NFL) 1971 season, the Dallas Cowboys and Miami Dolphins emerged as the final teams left standing and were scheduled to meet in Super Bowl VI on Sunday, January 16, 1972 to determine the world championship. Since this thoroughly hyped event was to be played in New Orleans, Louisiana, the 33rd Tactical Fighter Wing at Eglin AFB, Florida was notified by 9th Air Force Headquarters that should a flyby be requested, the 33rd Wing's geographical proximity would dictate that they be chosen for the task. The request came, the 33rd Wing responded, and the 81,000 fans in attendance of Super Bowl VI applauded the flyby and called it inspirational. What they didn't know was that the real air show had already occurred approximately one minute before the Eglin based F-4Es loomed into view over the east rim of Tulane Stadium on that Sunday afternoon.

Story

In 1972 I had the good fortune to be the D-Flight commander of the 58th TFS stationed at Eglin AFB, Florida. Located on the Florida Panhandle's Gulf Coast, Eglin's sprawling complex was surrounded by some of the world's most beautiful, sugar-white, sand beaches on the shores of the Gulf of Mexico. The

58th TFS was the only fighter squadron assigned at the time to the 33rd Wing and was equipped with the hard wing F-4E.[30]

As I arrived at the squadron early in the morning of the first week of January, 1971, my squadron commander, Lt. Col. John Downey, a truly great fighter pilot and leader, told me there was to be a meeting that morning at the wing conference room which would include the CBS Sports Crew covering the upcoming Super Bowl. At the appointed time, Downey, myself, and several others from the squadron rose from our seats around the conference table as Colonel Dick Henry, the 33rd Tactical Fighter Wing Commander entered the room. He was accompanied by a gaggle of rather sloppily-dressed civilians introduced as the CBS advance team that would be choreographing the pre-game and half-time activities in New Orleans. From the instant the team leader began to speak, it was patently obvious to the rest of us in the room, that these folks were definitely of the "show biz" ilk with absolutely no native intelligence of military operations in general, or fighter operations in particular.

In his opening remarks, the CBS Team Chief obviously felt his mission was to impress upon the assembled military audience the overriding importance of the event, as he seemed to suffix every other declarative sentence with the words, "because this is the Super Bowl." After about twenty of these naïve observations we all had definitely "got it." He concluded his inspirational remarks by saying, "So you see gentlemen, another one of those missing man formations simply won't cut it. We need something that has not yet been done. Something unique.

---

[30] The difference between a "hard wing" and a "soft wing" F-4 was, the former had boundary layer control and no leading edge slats. In contrast, the "soft wing" variant had no boundary layer air blowing over its leading edge, but did sport leading edge slats that programmed automatically on angle-of-attack. The soft wing version was the last of the variants, came only on the F-4E, and was developed under a project named "Agile Eagle." The advantage of the soft wing was that it gave the aircraft a much better slow-speed turning capability, and, as an aside, also greatly attenuated the adverse yaw effect which was responsible for so many out-of-control conditions (OCC) in the hard wing models. The down side of the soft wing was it "bled energy" much faster than the hard wing variant, and once the slats were out, that energy was hard to regain. The smart play with a "soft wing" equipped F-4E was to manage your energy just as you would in a "hard wing" model, using its superior turn capability only when required to affect a kill or to escape being killed.

Something spectacular that will really impress the crowd, for after all, THIS IS THE SUPERBOWL!"

Sensing that he was on a roll after such an inspirational speech, the CBS team leader announced he had already come up with an obvious solution. Since the missing-man formations always seemed to be real "crowd pleasers", why not simply stay with a winner, but with a twist. Instead of using the typical fighter type airplanes, why not have a missing man formation with B-52s? His disappointment was obvious upon observing the reactions

(Author)

Figure 24—Four ship diamond formation of F-4E Phantoms

of those around the table, and probably hearing more than a few "you've got to be shitting me" remarks. Colonel Dick Henry was obviously embarrassed and shot a "cool it" look around the table as he stood in an attempt to give the guests a little help. He patiently explained to the CBS team, the B-52 idea wasn't really a starter since the 33rd Wing flew the F-4E Phantom II, with "nary a BUFF[31]" to be found anywhere on the flight line. Also, after delicately pointing out that up to this point in the Vietnam War, no B-52s had been lost, the CBS team leader seemed somewhat crestfallen as he asked for suggestions from the floor.

Following an embarrassing silence my squadron commander, John Downey said, "I think I might have something here. Why not use the F-111, you know, the big fighter bomber with wings that sweep back and forth?" Encouraged by this overt display of cooperation, every member of the CBS team listened with rapped attention as this seasoned combat veteran and squadron commander, with a

---

[31] Like many other military aircraft, the names with which they are officially christened are often replaced with nicknames, some flattering and some not-so-flattering, as selected by those who fly the machines. For instance the F-100 Super Sabre was call the "Hun"; the F-105 Thunderchief, the "Thud"; The F-111 Switchblade, the "Aardvark"; and the F-16 Fighting Falcon, the "Viper." The B-52 Stratofortress has for many, many years been nicknamed the "BUFF," an unflattering acronym that stands for "Big Ugly Fat Fucker."

totally straight face, led them in "right down the garden path" as the rest of us tried to imagine where the hell John was going with this.

"Visualize this, as the last strains of The National Anthem are played, the crowd suddenly becomes aware of a distant but ever- increasing hum, which becomes a deep rumble and finally a deafening roar just as the four F-111s in perfect "fingertip formation" appear over the rim of the stadium. Then, just as the formation reaches mid-field, the number 3 aircraft folds its wings and falls out of the sky." As the rest of us nearly fell out of our chairs with laughter, the CBS team looked totally crestfallen.

Finally, after it was firmly established that the 33rd Wing could do no better than fly the "plain ole' F-4E", it was deemed, by the CBS spokesman, if one missing man formation was good, two such side-by-side formations would be different, and perhaps better, with the number 3 aircraft from each of the 4-ship formations pulling up simultaneously in 4th stage afterburner at midfield. After all, this was THE SUPER BOWL!

Over the course of the next few weeks, the flyby plan was reviewed and approved by 9th Air Force Headquarters at Shaw AFB, North Carolina. A message arrived stating that 9th Air Force would be sending two fighter experienced liaison officers to assist with the planning and coordination of the event. When a subsequent message arrived naming the two liaison officers, John Downey shook his head, laughed and said, "This is like having the fox watch the chicken coop." One of the two colonels 9th Air Force had selected for this "tough duty in New Orleans" was the famous "Fire Can" Dan Walsh.

Lt. Col. Downey had apparently served with him in previous years and knew what to expect. Like most of the younger officers, I had heard stories about the exploits of "Firecan Dan", and from all indications, he was universally liked, a hell of a fighter pilot and a wild man to boot. At any rate, Firecan Dan and his sidekick were due to arrive at Eglin on the Friday morning before the scheduled Sunday afternoon event to review our plan and establish a fool-proof communications scheme.

At the appointed time on Friday, Firecan Dan and the other colonel, whom I remember as a good-natured, Irish looking fellow about "Firecan's" age, arrived for the coordination meeting. Our mission was simple: Make certain the eight-ship formation arrived over the rim of Tulane Stadium at the precise moment the last stanza of The Star Spangled Banner, being sung by the 81-voice Air Force Academy course, rang out. To achieve this we had determined the length of time from the first "Oh, say can you see" to "and the home of the brave", selected an initial point (IP) and holding pattern approximately three miles out along the run-in heading, and worked down to the second, the precise time we would need to depart the IP to arrive overhead at the right moment.

Our plan was to be in the holding pattern at least 20 minutes prior to the scheduled beginning of the Nation Anthem with established UHF radio communication between ourselves and our intrepid liaison officers in the booth. It was simply then a matter of one of them pushing the transmit button on his UHF radio and transmitting to us, "First Note National Anthem." At that time, regardless where we were in the holding pattern, we could either extend or shorten a timing leg to depart the IP at the precise second to nail the arrival. I can vividly recall John Downey remarking to our 9th Air Force keepers that we could handle almost any contingency while in the holding pattern, but once we departed the IP inbound we would be committed, and the last thing, at that point, we wanted to hear would be "Delay one minute!" We were assured nothing like that could possibly happen and Colonel Walsh and his buddy departed Eglin for a no-doubt, eventful Friday and Saturday evening on Bourbon Street in New Orleans.

There was a lot of competition for the sixteen slots (eight pilots and eight WSOs), with everyone particularly hoping to be one of the two number 3 aircraft pulling up and out of the formations. Since John Downey was the squadron command with decision authority, he decided he would be number 3 in the formation on the right, while I would have the similar position in the formation on the left. Between the two of us it was decided our simultaneous pull up would be initiated by his countdown as we approached the stadium. He would transmit, "Five, four, three, two, one. PULL." At that time, both of us would select full afterburner while making a smooth 4G pull up until reaching a vertical climb. We practiced this maneuver several times while enroute to one of the range complexes for routine practice gunnery and found it worked best if John simply executed the maneuver, and I flew a parallel formation from my position to his left. After several tries, we had it cold.

The Sunday morning of January 16, 1971 dawned cold and clear with an expected temperature of 29 degrees predicted for the 2:30 PM kickoff time. Since our flyby was a part of the opening ceremonies, with the National Anthem being the last event before the team's captains met at mid-field for the coin flip, we gave ourselves plenty of time to checkmate "Murphy's Law" contingencies. To ensure we had all eight birds, we had two spares with crews which started engines and took off with us until it was certain all of the primary eight jets were operating properly. Major "Dutch" Horace was leading the right-hand, four-ship formation, and as I recall, Captain Vick Andrews was leading the formation on the left.

Everything went like clockwork with us arriving at our holding point precisely on-time, without need for the two spares who raced back to Eglin to watch the game on TV.

Dutch Horace took all eight birds over to the booth liaison UHF frequency where Walsh immediately responded with a strong, clear signal. By now, all eight birds had descended to an altitude of about 1,000 feet above the ground and decreased our airspeed to 250 knots for the holding/timing portion of the mission. The WSOs in the lead jets of both formations had detailed data on precisely how and when to "turn in" from the holding leg of the pattern, descend to 500 feet above the ground, and accelerate to 350 knots indicated airspeed to nail the timing. The two four-ship formations were at this point in a loose route formation with the second four-ship following the lead formation around in a staggered-trail position from which it would be a simple matter to pull up line-abreast on the lead formation and tuck in all of the wingmen to a tight fingertip position once we departed the IP.

Everything seemed to be going absolutely perfectly up to this point and I was thinking to myself that this almost seemed too easy. Dutch had continued to communicate on the UHF radio with our liaison officer and we had good situation awareness of the events leading up to the beginning of the National Anthem. We were informed when the Apache Belles began their performance, followed by the Silent Drill Team from Washington, D.C., followed by a special presentation of a 29 by 40 foot American flag from the Fifth Army garrison at San Antonio...then at last Firecan's transmission, "Stand by." Then, "First Note of National Anthem." Dutch "rogered" the transmission as the eight ships closed it up and Vic maneuvered our four-ship formation closer to a line-abreast position. The two lead WSO's confirmed with each other the precise second we should turn back toward the IP. As that turn was made, Vic brought our formation directly abeam Dutch's formation and we hit the IP precisely on time at 350 knots and 500 feet above ground level. The air was relatively smooth and there was nothing to do now but concentrate on flying perfect formation.

We had no sooner settled down on the final, run-in course when Firecan Dan's voice cracked over the UHF receiver, "DELAY ONE MINUTE." I didn't want to believe what I had just heard, as delaying eight jets in show formation from so close in would be almost impossible. There was too little distance left to slow down then speed back up. S-Turning would not buy enough time. The only way it could have a chance would be for the whole gaggle to do a 360-degre turn, which would be no big deal were it performed at a somewhat higher altitude with moderate angles of bank. In this instance however, none were viable options and

Dutch Horace reacted immediately as he transmitted "Everyone go fighting wing[32] and hang on" as he began a hard right-hand 360-degree turn. I am sure there were four-letter expletives coming from all sixteen cockpits as our once-tight, eight-ship formation collapsed into a gaggle of seven pilots weaving in and out of the 60-degree cone behind the jet to his right to avoid hitting anyone, or the ground.

As we completed the turn, we were still at about 350 knots airspeed when Dutch transmitted one last time for us to "tuck it in." I can remember seeing the stadium up ahead at what seemed less than one mile as I once again put "the light on the star"[33] for proper formation position and noted with pride, everyone had indeed somehow maneuvered themselves back into perfect fingertip formation. Almost immediately I heard John Downey begin his countdown and as he said, "PULL!" we both selected 4th stage afterburner and applied 4Gs. From where I sat everything looked perfect as we reached the vertical and relaxed G. At about 10,000 feet, on John's command, "Roll off now", I rolled left and pulled down to a wings-level attitude, while John did the same, except to the right, thus insuring good separation between us.

With the UHF radio now suddenly silent, the sight I saw on that Sunday afternoon has forever since been burned into my memory. Looking straight up through my canopy I saw directly below me a packed Tulane Stadium with the playing field totally covered by an American Flag held by hundreds of hands stretching from end zone to end zone. Now well past the west end of the stadium I could see the six-ship formation with perfectly formed spaces, which Downey and I had just occupied, begin a gentle right-hand climbing turn to the north as the UHF radio once again came alive with a transmission from the booth, "Beautiful, just beautiful!"

We quickly rejoined into separate, four-ship formations and wasted no time in returning to Eglin and racing to our individual homes to watch the remainder of Super Bowl VI, in which the Dallas Cowboys, led by the great Roger Stauback beat the Miami Dolphins 24 to 3.

---

[32] Fighting wing: A tactical formation for high "G" maneuvering.

[33] Light on the star: A close formation position whereby the navigation light on the F-4's wing is placed in the center of the insignia star on the fuselage.

The Run for the Roses

- 1972 -

Prologue

The Rolling Thunder and Linebacker bombing campaigns against targets in North Vietnam were conducted by integrated strike packages. Commonly known as "The 800 Pound Gorilla", these packages, specifically designed for "mutual support", were often comprised of more than one-hundred aircraft of various disciplines and capabilities. It was a fine idea which probably worked better than anything else which might have been tried. However, after this armada with its fighters, bombers, chaffers, jammers, tankers, SAR, radar intercept and intelligence support aircraft had wreaked havoc, someone had to go back in and get the pictures. Such was the thankless task of the long-suffering recce pilot.

(USAF File Photograph)
Figure 25—"Run for the Roses"
party suit patch

With a motto of "Alone, Unarmed, and Unafraid", the men who flew reconnaissance missions in Southeast Asia were a breed apart. Affectionately known as "Recce Pukes", they stoically went about their business despite a constant stream of good-natured badgering and abuse from their fellow, fighter pilots. I emphasize "good natured" because anyone who might have been serious in their barbs was either totally naive about the recce mission, or insecure in their own abilities.

Any lingering doubts about the dangers of post-strike reconnaissance or the tenacity of those who flew those missions came to a screeching halt during the latter portion of the Linebacker I campaign. Noting the vulnerability of the unarmed recce to MiG attack, it was decided future post-strike recce sorties into

Route Package VI would be escorted by an element of F-4s. The "shoe was now on the other foot", and passionate arguments arose from the fighter pilot community. It was noted by some that trying to escort an RF-4C which could "walk away" from the F-4E escorts would be counter productive.[34] Because the recce pilots passionately believed, "speed is life", the escorts would actually be a liability since the recce would likely have to slow down to allow the escorts to keep up. Still others pointed out that since the typical recce pilot was not used to flying in tactical formation, and had received little or no training in BFM, the entire 3-ship flight could be jeopardized.[35] However in the end when none of the arguments prevailed, most of the detractors lamented that the only reason they were along on such a mission was to give the recce a "warm & fuzzy feeling", and to provide two additional targets to soak up the AAA and SAMs.

---

[34] *The J-79-15 engines in the RF-4C produced 1,800 pounds less thrust than the J-79-17 engines in the F-4E. However the RF was lighter by over 1,200 pounds and had a more aerodynamically clean nose. Additionally, since its only drag consisted of the ALQ-119 jamming pod and fuel tanks (which were jettisoned when empty), it was fast as hell. The escorting F-4Es were not only heavier, but on a typical CAP mission had excessive drag in the form of 3 bags of gas, 7 missiles, and an ALQ-119 jamming pod in the left-forward AIM-7 cavity. The combined effects of this weight and drag became painfully obvious to the escorting fighters when they found themselves in 2nd stage afterburner just to keep up with an RF running at Mil Power. As "the fence" was crossed and the recce began to "push it up," things got progressively worse. It took almost full burner to keep up with an RF running in 2nd stage. Finally, as the target area was approached, the recce would often go to full burner, at which time the escorts would watch him "walk away" from them like they were parked. This of course had the unfortunate effect of dragging the escorts through the AAA and SAM envelope after the RF had gotten the pictures and was leaving the area at the "speed of heat."*

[35] *Although recce pilots could fly basic formation as well as anyone, it was true that they had received little or no training in tactical formations such as Fluid 4, fighting wing, et al. Additionally, many were not used to the R/T terminology and discipline that is required of a tactical formation. Concerning their abilities to maneuver if attacked, their training basically taught them how to use their speed to evade and escape from attacking fighters. Instead of the BFM training afforded to upgrading fighter pilots, they were taught DFM (Defensive Fighter Maneuvers) that were designed to "spit out" an attacking fighter and provide room to run.*

Appropriately named "The Run for the Roses", these missions soon merited commemorative patches from the local tailor shops which would adorn the "party suits[36] of those who had experienced the thrill of it all. The recce pukes simply smiled and continued to do what they had been doing so well all along. At the same time, they probably noted a marked decrease in the level of bombastic remarks directed their way at the bar.

The following story, as related to me by the leader of one of these flights, is a humorous affirmation that despite best laid plans, Murphy's Law can and will prevail.

Story

Having the day off, I had taken the squadron truck to meet a friend after landing. He had been leading Dodge Flight on one of the newly designed 3-ship Run for the Roses flights which followed the strike into Route Pack VI that afternoon. I was anxious to see how they had fared but got the idea something was not quite right when my friend taxied the F-4E nose first into the revetment and stop-cocked its engines. Next, I saw the GIB remove his helmet and toss it onto the left wing, where it rolled off the trailing edge and bounced off the ramp.

As he came down the boarding ladder, my friend who was a captain named Buddy, was tight- lipped and unsmiling. The GIB, looking even more distraught, simply said, "My God, are all of them like this?" as he collected his helmet from the crew chief, ignored the squadron truck and stalked off toward the maintenance line

---

[36] *A "party suit" was one of the first items you purchased upon arrival "in country," and wore every time you attended a squadron party or function. They looked somewhat like a flight suit in that they were one piece and zipped up the front, but the similarity ended there. They were tailor made and in the color of your particular squadron, short sleeved, with your name, rank, and wings embroidered on them. Any standardization ended at this point as they became the personal repository for every conceivable patch or personal statement the wearer elected to affix. Although there were dozens of tailor shops in the local communities, there always seemed to be one tailor at any particular base who cornered the market and cranked these things out by the hundreds, making a comparative fortune in the process. At Ubon, it was the OK Tailors. At Udorn, we simply called the guy "The Thief."*

shack. "How'd it go Buddy?" I asked nonchalantly. "Don't ask!" came the terse reply. I bided my time until he had completed the maintenance debrief and stowed his equipment before I pressed him again. By now he was ready to talk.

Buddy was a damn fine fighter pilot who was an F-4 "Target Arm",[37] and the squadron weapons officer. When he was assigned the task of escorting the recce on the post-strike mission, he had thought things out and presented a good plan at the flight briefing.

Recognizing this particular recce pilot, whom they would escort, was very green, he tried to make things as simple as possible. To further complicate matters, his own GIB was an "FNG" who would be flying his first mission north. Using the "KISS" principle, he concentrated his flight briefing on the tactical formations to be flown, mutual support, and radio discipline. His plan was to basically fly the mission as a standard two-ship, but with the recce as Dodge 03 flying a right fighting wing position prior

(USAF File Photograph)

Figure 26—McDonnell Douglas RF-4C

to initial point (IP). He reasoned this would reduce the recce pilot's task down to simply hanging onto his wing during all phases of the flight except the target run. From the "IP" on across the target, the recce (Dodge 03) would be on the point of a "Vic formation", with Dodge 01 and Dodge 02 line-a-breast 3,000 out and 3,000 feet in trail with the recce. Knowing that recce pilots were not used to flying with others, he also stressed the critical importance of strict radio discipline, particularly use of call signs throughout the mission. Finally, he briefed the recce that should they become engaged with MiGs, he need only maintain his fighting wing position and stay off the radio.

The mission was planned for ingress and egress from the west side with both pre-strike and post-strike refueling from a KC-135 tanker and all seemed to be progressing well through the tanker rendezvous. As was standard practice, the flight refueled in reverse order, with the Dodge 03 taking fuel first, followed by the

---

[37] *"Target Arm" was a slang term for a graduate of the USAF Fighter Weapons Instructor Course (FWIC). This school is often incorrectly referred to as "The Fighter Weapons School."*

Dodge 02, then the flight lead. Now air-to-air refueling is a mundane task easily accomplished by an orangutan given enough practice, and heaven knows we all got enough practice in SEA. However like most things which become routine, it is sometimes easy to become complacent and assume someone else is "watching the store."

Although the Peoples Republic of China was not officially in the war, they did provide supplies and sanctuary for their North Vietnamese buddies. Additionally, they had taken it upon themselves to build a large highway running through the northern part of Laos. It was well known this highway was very heavily defended with large caliber AAA, and the Chinese would shoot at anyone coming within range of their guns. Since no one was anxious to foster another "Chinese Enter the Korean War" scenario, you didn't chase MiGs past the China border, you didn't strafe Chinese ships in the North Vietnamese harbors, and you didn't fly over the "China Highway."

The refueling anchors on the west side generally hung around in the vicinity of the Laotian Barrel Roll combat sector, seldom venturing north of 20 degrees north latitude, which kept them well clear of the Chinese road gang. However on this day, although no less than nine rated Air Force officers (6 in the F-4s and 3 in the KC-135) could and should have been monitoring the tanker's position, no one was. And so as Buddy slid onto the boom as the third and final receiver, Dodge Flight and their tanker were squarely over the China Highway.

The first inkling Buddy had that something was amuck came when he overheard comments on the UHF radio such as, "Boy they are really shooting at us!" "God, that one was really close!" "Geez, he almost got you!" Speaking on the intercom to his GIB, Buddy said something to the effect that it certainly sounded like some poor SOB was getting "hosed down", and that it would be really nice if that guy on the radio would use call signs. After a few more increasingly-shrill declarations from the unknown source, the FNG GIB decided to check their six and made a startling discovery in the form of alarmingly close 85 and 100mm AAA bursts. "Holly shit, it's us" he screamed, to which Buddy looked in his side mirrors instantly seeing the tell-tale, large, orange-black air bursts walking squarely up their six o-clock. Telling the tanker to disconnect, breakaway and turn hard to the south, Dodge flight and its accompanying tanker turned instantly into a "gaggle" that did successfully evade the AAA as they beat a hasty retreat back to the designated tanker orbit. It now became painfully obvious to Buddy, the unknown voice using no call signs was that of the Dodge 03, their resident recce puke.

After topping off the fuel one more time, Dodge Flight got a fresh start and departed the tanker in the formation Buddy had briefed with a positive "can do attitude." Again things seemed to be going as planned until shortly after "crossing the fence", where Murphy's Law again reared its head. Because of the longer range of the AIM-7 (as opposed to the AIM-9), it was standard practice that in the F-4 they be selected and in priority after crossing the fence. The F-4 was designed so that if there were electrical failure or power interruption, the weapon selection would default to the heat missiles (AIM-9).

Under normal circumstances, this would be no big deal, and the situation could be assessed and the generator reset, etc. However on this day, sometime between the time the munitions arming crew at the departure end of the runway at Udorn conducted checks to ensure the missile circuits integrity, a ground fault developed in one of the heat-missile, firing circuits. This meant the AIM-9 in priority would receive a fire signal the instant "heat" was selected. So, when Dodge 01's generator dropped off the line, the weapons system defaulted to "heat", and a single AIM-9 leapt from Dodge 01's missile rail.

One can only speculate that at this point Dodge 03 was probably as "tight as a fiddle string." So when he saw the missile smoke trail immediately ahead of Dodge 01 he came quickly to a seemingly logical conclusion that someone had just fired a missile which had passed directly under his flight leader's aircraft. Reacting instantly, he punched the UHF transmit button and shouted: "Dodge Flight, MiGs!" This transmission came just as Buddy observed the missile smoke trail directly in front of him and could only conclude that a MiG had indeed fired at him from almost point blank range.

On Buddy's call, Dodge Flight broke left, went full burner, and jettisoned their fuel tanks. Now, with Dodge 03 holding a grim fighting wing position on his leader, Dodge 02 "split the plane" and went "counter flow" in an attempt to turn the tables on the attacking MiGs. Since everyone in Dodge Flight was now absolutely convinced they were under attack, and someone else in the flight had the MiGs in sight, a whole series of high-G maneuvers and informative radio transmissions ensued for the better part of a minute, "Your six is clear!" "I'm pitching back left!" and so on.

Totally frustrated because he could not pick up the MiGs, Buddy finally asked, "Dodge 02 do you have the MiG?" "Negative." came the answer. "Dodge 03 do you have him?" "Negative." "Dodge Flight this is Dodge 01, everybody come out of burner and roll out." "Dodge Flight rejoin to tactical."

One can only speculate by this time that the North Vietnamese radar controllers at the Phu Yen Airfield must have been falling out of their chairs as they laughed their asses off at the airshow occurring above their southern border. At any rate, knowing now that Dodge Flight was too low on fuel to fight, much less continue to the target, they launched a flight of three MiG-21s which in full afterburner chased Dodge flight like a pack of yapping dogs all the way back to the Thai border before turning around.

Fortunately, the perils of Dodge Flight were the exception, and as time passed the recce types integrated very well into the post-strike tactical formations. It did take more than a few drinks that evening before Buddy could find anything humorous about the whole affair. I'll bet when he now hears the term "Run for the Roses", he doesn't immediately think about a horse race in Kentucky, but smiles to himself as he recalls the events of an afternoon sortie flown in the late summer of 1972 at Udorn RTAFB, Thailand.

Supersonic Deflection Shot

- 1972 -

Prologue

This story involves the scenario surrounding a high-speed, gun kill achieved by Brenda 01, a hard wing F-4E on Combat Air Patrol northwest of Hanoi, North Vietnam, on the afternoon of 2 June 1972. The end game of that engagement is shown on the cover of this book through Canadian artist Rich Thistle's magnificent and technically accurate painting, Rhino Charge.

At the time of the kill, the estimated flight parameters were: F-4 speed over 1.2 mach (800 kts); MiG-19 speed mach 0.77 (500 kts); altitude above terrain 500 feet; slant range 200-300 feet; and flight path crossing angle 90 degrees. This was the only MiG-19

(Rich Thistle)
Figure 27—Rhino Charge Painting

shot down by cannon fire during the course of the war in Southeast Asia, and is believed to be the highest-speed, gun kill in the history of aerial combat.

I was the pilot of Brenda 01. Sitting seven feet behind me was 1/Lt. Jack "Karst" Smallwood, the best weapons system officer (WSO) I ever knew and the last USAF flyer to die in the Vietnam War.

The reconstruction, visualization and understanding of air-to-air engagements are not particularly difficult for experienced fighter pilots. However, that same visualization and understanding by those not employed in the field of tactical aviation can more often than not prove to be a daunting task.

To facilitate understanding of the engagement, the following overhead view accurately depicts the relative position of the aircraft within a block of airspace that is 5 miles long, 3 miles wide, and 3 miles deep. On this diagram, the time lapse between starting position "1" and end game position "5" is one minute and forty-two seconds.

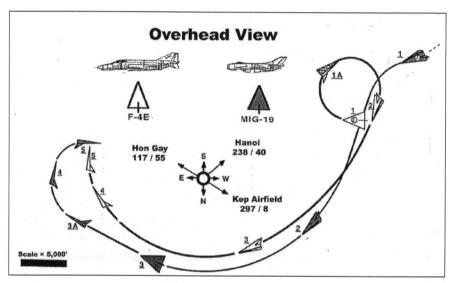

(Author)

Figure 28—Overhead view of air-to-air engagement

To "set the stage" of how that one minute and forty-two seconds period would have appeared, pretend for a moment you were an observer on the ground at a point directly beneath point 5 of the diagram...then visualize the following hypothetical scenario which I sent to Rich Thistle during one of the numerous email exchanges of technical data he used to create his painting, Rhino Charge.

"Can you imagine Rich what an air show this would have been to a North Vietnamese farmer in one of the rice paddies directly below this scene? Jaded by years of watching numerous flights of MiGs and American fighters overhead and hearing the distant rumble of heavy bombing, he had learned to mostly ignore the continuing saga he wished would go away. However, just over a minute and one-half earlier an echoing, muffled boom had attracted his attention as Brenda 01 accelerated through the mach, two miles above and five miles southwest of the field in which he stood.

Focusing upon the rapidly turning and descending F-4, his eyes also picked up a second F-4 which was climbing upward and turning slowly left. Soon he saw two more silver aircraft descending and turning to the north. Continuing to watch, he saw a streak come from the F-4 in the direction of the silver aircraft, but it seemed to simply fly harmlessly upward. As his gaze passed northwest, he could not believe how fast all three of the airplanes seemed to be going. Just then a second streak left the brown airplane and flew behind the silver planes. He now realized all of the airplanes were going faster than he had ever seen, and they were very, very low.

As he now faced directly north, he looked to the northeast to see two rapidly approaching silver aircraft, and back to the north to see the brown airplane. He suddenly realized all of them were going to pass directly over his head. He snapped his head to the right as his ears sensed the high-pitch squeal of the four afterburning engines of the MiGs and noted that there was some sort of fog streaming off both the rapidly turning silver airplanes.

Quickly checking back to the north, he saw the same fog streaming from the big brown airplane, but oddly, could hear no noise from its direction. Just then, a long streak of red fire shot from the nose of the brown airplane and his ears heard the staccato cracks of one-hundred 20mm rounds per second breaking the sound barrier over his head at over mach 4.5.

Now, in less than one second both of the silver airplanes screamed directly over him in a westerly direction amidst the loudest roar he had ever heard. At the same instant, he thought he saw some sort of sparkles and puffs on the second silver airplane, but had no time to reflect on it, for as the brown airplane passed directly over his head in less than 1/100th of a second, the air in his lungs was suddenly expelled as if hit with a bat when the mach-Y stem of the F-4's shock wave swept over him, knocking him from his feet.

Now crouching on the ground and looking directly south, his eyes followed the brown airplane which had snapped out of its right turn and was pulling rapidly into a vertical climb. As he looked back to his right he saw the second of the silver airplanes streaming fire, with its wings rocking and nose dropping. He continued to watch as within seconds, it crashed into one of the neighboring rice paddies, exploding into a huge orange ball of fire. He dropped his rake and began to run toward the distant, billowing black smoke.

Story

As I write this, the events of that June afternoon, more than thirty-three years ago, including the smallest details of that one minute, forty-two second engagement remain indelibly burned into my memory.

The Mission: On 10 May 1972 Oyster 01, an F-4D from the Triple Nickel (555th Tactical Fighter Squadron) was shot down by a MiG-19 near Thud Ridge northwest of Hanoi. Only the WSO, Captain Roger Locker survived, and for the next twenty three days successfully evaded capture by NVA troops. When on June 1st a flight of Triple Nickel F-4s made positive voice contact with him and pinpointed his location, it was immediately determined an SAR mission would be launched the next day, June 2nd to bring him home. Since the pickup would have to occur at the very doorsteps of Hanoi, a large diversionary raid on multiple rail yards, airfields, and other targets was planned to hopefully give the slow-moving HH-53 Jolly Green Giant and her A-1 Sandy escorts some degree of cover. On this day, I was the leader of the four F-4E aircraft comprising Brenda Flight, a MiG CAP anchored northeast of Hanoi between the Gia Lam and Kep enemy airfields.

The Flight: On my wing as Brenda 02 was Captain Buddy Green with 1/Lt Doug Eden in the rear cockpit. The element leader, Brenda 03, was my squadron commander, Lt. Col. John Downey with Captain John Leach in the pit, while Brenda 04 was flown by Captain Bob Ellis with 1/Lt Ed White as his GIB. Our spare aircraft was manned by Captain Ron VanMeter with Captain Ron Sacre in the pit.

The Briefing: For some time I had become increasingly concerned about the viability of the current USAF tactical formation, fluid four, because of the excessive time required to turn the formation and the fact, "welded wingman" were being eaten alive by attacking MiGs. My theory was although fluid four had been well suited for F-86 Sabres at high altitude in the skies of Korea, it was simply not viable in the medium altitude, high-G, high-indicated, airspeed environment of Route Package Six. I believed formations were most vulnerable during turns when wingmen were forced to spend valuable time flying formation off their leader instead of looking in earnest into the block of airspace from which an attacking MiG would appear. With this in mind I had drawn out some simple tactical formations allowing the four ship flight to change course 90 degrees left or right, as well as a cross turn to reverse course 180 degrees, all at very high turn rates involving upwards of 4Gs. Such free lance thinking was heresy at the time but nevertheless I briefed these tactics, which I had named the "called turn", as those to be used by Brenda Flight on this mission.

The Aircraft: We stepped to the aircraft for pre-flight inspection, at which time I was disappointed to find I had the only bird in our four ship flight carrying three external fuel tanks. Unlike my jet, which had two 370 gallon tanks on the outboard armament pylons and a 600 gallon tank on the centerline, the other members of my flight had only the outboard tanks. In addition to that, none of the birds carried the full complement of missiles. My jet had only two AIM-7 Sparrow missiles in the aft fuselage cavities and one AIM-4 Falcon IR missile on each of the inboard armament pylons. A check of the aircraft's log showed however that my bird had the full load of 640 rounds of 20mm ammunition.[38] Start and taxi were uneventful and we took off on schedule at 1105 hours.

The Ingress: Everything preceded smoothly through our scheduled 1215 hours rendezvous at 17,500 feet with Tan 104, our designated KC-135 tanker. All our jets topped off their fuel tanks without incident and Brenda Flight departed the Tan Anchor on schedule, heading north up the eastern coastline of South Vietnam to a point near the island of Hon Gay. There we would turn left and proceed to our designated CAP orbit just northwest of "The City on the River." As per normal, the RWAH (Radar Warning and Homing) scopes became increasingly active with the various strobes and tones showing the energy and direction of enemy threat radar which "painted" our flight. I jettisoned the 600 gallon "bathtub" centerline tank as it fed out just prior to reaching our turn point at Hon Gay. Since the other members of my flight had been feeding from their 370 gallon tanks, a quick fuel check at this point predictably showed my jet had almost 4,000 more pounds of fuel than the rest of the flight.

The *CAP*: We arrived at our designated CAP orbit point on schedule and contacted Red Crown, a U.S. Navy cruiser operating in the Gulf of Tonkin with powerful radar monitoring the MiG activity in the Route Package V & VI areas. The UHF connection was loud and clear and we were advised that the controller

---

[38] The aircraft's log was in error concerning the number of 20mm rounds loaded. In all probability one of the previous crews which flew this aircraft had fired the gun but failed to report it in the post mission debriefing. This was discovered when I landed from the current mission and the armament personnel told me only ten rounds remained aboard the aircraft. Since I had only fired a three second burst (approximately 300 rounds), the bird actually had only approximately 310 rounds aboard when I took off.

who would monitor our flight had the call sign "Worm." As planned, we set up on a 10-mile leg racetrack orbit with axis pointing our nose directly at the Ghu Lam Airport in downtown Hanoi on the inbound leg, then the Kep Airfield to the northwest on the outbound leg. Using the "called turn" tactical formation I had briefed earlier, everything proceeded with neither SAM nor MiG activity throughout the first two orbits. At the southeast end of the third orbit, things changed drastically.

The SAM Rouse: *(Times below indicate elapsed time in minutes and seconds between the radio transmissions as recorded on Smallwood's tape recorder in the map case of the back seat of Brenda 01.)*

Time 0+00: I transmit "Brenda Reverse" and the flight began a 4G cross turn back to the northwest.

Time 0+07: As the RHAW scopes came alive in all four of Brenda Flight's cockpits. I transmitted to the flight that Brenda Lead had the E-SAM Hi warning and continued the reversal turn.

Time 0+21: When the red light on the console illuminated, indicating a SAM launch, accompanied by a piercing 1,000 Hz tone I transmitted "OK, we've got a launch light…Brenda let's turn into it. Neither Smallwood nor I could visually acquire the missile, which led me to believe it could be a false launch signal to distract our attention while MiGs attacked.

Time 0+30: A Red Crown controller with the call sign "Bing" advises "Fletch", another F-4 MiG CAP that they have a possible bandit (MiG) on a bearing of 058 degrees from "Bullseye" (the center of Hanoi) at 15 miles.

Time 0+35: I call for all members of Brenda flight to turn on their radar jamming pods. At the same time, Brenda 03 advises, "Brenda 03's going to turn east bound, I lost you in that break." I acknowledged and immediately transmitted, "OK Brenda, let's reverse course back to the east."

Time 0+57: Worm's voice cracks over the UHF, "Brenda, Worm, Bandit will be on your 167 at 8 (which meant he would be on a bearing of 167 degrees from our position at 8 miles)." I acknowledged Worm's call and brought our now two-ship element to a heading of 167 degrees with Brenda 02 flying tactical formation, line-abreast and 6,000 feet off my left wing. With Buddy Green and I straining to visually acquire the MiGs visually, Jack Smallwood in my pit and Doug Eden in Buddy's pit were having no better success with radar acquisition.

Time 1+20: Red Crown transmits, "Brenda, you're in the dark (meaning that they had lost our RADAR blip), Bandit is 047 Bullseye, 14."

Time 1+38: I transmitted, "Red Crown, Brenda 01, where's the bandit?" Before Red Crown could reply, Brenda 02 declared "Bingo Fuel", which meant he had reached the pre-determined fuel level required for him to safely reach the refueling anchor. It was time to "get out of Dodge." This was precisely what I didn't want to hear, but said to Smallwood, "OK, give me egress heading", as I continued to look as hard as my 20:10 eyes could muster for the MiGs I was certain we were being vectored for attack on our element.

Time 1+48: Red Crown once again attempted to advise me of the MiG's position but was cut out by Brenda 02's repeated transmission, "Brenda 02 is Bingo." Reluctantly, I transmitted, "OK Brenda, let's Bug Out, Bug Out" (meaning to disengage and exit the area). Smallwood gave me an egress heading of 100 degrees as I brought the element to that heading with a modified "90 left" called turn. This now placed Brenda 02 off my right wing, line abreast approximately 4,000 out as we proceeded to the "feet wet" environment of the Gulf of Tonkin at 450 knots indicated airspeed. All eight eyeballs inside the cockpits of Brenda 01 and 02 were scanning the hemisphere behind our element for the yet to be seen MiGs we knew must be near. We continued on this easterly course amid numerous RHAW warning signals for AAA and SAM, as well as UHF transmissions between friendly flights in the area. I advised Fletch Flight, the egress CAP which would give us cover as we exited the area, that we were coming out, to which Fletch 01 replied, "Roger, we're on station."

Time 3+15: The strong "rattlesnake" tone of a Fansong tracking radar in high PRF (pulse recurring frequency) focused our attention immediately on the RHAW scope. Jack Smallwood called, "E-SAM Hi at 5 o'clock" from the rear cockpit as I looked immediately into the airspace at the formation's right rear quadrant.

Time 3+19: As my eyes swept behind Brenda 02, I saw a reflected glint of sunlight beneath the scattered cloud layer at 10,000 feet. Knowing most of the MiGs were polished aluminum, I strongly suspected I had finally achieved a "tally-ho" on the bandits and transmitted, "OK, I've got a MiG-21 at our 3 o'clock low down there Brenda two, cross to the other wing, he may try to pop up on us." I don't know why I called the bandit out as a MiG-21 other than the fact they were usually more numerous in Route Package Six than the MiG-17 and MiG-19, and simply made the logical assumption. Buddy Green replied, "Roger." and turned immediately left as I turned right in a weave placing him off my left wing in tactical formation. I checked our fuel and said on the intercom to Smallwood, "We've got 95 fuel (9,500 pounds)", to which he replied, "Roger." as I mentally noted that while I was fully 3,500 pounds above Bingo fuel, Brenda 02 had none to spare. With my eyeballs almost sticking out of the cockpit to scan the position from which I had seen the flash of light, I became aware of the faint tone of a "golf band" radar and noted a short, one-ring strobe on my RHAW at the 5 o-clock position. Somewhere in the recesses of my mind I recalled that some of the older MiGs used the golf band for radar ranging and twisted around to look further aft of our flight. There they were, plain as day, low, just right of our six o-clock position, at a range of about 8,000 feet. It was a two-ship formation of silver MiG-19s flying a Russian style "sharp bearing" tactical formation in a curve of pursuit which would shortly have brought them into firing position at our six o-clock low position.

The Kill:

Time…the final 1+42: Punching the mike button I transmitted, "OK, I'm going to take one quick run at him 2, you continue on out." To his undying credit, Captain Buddy Green replied in an almost casual voice from the cockpit of Brenda 02, "I'll stay with you." He then immediately pulled sharply up in a steep climb to conserve fuel and come to my aid if required. In retrospect, Buddy's sudden move probably set the stage for the kill.

As I released the mike button, I broke hard right into a 135 degree bank slice turn as I slammed both throttles of the General Electric J-79s into 4th stage afterburner and snapped just over 9 Gs on the F-4. (The tell-tale needle in both the front and rear cockpit recorded this over-G condition, but the bird was so strong it only popped about one-half dozen rivets on the upper surface of both wings where they joined the fuselage.) At this point, I was so full of adrenalin I simply don't recall feeling any G forces. In contrast, Smallwood in the rear cockpit told me later he went to instant blackout but was able to retain consciousness until I slacked off on the Gs a few seconds later.

Aided by radial G, I passed the 90 degree point of the slice turn in seconds and noted from the characteristic "mach tuck" of the F-4 as it goes supersonic, we had indeed slipped through the mach at that point and were accelerating at a rapid rate. Looking intently at the two MiGs now at my right 2 o-clock low position, I expected them to pull up and pass me "close aboard" denying me turning room, which would have placed them in a position above me with their nose up and mine buried. Had this been the case, I would have had no choice but to extend out of the fight as the MiG leader would have had radial G working in his favor with endless options, none of which I liked.

As I continued in an approximate 7G slice turn, I was dismayed to see the MiGs turn left to a southerly heading and level off before beginning a right turn at an altitude of approximately 5,000 feet. It is my belief that the MiG leader had been focused on Brenda 02, and upon seeing Buddy zoom sharply up, turned left to position himself for a six o-clock curve of pursuit. Although at no time during the slice turn did I take my eyes off the MiGs, by the 300 degree point of the turn I found myself exactly tail-on to the tiny MiGs at a range of approximately 2 miles, at which point they simply disappeared before my eyes.

I let off the G to lag to the outside of the perceived turn circle and almost immediately, visually reacquired the MiGs again as they began to show some planform view due to their continuing right turn. Pulling the nose to pure pursuit, I asked for and got "five mile boresight." Now able to see once again, Smallwood replied in a voice strained by the heavy G load, "You've got it." Placing the pipper (a 35 mil projected aiming circle on the combining glass) on the trailing MiG, I punched the auto acquisition button on the right throttle and was instantly rewarded by a radar lock-on, as indicated by the analog bar which appeared on the pipper to indicate a slant range of just over 4,500 feet.

After four seconds of settling time to allow the aircraft's fire control system to input data to the radar missiles, I squeezed the trigger twice, and then held it down to ripple fire my two AIM-7 Sparrow missiles. The first missile's rocket motor apparently did not ignite after it blew from its fuselage cavity, and the second failed to guide, arching harmlessly straight ahead of the aircraft. Brenda 02 transmitted, "It went ballistic, Lead!" as I did a lag pursuit roll to the left to reduce angle off and slapped the four inch piece of plastic tube attached to the missile select switch on the weapons select panel down to the "heat" position to select my IR missiles. The heat missiles we carried that day were the notoriously ineffective AIM-4E Falcon, commonly referred to as the "Hughes Arrow in the Heart" missile because of its tiny warhead, lack of a proximity fuse, and the "Rube Goldberg" procedures required to launch them within ideal parameters.

As soon as I knocked the weapons switch to heat, the familiar Norelco razor tone of the AIM-4E buzzed in my headset indicating the missile was indeed online and looking forward, but its cryogenically-cooled, seeker head was seeing nothing beyond background IR. As I pulled the F-4's nose into pure pursuit and placed the pipper on the trailing MiG-19's twin afterburner plumes, I was rewarded by a change of missile tone from the Norelco razor to the sizzle tone indicating the missile's IR tracking heads were looking directly at the heat source. I punched the missile uncage button on the stick allowing the missile heads to continue to track the heat source, regardless my nose position. I then pulled approximately 20 degrees of lead on the trailing MiG to give the missiles a lead-turn advantage after they began to guide at safe separation clearance, then pulled the trigger twice and held it down to ripple fire the missiles.

The fist missile went ballistic and the second never left the right inboard, pylon-launcher rail. The MiG leader, apparently seeing the smoke trail from the first AIM-4 broke hard right, turning both MiGs into balls of condensation in the humid SEA air. By now the fight was descending rapidly through approximately 2,000 AGL. The slant range to the MiGs was shrinking quickly from about 3,000 feet, with angle off increasing dramatically as the low wing loaded MiGs turned into me at maximum G. Knowing there was absolutely no way I could maintain nose-tail separation, my only option at this point would be a very high angle deflection shot from the plane of motion.

Without looking into the cockpit, I selected guns, pulled the nose into lead pursuit, carrying the trailing MiG in the left quarter panel of the windscreen to keep him in sight just above the F-4E's long nose. Although I was now pulling 7 Gs to hold the MiG in lead pursuit, while traveling at a rate of three football fields per second with the slant range closing at an alarming rate, I felt no Gs whatsoever. Additionally, everything seemed to be moving in slow motion. At a point where it appeared my flight path would pass just behind that of the trailing MiG, I rolled slightly left then back right and down into the perceived plane of motion to align the axis of my aircraft with that of the target.

With the long nose of the F-4E now obscuring my ability to see the MiG, I held down the trigger, and for just a fleeting moment as the General Electric M-61 gatling gun wound up to its 100 round per second rate, I had the dread feeling that I was too close and would collide with the MiG. However the thought passed quickly as the trailing MiG once again appeared directly above my nose and seemed to move no faster than a car traveling at a right angle through an intersection one-half block away, at no more than 70 miles per hour. As the MiG flew through the 20mm bullet stream, I observed multiple hits down its longitudinal axis, and in particular on the canopy and right wing root. As I passed behind the MiG I rolled 90 degrees left and held the G to begin a quarter-roll-and-zoom maneuver while continuing to watch the MiG, now at my right 4 o-clock low position. It was now in heavy wing rock with fire, smoke, fluids and pieces of the aircraft streaming from its right wing root. Its' nose continued to drop and it crashed into a green meadow, exploding in a huge orange ball of fire approximately 10 seconds after I had fired my 300 round burst.

The Egress: During those last three seconds before the MiG crashed, I inadvertently pushed the UHF transmit button as I shouted to Smallwood, "He's going down! You see 'em? I got him, I got him! He hit the ground!" This was followed by immediate cheering on the UHF by what sounded like a dozen transmitters and ended with a voice I recognized as that of my squadron commander, John Downey saying, "Way to go!"

The next voice I heard however was Buddy Green in Brenda 02, who remarked in the same off-handed tone he had used two minutes earlier, "Let's get out of here Brenda Lead. Right now, he's closing at six." (Referring of course to the leader of the MiG-19 formation.) The lead MiG actually didn't close an inch at my six for as I pulled down hard to an easterly heading at 15,000 feet, I looked into the cockpit and saw an indicated airspeed I can't precisely recall, but remember noting it was still incredibly high and well above the speed which any pursuing MiG might achieve. Since Brenda 02 was still well above me and further to the east, I told him to continue on toward the coast in hopes of preserving precious, remaining fuel.

As we passed the coast I directed everyone to climb and set course for our scheduled post-strike refueling Tan Anchor. Red Crown passed us a current UHF frequency for the Tan Anchor but I got no reply until a lone tanker from the Purple Anchor advised us that everything had been screwed up with the refueling anchors and asked if he could help. After I told him my wingman was critically low on fuel, he advised that he would be waiting for us at the northern extreme of his orbit, just short of the 20 degree north latitude limit as set by command directives. After Smallwood's radar painted the tanker at 80 nautical miles on the nose I asked the Purple tanker to press on north an additional 25 miles. "If you've got an emergency, we'll come." was his reply. "We've got one." I answered. "We're on the way." was his immediate transmission.

The rendezvous was successful with Brenda 02 the first to hit the boom with "only fumes remaining." After we all topped off our fuel tanks, Brenda flight proceeded back to Udorn RTAFB, where I executed the traditional "victory roll" I had dreamed of executing since I was a young boy drawing pictures of P-51s.

(USAF File Photograph)
Figure 29—Maj. Phil Handley & 1/Lt. Jack Smallwood after landing at Udorn RTAFB, Thailand

(USAF File Photograph)
Figure 30—1/Lt. Jack Smallwood, WSO, Sgt. Steve Accup, Crew Chief, Major Phil Handley, Pilot

Postscript—Cover Art

The painting shown on the cover is from the easel of noted Canadian artist, Rich Thistle. Working from charts, diagrams, pictures, models and innumerable exchanges with the author, he dramatically captured a historically significant instant of aerial combat with stunning accuracy.

Appropriately named Rhino Charge by the artist, the painting places the viewer in a "fighting wingman's position" behind and to the right of the attacking F-4E at the instant of the kill. Details accurately depicted include: Underlying terrain, cloud layer, sun angle, bullet ballistic path, angle-off, slant range, plane of motion, afterburner plumes and shock rings, M-61 gun gas exhaust, lift induced vaporization, wingtip vortices, and 20mm bullet strikes.

I will always be grateful to Rich Thistle for the tenacity, dedication and patience he showed in the creation of this painting which hangs proudly over my bar, and shall forever be a treasured possession.

(Rich Thistle)
Figure 31—Rich Thistle at his easel in creation of Rhino Charge.

(Author)
Figure 32—Suspended scale models of aircraft and bullet stream used by artist.

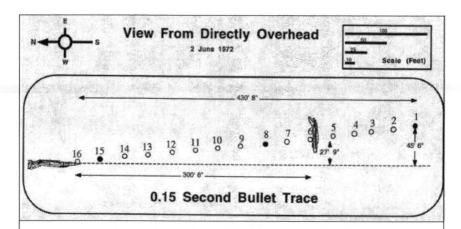

This drawing is to exact scale. It shows the relative positions of the aircraft as well as the bullet stream for a 0.15 second interval (during which time the MiG flew through that bullet stream).

The F-4 is 63' long and is traveling at 1,363 feet per second. The MiG-19 is 42' long and traveling at 833 feet per second.

Fifteen bullets are in flight, with bullet #16 just leaving the muzzle of the M61 cannon which is firing 100 bullets per second. Bullets #1, #8, and #15 are tracer rounds and should be visible on the painting.

At the instant shown, bullet #6 (the 3rd to hit) is just striking the MiG in the right wing root area. 1/100th second earlier, bullet #5 explodes the canopy, and 2/100th second earlier bullet #4 hits the left tip of the MiG's nose. 1/100th second after the instant shown, bullet #8 will hit the right fight stabilator.

(Author)

Figure 33—Geometrically accurate drawing used to depict visible tracer rounds on painting.

A Sobering Call to Spike

- 1972 -

General William W. ("Spike") Momyer was the Commander of Tactical Air Command from 1968 until his retirement in 1973. Prior to his stewardship of TAC, he was the Commander of 7th Air Force in Vietnam at the height of the Rolling Thunder Air Campaign of 1966 to 1968. He was a distinguished airman of three wars (WWII, Korea, and Vietnam), and widely acknowledged as a preeminent expert in the employment of airpower, in particular tactical airpower. In summary, he was a serious, intellectual, no-nonsense officer who was respected by all who knew him. "Spike" Momyer was definitely not inclined to frivolity and a man with whom only a fool would dare engage in a practical joke.

On the evening of 2 June 1972, patrons of the Udorn Officers Open Mess had been in full celebration mode since late that afternoon. The main celebration centered on the rescue earlier in the day of Captain Roger Locker who had been shot down some 21 days earlier and was picked up by SAR forces and returned to Udorn. A collateral, but no less enthusiastic party was occurring among members of the 58th Tactical Fighter Squadron, in celebration of the MiG kill Jack Smallwood and I had scored near Hanoi that afternoon. Needless to say, after all the champagne, beer and hard liquor we had consumed, no one was feeling any pain.

For some reason the O-Club at Udorn had a telephone booth right there in the bar. Since the telephone installed in the booth connected only to the military telephone voice network (Autovon) through the local command post, one can only speculate its purpose was to provide instant communication for the Wing Commander and his immediate staff during those times they were at the bar.

Because of the twelve hour time differential between Udorn and Langley AFB, Virginia, 2130 hours (9:30 PM) at the Udorn O-Club bar coincided with 0930 hours (9:30 AM) at Langley AFB, Virginia, where General Momyer would have been thirty minutes into the morning's Command Staff Meeting. The military telephone voice network is reserved for "official business" with orders of precedence established to ensure that increasingly important calls have priority over those of lesser importance. At the top of this "food chain" is FLASH Precedence, reserved for only those emergency calls involving national security, such as nuclear attack, etc. A FLASH precedence call will therefore preempt (or bump off) all other calls working on the network to ensure a clear channel for the vital FLASH communication.

At approximately 2130 hours one of the 58th TFS "hair-on-fire" fighter pilots, Captain Mac Poll lifted the receiver of the telephone in the O-Club bar booth and announced to the autovon operator he was placing a call to the commander of Tactical Air Command at Langley AFB, Virginia. When questioned as to the precedence of the call, he naturally answered, "FLASH." When the autovon line in the TAC Commander's office, adjoining the command briefing room where General Momyer was presiding over the morning, command briefing, rang, his aide answered immediately. He was greeted by the voice of Captain Poll, saying it was imperative he speak with General Momyer. "Are you certain you want me to interrupt the command briefing and have him come to the phone?" the aide asked. "Absolutely." was Poll's reply. "OK, standby." came the reluctant reply.

From across the room I saw Captain Poll motioning to me from the telephone booth. As I approached he said I had an urgent call as he handed me the receiver and headed directly back to the 58th gaggle at the bar. Assuming it must have been someone in the wing command post passing along a congratulatory message from back home, I grabbed the receiver and said, "This is Major Handley." "This is General Momyer came the stern reply." The ethyl alcohol which had been absorbed into my blood stream during the preceding five hours of celebration evaporated in an instant as I was immediately stone cold sober and literally snapped to attention as I realized the voice on the other end actually was the TAC Commander. I became painfully aware all eyes of my squadron mates, most of whom wore a silly smile, were fixed squarely upon me and it had become suddenly quite.

Since running didn't seem to be a viable option, I began, "General Momyer, this is Major Handley, and this call is a big mistake. All of my squadron is here in the bar at Udorn celebrating and one of my buddies apparently placed this call. I know this was a bad idea for which I apologize." After a short silence he said, "What is it you are celebrating?" I replied, "It was a MiG kill Sir. We shot down a MiG-19 northwest of Hanoi earlier this afternoon." Another longer silence, during which I feared the worst. "Well, why don't you tell me about it" he asked.

So for the next several minutes I described the engagement with General Momyer asking logical and informed questions concerning the parameters of the kill. He concluded the conversation by saying, "Well Major, I'm damn glad you called. You tell those men there with you I'm proud of every one of you and to keep up the good work. You just continue to take care of business there on that end, and I'll do my best to handle things back here in the States." "I certainly will do that,

Sir." I replied as the line went dead. As I replaced the receiver, I felt the weight of the world had been lifted from my shoulders, but only hesitated for a moment before I took off in a dead run after Mac Poll.

Some eight years later while I was a student at the U.S. Army War College at Carlyle Barracks, Pennsylvania, General Momyer was scheduled to deliver a lecture on tactical airpower. As I arrived that morning and was walking to Root Hall where the lecture would be given, I saw General Momyer emerge from the Distinguished Visitor's Quarters for the short walk to Root Hall. Joining him, I introduced myself and exchanged pleasantries for a short time. Before reaching our destination, I asked, "Sir, do you remember the time you were called from the morning staff meeting to take a call from a fighter pilot at Udorn Air Base?" Looking at me he smiled and said, "Was that you?" "Yes sir it was." I replied. "Well I certainly do remember it, and I'm still damn glad you called."

This was the precise terminology he had used on that evening some eight years earlier to assuage my embarrassment over the ill-advised phone call. It is also worth noting, despite his reputation for never uttering a word of profanity, he took the unusual step of inserting the word "damn" on both occasions.

Eagles to "The Bush"

-1976 -

Prologue

For some reason I never really understood, Bitburg Air Base, Germany, home of the 36th Tactical Fighter Wing, was commonly referred to as "The Bush." I assume the nickname was the result of what us Americans thought the native Germans were saying when pronouncing the last half of the word "Bitburg." In the fall of 1976 a great old fighter pilot named Fred Kyler commanded The Fight'n 36th. The wing had three fighter squadrons, the 22nd, 53rd, and 525th, equipped with the F-4E Phantom II. I was fortunate to be commanding officer of the 22nd TFS (The Big 22). The transition from the Phantom to the Eagle brought with it, not only ponderous changes of maintenance and operational procedures, but also a major downsizing of the wing's rated force since the F-15 did not carry a weapons system officer (WSO). This is a story of my recollections of the 36th Wing's conversion to that big, beautiful machine, and in particular the events of the afternoon of 26 January 1977. It was on that day I flew F-15A, tail number 76-049, the Fight'n 36th's very first F-15 on its maiden voyage from "The Bush."

Story

Perhaps in the annals of USAF history there had been a more eagerly antici-pated delivery of a fighter than the F-15 Eagle, but not in my time. From the moment details began to leak out about its design, every fighter pilot in the world wanted to get his hands on this jet. With a design motto of "not a pound for air-to-ground", the F-15's specifications and performance capabilities were to be articulated by a hand-selected team of experienced fighter pilots, not engineers. Who couldn't love the rumors that this aircraft would have a big bub-ble canopy affording visibility not seen since the F-86? That its thrust to weight ratio would exceed one-to-one in afterburner and the engines would not smoke at any power setting? That its wing loading would dictate a corner velocity[39] fully one hundred knots lower than that of the F-4? That it would out-accelerate and out-turn anything in the air? That its computerized flight controls would effectively negate the adverse yaw[40] effect common to swept-wing fighters such as the F-100 and F-4? That its pulse Doppler radar could actually look down into "ground clutter" and see only targets? That its internal 20mm gatling gun would be canted up two degrees to make high-G tracking easier, and would be coupled with a state-of-the-art, lead-computing sight that actually knew where the bullet stream was going? What was there not to like? By the time the famous aviation artist Keith Ferris' beautiful oil painting of a sky blue F-15A appeared on the cover of Air Force Magazine in 1973, our collective anticipation had reached fever pitch. God, as great as the slatted F-4E was, we couldn't wait.

In 1973 pilots who would form the "initial cadre" for the F-15 were selected and I was delighted to learn one of the really sharp captains in my flight at the 58th TFS at Eglin AFB, Florida was one of them. His name was Bob Ellis and he would later be my instructor pilot when I checked out in the F-15 at Luke AFB, Arizona. He would also be, not only the top graduate of the first class for F-15 pilots at the Fighter Weapons Instructor Course (FWIC), but would also receive the prestigious Robbie Risner Trophy, an award presented to the top weapons officer (all systems) in the field for the past year.[41]

While all of this was happening in 1973, I was selected to attend Air Command and Staff School (ACSC), a nine month course conducted at Maxwell AFB, Alabama. Sometimes referred to as "Command and Golf", this "square filler" was a must if promotion to higher rank was among one's career goals. If not selected to attend the school in residence, your alternative was to take the course by correspondence. At one point during the course I recall a speaker reading a letter from some commander in the field saying, in essence, that graduates of the Command and Staff School were fully six months ahead of their peers who did not attend. Predictably, the first stu-

---

[39] "Corner Velocity" is the slowest airspeed at which a fighter can pull its established "maximum G," thus resulting in the quickest, tightest turn possible.

[40] Adverse yaw is the tendency for a fighter to yaw in a direction opposite that of aileron input at high angles-of-attack and usually resulted in an out-of-control (OOC) situation.

[41] Annually, each USAF fighter wing, worldwide, has an opportunity to nominate one of their weapons officers for the Risner Award. The Weapons School at Nellis AFB, Nevada evaluates these nominations and picks the best. So, Bob Ellis was the best of that year.

dent who could grab the "question microphone" in the auditorium inquired about the three lost months since ACSC was a nine-month course.

Following graduation from ACSC in June 1974, I was assigned as the assistant operations officer of the 53rd TFS at Bitburg Air Base, Germany, and subsequently became the 22nd TFS Squadron Commander approximately two years later. The announcement in the summer of 1976 that the 36th wing at Bitburg would be the first unit in Europe to equip with the F-15 created a lot of activity among pilots within the wing as they scrambled to ensure their longevity for the transition. Those pilots with little time remaining before they would normally have rotated back to the States were automatically excluded, and of course all of the F-4 WSO's would no longer have a seat in the "pilot only" F-15.

At the same time many of the pilots arriving from the States had been specifically assigned to the wing to grab one of the prized slots. Most of these officers were highly qualified and had been picked as a reward for previous jobs well done. A few were quite simply someone's "fair-haired boy", but they were by far in the minority among the well qualified "new guys" that began to show up. Personally, I was able to hang on to the finest ops officer with whom a squadron commander was ever blessed, Major Tom Goldman. "Goldie" was a big, tough, smart, cigar chomping old fighter pilot and disciplinarian who made my job a breeze and The Big 22 "ran like a Swiss watch."

Within the next few months TAC and USAFE personnel handpicked the rest of the pilots forming the initial cadre of approximately 85 pilots to man Bitburg's three fighter squadrons. In addition to a core of qualified F-15 pilots from the 1st TFW at Langley AFB, Virginia, the remaining pilots represented the "cream of the crop" of those eligible. So the end result saw the Fight'n 36th end up with a whole wing full of "ringers." 42

---

42 Among those "ringers" was a group of slick wing first lieutenants that had just completed their F-15 tactical qualification at Langley AFB, Va. Through manipulation and "luck of the draw", the Big 22 ended up with "the pick of the litter." Under the tutorage of great flight commanders and my "iron fisted" ops officer, Tom Goldman, "Cobra" Holmes, "Knife" McAllister, "Skeet Fraser", "Tony" Mahoney, and "Hawk" Hill rapidly developed into superb fighter pilots who were a great source of pride for the squadron. I was always amused by the lengths to which they went to avoid one-on-one contact with Major Goldman, since they had quickly learned that any such chance encounter within the confines of the squadron building would usually result an assignment or task of which

In October of 1976 the first groups of Bitburg pilots departed for Luke AFB, Arizona to check out in the Eagle. This was a wonderful time of year to be at Luke since the weather was absolutely perfect, especially when contrasted to the drab, cold climate of a typical German winter. The school itself was a pleasure because it was staffed with an outstanding group of instructors teaching a well-structured syllabus. At that time the wing commander at Luke was a flamboyant and popular old Brigadier General named Fred Haeffner. He was an officer who was unafraid to make decisions within his command, including experimentation with the paint schemes of the F-15s under his operational control.

---

they had not conceived. Accordingly, they learned that since "Goldie" walked around with a lot of keys and jangling coins in his flight suit pocket, sharp ears could hear him approaching in time for them to beat a hasty retreat. In addition to their outstanding flying skills, they were also "smart as a whip", which Goldie and I used to our advantage to sell the virtues of the newly introduced cockpit procedures trainer (CPT) to the USAFE Stan/Eval team. The CPT was a simple mock-up of an F-15 cockpit in which the pilot sat and actually "acted out" emergency and normal procedures as quizzed by another pilot or evaluator, as opposed to rote recital of answers to emergency situations. We knew that it was far better than the old "bold face" memorization, but the USAFE team was unconvinced and had come to Bitburg to "drive a wooden stake" through the heart of the concept. So when the USAFE evaluators arrived at the squadron, Goldie and I had purposefully arranged for our most senior flight commanders to be hanging around the CPT and available for immediate testing. We also arranged for our "ringer lieutenants" to be "not quite out of sight" at the far end of the room. Since Lt. Col. Bart Crews of the Stan/Eval team had been around, he quickly saw through this setup and announced that he wasn't interested in evaluating our flight commanders...but wanted to test "that lieutenant" over in the corner. "That lieutenant" happened to be the diminutive "Cobra" Homes, future outstanding graduate of the F-15 Fighter Weapons Instructor Course at Nellis AFB. When Cobra effortlessly began to answer every question and situation posed, Bart "smelled a rat" and went for another lieutenant. So it came to pass that he ended up with "Knife" McAllister, an Air Force Academy graduate with an absolute photographic memory in the CPT chair. Beginning with the critical, immediate action procedures, McAllister flawlessly recited them word for word while deftly acting out the procedure in the CPT. Crews then proceeded to smaller and smaller details in the Dash-1 until he was down to the mundane, small print "notes" sections. Not only did McAllister recite every word of the procedures verbatim, he prefixed and suffixed every response with "Sir." The USAFE team left the building shaking their heads in disbelief and the CPT has forever since been the training aid of choice for emergency procedure testing and training within the fighter community.

Originally the F-15 designers had rationalized, since it was to be a pure air-to-air fighter, what better color for it to blend with the blue sky in which it would operate than sky blue? Unfortunately this beautiful color, which the Air Force named "air superiority blue", made the big fighter shine like a mirror in the sky. So General Haeffner used his fleet of Eagles as "a canvas" in search of the perfect paint scheme to make the aircraft less visible in a combat environment. Affectionately know as "Fat Fred's Flying Circus" (General Haeffner bordered near the top end of the maximum gross weight for officers) the F-15s parked on the Luke ramp were indeed a colorful and eclectic collection.

There were the original, beautiful Air Superiority Blue planes, some with WWII invasion stripes, some lizard-colored, some with Keith Farris jagged lines on the sides as were seen on Japanese battle ships during WWII and others with canopies painted on the bottom. If nothing else, the multiple colors and patterns made it a lot easier to ascertain "who was who" during multiple aircraft engagements. It was ultimately determined the quintessential paint scheme would be the flat, mottled-gray color currently seen on almost all fighters today. Flawlessly

In an impressive demonstration of just how effective the gray color really was, I remember watching a film which delved into the methodology used to determine the color most difficult for an adversary to see. After discussing the advantages of various approaches, the film showed an echelon of four F-15s coming up initial approach, with the narrator asking, "Which of these four aircraft do you think is hardest to see?" As the formation drew closer, the narrator said, "If you picked any of the first four aircraft, you would be wrong." Just then, a fifth Eagle at the end of the echelon faintly appeared, painted in the mottled-gray scheme which would replace the original, beautiful, but totally, ineffective "air superiority blue" paint job.

After a week or so of academics we took our first ride in the F-15. In the backseat of the F-15B I flew was my old wingman, Captain Bob Ellis. I had heard all the stories relating how well the Eagle flew, but was nevertheless stunned by how truly superior it was to the great F-4. Not only did it have dazzling performance, but it was beyond doubt the easiest airplane to fly that I had ever piloted. I have told many people over the years I would have absolutely no hesitation in giving my wife, who flew a Cessna 150, two hours of instruction in the traffic pattern, then let her solo the aircraft with a takeoff and landing. The plane is really that forgiving and easy to fly.[43] Doing the same thing in an F-4 would be like signing her death warrant.

---

[43] Although the Eagle is really that easy to fly when doing something as routine as take-offs and landings, it is not so easy to learn to tactically employ, specifically when flown against equally capable aircraft whose pilots are obsessed with your demise.

So on my very first ride I did a triple immelmann, a truly vulgar display of raw power. We followed this with a level acceleration run from 200 knots indicated to 600 indicated at 10,000 feet in 23 seconds, during which time the airplane's amazing flight control system kept the stick trim dead neutral. I couldn't believe it. Upon return to the Luke traffic pattern Ellis demonstrated the first overhead pattern. After the left overhead break I was looking at Runway 30 Left so close aboard my left wing, I said to Ellis, "You'll never make this base turn." It wasn't even close as Ellis easily slid around the corner and rolled it out right on the numbers.[44] Unlike the F-4 this bird had a very light nose that could be held up for aerodynamic braking after touchdown all the way down to approximately 70 knots, thus eliminating the need for a drag chute. The high lift wing also allowed the aircraft to float effortlessly in idle power above the overrun to touchdown with perfect control.

Although this was a very large fighter, it did not feel so on the stick. It was absolutely as light as a feather and responsive beyond belief. Six years later when I commanded the 405th Tactical Training Wing at Luke, I routinely flew sorties in both the F-15 and the F-5Es stationed across town at Williams AFB. In direct comparison, the Eagle handled like a fighter about one-half the size of the tiny Northrop fighter.

Checking out with us at Luke was our wing commander, Brig. Gen. Fred Kyler, a personal acquaintance of Brig. Gen. Haeffner. On the second sortie the training syllabus called for a full afterburner takeoff in a "clean" F-15.[45] The stories about the takeoff acceleration were of course exaggerated by such claims as, not pulling the nose straight up after rotation would cause you to exceed the gear door speed, etc. This was of course BS, but Gen. Kyler apparently took these tall tales to

---

[44] "The numbers" refers to the large two digit numbers that are painted on the end of the runway to denote its direction. For example, the numbers 35 would indicate a runway aligned to a magnetic heading of 350 degrees. Since these numbers are painted on the very ends of the runway, an ideal landing in a fighter aircraft touches the aircraft down on these numbers, leaving the maximum amount of runway to stop the aircraft. Similarly, "rolling it out" means that the touchdown was exceedingly soft.

[45] A "clean F-15" referred to one without external tanks or armament pylons. In this configuration, the bird is not only lighter, but also more aerodynamic, making it perform exceptionally well. Since the F-15 had approximately as much acceleration in non-afterburner operation (military power) as the great F-4 had in full afterburner power, takeoff in the F-15 was typically made without the afterburner, thus saving fuel for other mission aspects.

heart. So when he performed his max performance takeoff he did precisely what he had been told was required to prevent overstressing the gear doors. Immediately after rotation he sucked up the gear and continued his pull to a near vertical attitude as the undercarriage retracted.

General Haeffner apparently witnessed this as he was driving in his staff car somewhere on the base and nearly ran off the road.[46] He immediately got on his radio to the command post and demanded that the "hot dog" that had just pulled the juvenile stunt be in his office immediately upon landing. It was a damn, good thing it was Kyler rather than any of the rest of us, as we would surely have received both barrels of his Haeffner's wrath.

The duration of our sojourn to Luke was about ninety days, running through the Christmas holidays of 1976. It was during the week before Christmas that our class's syllabus called for dissimilar air combat training (DACT) which would pit the F-15 against some other type of fighter. This was an important part of the training, since maneuvering against aircraft of different size, performance, and tactics as opposed to the one you fly is absolutely essential in the development of a pilot's air-to-air combat skills. Constantly fighting against an aircraft identical to the one you are flying develops bad habits in the form of miscalculation of range, energy, and turn radii. There is a wise proverb saying, "Flying only against similar aircraft is like inbreeding hogs. You end up with nothing but hoofs and snouts."

Normally, Air Force, Navy and Marine squadrons throughout the States would jump at the chance to come to Phoenix, especially with its chamber-of-commerce, winter weather. However, the wing scheduling officer was having trouble filling our requirement because everyone seemed eager to stay close to home over the holidays. However, when he called the 163rd TFS, an Air National Guard unit stationed at Tucson, Arizona, they said, "You're damn right we'll come. When do you want us there?"

Popularly known as the "Taco Guard", the 150th TFS was still flying the venerable old F-100, with many of the assigned pilots having thousands of hours in the aircraft. Among the pilots who showed up was Major Bob "Cass" Cassaco who happened to be one of the highest flying-time F-100 pilots in the

---

[46] The "white-knuckled" instructor pilot (IP) sitting in Kyler's back seat was then Captain, now Lt. Gen Paul Hester.

[47] Later, Cassaco became the oldest fighter squadron commander in the USAF Air National Guard as the A-7 equipped 150th Tactical Fighter Squadron, and subsequently the Guard's oldest F-16 pilot.

world.[47] I had the pleasure of flying against him on one of the several DACT missions we flew. On one mission Bob Ellis and I flew two Eagles versus two F-100s, with all aircraft simulating ordnance of heat seeking missiles and guns.[48] Although the F-100 was by no means a match for the F-15, I have never seen a Hun[49] maneuvered more successfully than by this guy Cassaco.

Because of its severe adverse yaw characteristics, the F-100 would depart controlled flight in the form of a snap-roll, opposite direction of turn when "pro-turn aileron" was applied at very high angles of attack. In the hands of a skilled pilot, this controlled departure could effectively be used as a "last ditch" maneuver creating an overshoot by a gun-tracking adversary. When executed properly the maneuver could, in a heart beat, snap-roll the aircraft opposite to the direction of turn, while shedding well over 100 knots of airspeed. If you, as the attacker, were just beginning to pull lead for a gun shot it looked almost like the plane stopped right in front of you and you were going to run over it.

Without exception this "air show" would spoil even your best tracking solution for the time being. The counter for the "spit out" attacker was a quarter-roll and zoom maneuver to reposition, which was relatively easy to do and very effective in the Eagle (thanks to Pratt & Whitney). The far more difficult task was for the Hun pilot to recover to controlled flight, extend away, and live to fight another turn. I'll never forget how really well Cassaco flew that pretty old fighter and I told him so at the debriefing. I haven't seen him since, but if you ever hear stories about how good he was in a Hun, believe them.

Our group completed checkout in January 1977 and returned to Bitburg where the remaining pilots who had not been selected for transition to the F-15 were flying the F-4E.[50] It would be our plight to remain at Bitburg in non-flying status until all of the wing's pilots had completed the basic checkout F-15 program at Luke, and then proceed to Langley AFB, Virginia for tactical qualification and

---

[48] Commonly referred to as "heaters and guns," these were stern only ordnance that required the attacking aircraft to maneuver into the target's vulnerable six o-clock position to reach the weapons employment envelope, thereby almost always ensuring a close-in turning engagement

[49] Although the F-100's official name was the Super Sabre, it was commonly called "The Hun."

[50] The "staggered" classes attending the upgrade training at Luke AFB were comprised of about six pilots, with these classes spaced approximately three to four weeks apart.

combat readiness certification. Since we were no longer allowed to fly the F-4 (why, I don't know), we spent our time doing staff work in preparation for the arrival of our aircraft in the spring.

So one morning in late January 1977 at the wing commander's morning staff meeting, Colonel Gene Harrell, the wing's Deputy Commander for Maintenance proudly announced the first F-15 would be arriving within a few weeks. He quickly added that it was important for the pilots to realize the aircraft was to be used strictly for maintenance training, not flying. "What do you mean this airplane isn't for the pilots to fly?" demanded General Kyler. Harrell launched into a logical explanation saying, flying the aircraft would seriously disrupt the really tight maintenance training schedule which had been structured around its availability. Kyler listened closely, and retorted, "Nonsense! Everybody on this base has been waiting now for over a half year to see this airplane fly and we're damn well going to fly it the day after it arrives." Then turning toward me he added, "And Officer Handley is going to fly it. Put the word out." I was delighted and replied, "Yes sir! You bet I will."

As the briefing ended Gene Harrell made a beeline for me. He said he had been talking with his counterpart at Langley (from where the aircraft was coming) who had told him the bird would indeed be a good maintenance trainer since it would require "a lot of tuning up." "What does that mean?" I asked. He said he wouldn't know until they "got into it." I pointed out, if it could fly all the way across the Atlantic Ocean, it must surely be able to fly a routine mission in the local area. So when the aircraft arrived on the following Tuesday afternoon, Gene Harrell once again contacted me. He said the pilot who flew it in had told him the engines were in absolutely horrendous tune, and the left engine's afterburner operation was marginal at best, while the right one's operation was all but impossible.

My ear perked up at what Gene was telling me since he was not prone to exaggerate and was a fine pilot in his own right. During the few hours I had flown the F-15 at Luke, I had learned first hand that unlike the General Electric J-79 engines in the F-4, the Pratt & Whitney TF-100 engines in the Eagle simply would not tolerate the "slam-bang" throttle technique that could be routinely used in the Phantom, mainly because of the fan on the front of the engine.[51]

---

[51] The P&W TF-100 was the fan-jet engine to be equipped with an afterburner. This created problems since the pressure spike created by the ignition of the afterburner was prone to travel forward to the freely spinning fan on the front of the engine where it would disrupt laminar airflow through the engine to the extent that a compressor stall would result.

Even when the P&W engines were perfectly tuned, moving the throttle rapidly from some intermediate setting into the afterburner range would almost always invite trouble in the form of a compressor stall, with subsequent loss of power on the engine.

This probability for trouble was exacerbated by slow airspeeds and high angles of attack (precisely those routinely encountered during an air-to-air mission). At best, if you quickly pulled the throttle out of the afterburner range at the very onset of the compressor stall it would usually "self-clear." At worst, the engine would continue to stall regardless of your actions, the RPM would roll back, the FTIT (Forward Turbine Inlet Temperature) would rise, and the engine would have to be shut down and a wind-milling airstart performed to clear the stall and regain power from the engine.[52] A wind-milling airstart was the only way to restart an engine in the original F-15A when airborne. The procedure required sufficient airspeed to cause the slipstream passing through the dead engine to spool it up to a minimum of 12% rpm, at which time fuel could be introduced and the desired restart accomplished. The procedure was both time consuming and demanding of the pilot's attention. One dead engine to be restarted using this procedure was feasible, but attempting to restart both engines in this manner, without sufficient altitude to trade for airspeed (450 KCAS minimum needed) could quite simply be disastrous.[53]

These thoughts jangled around in my mind as I approached the newly arrived gray F-15 parked squarely in front of the Bitburg control tower slightly past noon on 26 January 1977. Since the event had been advertised in the Bitburg Baron base newspaper, a considerable crowd of base military personnel and their dependents had assembled to watch the launch. I noted there was a red carpet leading up to the crew boarding ladder, and the launch crew was wearing newly purchased powder blue jump suits with a big eagle stitched on the back for the occasion. Since it had been some time since I had flown the bird I though to myself, "Whatever you do, don't screw this up."

I decided since there was plenty of time before I was to meet a flight of four F-4s in the arming area for takeoff, I would carefully use the checklist to make damn

---

[52] When the Fan Turbine Inlet Temperature (FTIT) hit 1000 degrees C, you had to shut down the engine to clear the stall and prevent heat damage to the engine.

[53] As a matter of record, during the first year of the Eagle's operational employment, two were lost due to this scenario. These losses were the impetus for the Air Force to fund a modification of the Jet Fuel Starter (JFS) so that it could be used to restart an engine after airborne shutdown.

certain everything was done properly, and also re-familiarize myself with the cockpit environment. Using the checklist in this manner was not the mode of operation normally used by pilots who are exceedingly familiar with their craft. The procedure of pushing all the "sharp and shinny" switches forward and leaving the rest alone works pretty well, with the checklist simply used as a backup to make certain all required actions have been accomplished.

After exchanging pleasantries with the half-dozen or so members of the launch team, I examined the aircraft's log (Form 781). Although it was devoid of any "Red X's" or other discrepancies which would have grounded the aircraft, I noted that a host of previous write-ups concerning the engines operation had been cleared. Since the majority of them concerned afterburner operation, it really didn't concern me much since the F-15's performance without use of afterburner exceeds that of the F-4 at full power. I rationalized I would neither require nor use the afterburners anyway. After a scrupulously thorough walk-around inspection, I was still fully thirty minutes away from the F-4's scheduled start time, so decided to follow through with my plan to meticulously run the checklist up to engine start, then spend the remaining time familiarizing myself with switch and gage locations.

After the crew chief helped me strap into the cockpit and removed the boarding ladder, I balanced my helmet on the windscreen and directed my attention to the yellow checklist strapped on my left leg. However, before accomplishing even the first checklist item I noted the rudder pedals were positioned too far forward for my preference and immediately reached down to adjust them. At this point two thousand hours of F-4 "muscle memory" apparently came into play.

The rudder pedals were adjusted in the F-4 by pulling out a lanyard unlocking them from their track, permitting them to spring inward toward the pilot who could then push them forward to the desired position, release the lanyard, and lock them in place. Unfortunately this was not the way the rudder pedals were adjusted in the Eagle…and even more unfortunately, the F-15 had a lanyard I mistakenly pulled in my attempt to make the adjustment. Suddenly I was aware of the ear splitting howl of the aircraft's jet fuel starter (JFS) winding up! In my haste to ensure the throt-

(USAF File Photograph)

Figure 34—The first F-15A Eagle, 76-049, delivered to Bitburg Air Base, Germany and flown the author on its initial sortie.

tles were off, I inadvertently raised the finger lift on the right throttle, engaging the right engine to the JFS, which then applied hydraulic pressure to the aircraft's systems as the engine spun up to starting RPM.[54]

In my peripheral vision I became painfully aware of several, blue-clad, crew chiefs scattering like a covey of quail from underneath the aircraft where 3,000 pounds of hydraulic pressure were now slamming various gear doors shut. After quickly looking about and noting there still seemed to be a complete inventory of the launch crew, none missing any arms, I felt instant relief no one had been seriously injured. However, I was now faced with a real dilemma as I sat there, sans helmet, with this two-hundred decibel screaming JFS engaged to a rotating right engine. The choices, as I saw them, were to quickly shut it down, apologize to everyone concerned and look like a total fool, or to boldly bluff my way through.

Deciding on the latter, I moved the right throttle to its idle position, offhandedly retrieved and donned my custom Lumbar helmet from the windscreen, and completed the right engine start sequence. As I was bluffing my way through this charade, the lead crew chief was scrambling to plug his headset into the intercom receptacle on the left side of the aircraft. His first out-of-breath statement was, "Sir, I really wish you'd let us know when you are going to start up like that!" In as informal a voice as I could muster I replied, "Sarge, we always start 'em that way."

Thankfully the rest of the start procedures went smoothly, and judging from the inquisitive faces of the crowd, all with fingers sticking in their ears to attenuate the din of the screaming jet engines, no one seemed to realize anything abnormal had occurred. The only remaining embarrassment came when, even after running every imaginable built-in-test (BIT) for the aircraft's avionics suite, it would be at least another twenty minutes before the F-4s showed up. I therefore decided to taxi on down to the arming area for runway 05, which was far enough away from the crowd to allow them a break from the engine noise. As I awaited the F-4s in the arming area I thought to myself, "What else on earth could possibly go wrong?"

The F-4 flight showed up right on schedule and after a final "quick check" by maintenance personnel in the arming area, made twenty-second element trail departures ahead of me into an 800 foot overcast ceiling with forecast tops at

---

[54] Jet engines are started by bringing their rotational speed up to a certain minimum rpm, then introducing fuel to the combustion chambers. In the Eagle the start sequence was quite simple. Once the JFS was running, either engine could be mechanically coupled to it by simply raising and releasing a tab on the front of the throttle called "the finger lift." When the engine spun up to 18% rpm, moving the throttle to the "idle" position provided fuel to the engine for the start.

4,000 feet. I took twenty seconds spacing on the second element and made a nor-mal non-afterburner takeoff, locking on to the trail F-4 element with my radar immediately after gear retraction. After breaking out on top, the F-4s joined into a fingertip formation, while I, at the strict insistence of USAFE Headquarters, joined to a conservative route formation position since the USAFE staff had decided that flying an F-15 in close formation with an F-4 might be unsafe. I couldn't believe it.

The F-4 flight lead and I had briefed a series of one vs. four engagements, begin-ning from beyond visual range (BVR) at a distance of approximately twenty miles. As I was positioning for the first engagement I decided to gently and indi-vidually test the first stage of afterburner operation of each engine. The left engine's burner worked fine with very slow throttle movement and a pause for the engine to stabilize after the first of the five stages of afterburner lit off. The right engine's burner operated precisely as Gene Harrell had described, in that, any attempt to gently slip the throttle over the afterburner throttle gate was immedi-ately met with the staccato-like explosions of a compressor stall. Since I retarded the throttle quickly at the onset of the stalls, they "self-cleared." My curiosity sat-isfied, I reminded myself the remainder of this flight would be totally without afterburner operation.

The simulated engagements went well and after the F-4s reached their "bingo fuel" and set course for Bitburg, I still had several thousand pounds of JP-4 remaining, so I stayed in the area to do some aerobatics. As I approached Bitburg for recovery, the weather was basically the same as when we had departed. After handoff from Eiffel Control to Bitburg Approach, I began a totally routine radar approach which I had accomplished hundreds of times. Entering the thick 4,000 foot ceiling I instinctively checked my pitot heat as I was vectored for the GCA radar approach.

Stabilizing on the downwind leg I noted that my desired 250 knot airspeed seemed to require more power than I had remembered at Luke. Suspecting the pitot tube might be icing up, I looked down at the left console once again to ensure the pitot heat switch was indeed on. Despite this, as I approached the base leg turn I found myself adding more and more power in an attempt to maintain the desired airspeed. I knew something was definitely not right but simply could-n't think of anything other than an iced pitot tube, or possibly a burned-out, heating element in the pitot tube. The latter convinced me I needed to get back up into the VFR conditions above the clouds so I could join with a Bitburg F-4 and fly a formation approach to beneath the clouds on his wing (USAFE forma-tion orders be damned).

Before I could punch the mike button and advise Bitburg Approach of my request, they called for a right turn to the base leg. Almost simultaneously the airspeed began to decay precipitously, despite the fact that my gear and flaps were up and I was near military power.[55] As the airspeed rapidly dropped through 150 knots toward zero, the light in the gear handle came on, the gear horn sounded, and the master caution light illuminated as the central air data computer dropped off the line. Staring at an airspeed indicator now reading zero and with glowing red and amber lights throughout the cockpit, my instincts once again took over. Using my fully engrained F-4 power-management technique, I rammed both throttles into 5th stage afterburner. There was an immediate explosion which blew my feet off the rudder pedals and a ball of fire, which seemed as big as a house, shot out in front of the jet. Jerking the throttles to idle as I realized what I had done, I was gripped with an overwhelming sense of anxiety that I was actually going to lose this airplane.

While staring at the zero airspeed indication and trying to assess whether or not either engine had self-cleared the compressor stalls, I had an overpowering urge to pull back on the stick. I did. Four plus positive G's pushed me down into the ejection seat like a big hand and within seconds I shot from the 4,000 foot overcast ceiling at a forty-five degree angle like a NASA Saturn Rocket. I now found myself in the bright blue sky of Eiffel Control airspace with no clearance, while Bitburg Radar was no doubt wondering what the hell I was doing. I was still thinking clearly enough to realize that given the angle and velocity with which I had just departed to the tops of the clouds, I certainly did not have zero airspeed. I also realized I damn well better declare an emergency least Eiffel Control violate me for flying into their airspace without clearance.

Doing so, Eiffel asked me the nature of my emergency and how they could help? Asking them to standby, I reassessed my situation, now infinitely better than it had been moments ago. I was now totally convinced the heating element in the pitot tube had to be burned out. As I checked the tube's heat switch one more time, I was amazed at what I saw. It was indeed in the OFF position with the adjacent ENGINE HEAT switch[56] positioned to ON.

---

[55] "Military Power" refers to full engine power available without use of afterburner.

[56] Just as the pitot heat electrically warms the pitot tube to prevent ice blockage during atmospheric icing conditions, the engine heat introduces hot bleed air throughout the front faces of the engines to prevent ice accumulation under icing conditions.

As I flipped on the pitot heat switch, the airspeed immediately climbed rapidly to 450 knots. I couldn't believe I had overlooked this at least a half-dozen times since I began the ill-fated approach. Looking more closely, I realized the locations of the pitot heat and engine heat switches, which sat side by side on the left console in both the F-4 and the F-15, had been reversed in the Eagle. I had been turning on and rechecking the engine heat switch, not the pitot heat. Informing Eifel I no longer had an emergency, I reentered the pattern and made a totally routine approach and landing.

I was delighted no telephone calls from Eiffel had been received at the Wing Headquarters, and the entire "goat rope" scenario remained securely locked within the fertile gray matter between my ears until weeks later at a 36th Wing dining in. During the cocktail hour which always preceded such gala affairs, I was at the bar and feeling little pain while discussing the 36th wing's good fortune with its amiable commander. Since I knew Fred Kyler was indeed a man who could be trusted, I now viewed the whole nightmare incident with a degree of humor and felt confident that my secret would remain safe with him. What a mistake! Kyler thought it so funny he proposed a toast during the formal mess, told the entire story in painful detail, and ended with his conviction I should be put in for a Distinguished Flying Cross.

At this writing, more than a quarter century has passed since that flight and many of those at that dining in have departed the scene, including the great Fred Kyler. To this day I still run into attendees of that evening who "bring it up" one more time to relive the humor of the moment, which I genuinely enjoy. Although the whole story is quite entertaining to me now, rest assured there was absolutely no hilarity within the cockpit of F-15, tail number 76-049 that Wednesday afternoon, spring day of 1977 at "The Bush."

Mach & Career Busting

- 1978 -

Whaen my two year tour as squadron commander of the 22nd Tactical Fighter Squadron, The Big 22,[57] at Bitburg Air Base, German was up in 1978, I was reassigned to Ramstein Air Base, Germany as the Chief of USAFE Standardization and Evaluation. Since the job required I remain current in the F-15 Eagle, I would drive back to Bitburg almost every other week to get in a few sorties. I never minded the two-hour drive back and forth, and as a matter of fact really enjoyed it because of the car I was driving.

(Author)
Figure 35—1973 Chevy Z-28 "Mercedes Eater"

It was a 1973 Chevy Z-28 which had come into my possession just before I left Bitburg. One day while I was sitting Zulu Alert[58] one of the NCOs at the alert hangar with whom I frequently visited told me he had an emergency situation back in the States requiring his immediate return. He wanted me to purchase his Z-28, which was his "show room new", pride and joy. I told him that as much as I would love to have it, I already had a couple of cars. He insisted he didn't want to sell it to "just anybody" and would make me a deal I couldn't refuse. He did and I bought it.

Since the stock Z-28's engine of 1973 suffered from the same smog control devices found at that time on all American cars, I made a decision to convert this to a strictly "European based machine" which I could never send back into the

---

[57] The Big 22: The 22nd Tactical Fighter Squadron, "The Last of the Red Hot Fighter Squadrons" stationed at Bitburg Air Base, Germany.

[58] Zulu Alert: Aircraft sitting on five-minute runway alert for the purpose of air intercept. This is opposed to Victor Alert, where the birds are sitting five-minute nuclear alert with a nuclear device on the centerline station, for delivery upon a designated target, which the pilot of each alert aircraft knows "like the back of his hand."

States. I figured correctly that the NCOs at the jet engine shop, who could rebuild small block Chevy V-8s in their sleep, just might get a kick out of hot rodding this great looking car. When I asked them if I were to supply a Midwest Automobile Parts catalog along with carte-blanch authority to modify the drive train and suspension of the car, could they turn it into a "Mercedes Eater?" Their immediate answer was, "You better believe it!"

It wasn't long before all the air pumps and smog devices which make the engine look like a heart-and-lung machine were replaced with high-rise manifold, Holley double-pumper carbs, side-exit dual-exhaust pipes, special ignition, Hurst shifter and a dozen other goodies. The car's straight line and highway performance became immediately remarkable and provided real entertainment while transiting Germany's vaunted autobahns. My personal opinion of these autobahns is they are greatly overrated and don't even come close to the freeways found in the States, particularly in Texas. Their reputation is mainly based on the perception there are no speed limits, which is not quite true. Certain portions do have speed limits, which are pretty closely enforced, but there are a lot of long stretches where no speed limits exist. It is on those sections the super cars with lights flashing to warn everyone to get out of the way typically cruise along well above 100 miles per hour. For a rich German, there are few greater pleasures in life than owning one of the big Mercedes or BMWs and passing everything in sight on the autobahn.

So, during my trips back and forth to Bitburg I would cruise along at a reasonable speed, around 80-90 miles per hour, until I spotted flashing headlights in my rearview mirror indicating a rapidly approaching Merc or BMW in the passing lane. As he passed with an overtake of 30 miles per hour or so, I would immediately insert this unworthy looking American Chevy squarely in his draft and watch for the look of surprise in his rearview mirror. At this point, his reaction was almost scripted in that he would keep accelerating in a vain attempt to shake this totally ordinary looking piece of American iron.

When I was certain his engine was totally wound out, usually around 150 MPH, I would pull out and pass him in a routine manner with a good 15 knots of overtake, smiling and casually waving as I went by. The real fun now occurred when looking back to see the smoke coming from the driver's ears. To this day, although I have owned and raced a lot of high-performance sports cars, I have never gone faster in a car than the 180 mph I saw in that old Z-28…and it still had some left.

So, after another satisfying drive to Bitburg on a pretty fall morning in 1978, I parked in front of my old squadron, "The Big 22" around 9:30 AM for the two-ship BFM (Basic Fighter Maneuvers) mission I was scheduled to fly with Major

Charlie "Chopper" Price, the squadron's operations officer. Our mission was a basic 1v1 training flight with both of us flying a single seat F-15A in a designated block of airspace named Area 204 situated north-northeast of Bitburg. Like most of the fighter pilots at Bitburg, I had flown hundreds of sorties in this training area which overlaid the lovely fields and vineyards along the Mosel River Valley, with Koblenz at the southern end and Koln-Bonn to the north.

The area was bounded at the top at 24,000 feet with a floor of 11,000 feet as its base. As the flight leader, I briefed we would make a formation takeoff and proceed directly to the center of the area at 24,000 feet, where we would then do "butterfly start[59]", non-afterburner engagements until reaching "Bingo Fuel.[60]" This would be followed by a routine formation return to Bitburg for landing. When covering the rules-of-engagement during the briefing, I stressed that the 11,000 feet bottom of the area was a "hard altitude floor" beneath which we would not descend, and any engagement approaching that floor would be "knocked off" in time to recover above the floor.

There is a vast misconception that aircraft possessing great thrust-to-weight ratios, such as the F-4 or fighters the ilk of the F-15 would have little trouble maintaining enough energy to remain within the confines of two and one-half miles of vertical airspace such as that of the 204 Area. These aircraft would not have a problem were they not maneuvering against each other in efforts to achieve a rear quadrant position for a gun or missile shot. In such a situation, equally matched fighters will "burn" that excess energy as each of them strive for firing position using high-G maneuvers which continually drive down the aircraft's airspeed because of the excessive "induced drag" generated at extreme angles-of-attack."

The ability to "get on the opponent's tail" is basically driven by the fighter's energy, its ability to turn, and the skill of the pilot to maneuver the aircraft. When both aircraft are equal, only the human third of these factors will determine the winner. All aircraft have an airspeed at which the quickest, tightest turn may be performed.

---

[59] Butterfly start: A scenario whereby the two aircraft begin line-abreast at 350 KIAS, then turn 45 degrees away from each other and hold that heading until the radio transmission, "Fight's On," at which time they can do anything they wish to shoot down the adversary.

[60] Bingo Fuel: The pre-determined volume of fuel required to proceed to home base, execute a missed approach (if necessary), and then proceed to an alternate airfield and land.

It is called "corner velocity" and is predicated upon the minimum airspeed at which that particular fighter can pull the maximum allowable Gs without over-stressing the bird. So although it would seem logical that the best tactic would be to always stay near "corner velocity" during an engagement, it simply doesn't work that way as both aircraft strive for firing position. The old adage "Speed is life but rate kills", (where rate refers to turn rate) is proven every time fighters of equal ability engage in a turning engagement. Airspeed will be traded for energy to turn, and then altitude traded for energy to keep the airspeed up, resulting in a continu-ally descending fight. So in a stalemated fight where neither aircraft can bring their ordinance to bear, the aircraft will inevitably end up at the floor of the practice area at low airspeed and high angle-of-attack, at which time the engagement must be terminated for safety concerns as per the rules-of-engagement.

Weather was not a factor and our mission, which lasted just over an hour was totally routine. After recovery back at Bitburg and maintenance debrief, Chopper and I were sitting in one of the small briefing rooms with a cup of coffee going over the six engagements we had done when the squadron duty officer softly knocked on the door and asked if by chance we had done any supersonic maneu-vers during the mission. I replied off-handedly that we were barely sonic, much less supersonic. Shortly thereafter, another knock at the door produced one of the squadron's flight commanders who also asked if I was certain we couldn't have gone through the mach at any time. I told him absolutely not and asked why he wanted to know? He replied there had been some sort of complaint through the command post and they were checking to make certain it was not us. I assured him it had not been us. No sooner had we started to get back to the debriefing when the 36th Wing DO, Colonel "Storm'n" Norm Campbell came in and sat down with us at the table. "Hands", he said, "we've got a big problem here."

He told us there were all kinds of reports out of Köln-Bonn that a supersonic boom had shattered windows, including those of some very important cathedral on the Mosel. Apparently, dozens of people had been injured by flying glass. Worst of all, he added, was Rhine Control, the German radar agency monitoring the area, had reported that our two-ship flight was the only flight of fighters air-borne at the time of the incident and the damage was located squarely beneath our radar tracks. I couldn't believe what I was hearing but had little time to reflect on it as the duty officer announced I had an urgent call from the USAFE DO, who asked the same questions and was obviously upset.

This was followed immediately by yet another call from the American Embassy in Köln-Bonn. The voice on the other end of the telephone was that of a full colonel assigned as the USAF liaison officer. He asked me the same questions I had previously heard and told me Rhine was sticking to their story that my flight was the only one in the area. I told him I was absolutely certain it could not have been us. He said he believed me and would continue to dig for details as the reports, which seemed to get increasingly worse, continued to come in. He suggested Chopper and I immediately begin to document any and every shred of evidence to prove we were not the culprits. Returning to the briefing room, Chopper and I sat down with yellow tablets of paper and while "sweating bullets" we began to write!

Over the next half-hour we had written about twelve pages each, and were interrupted by a call from the colonel liaison officer at Bonn, who now had estimates of the tens of thousands of dollars damage which had occurred. I really dreaded picking up the telephone on the duty desk when the third call from Bonn came in. "Colonel, are you ready for some good news for a change?" the voice of the liaison colonel asked. "You better believe it!" I replied. He reported, "Well, it seems there was a witness to all this. The trouble is, it's a very young German boy who can't tell one aircraft from another. However, he told the police that as he was walking along the Mosel River he saw three airplanes coming at him very fast and very low, making a lot of noise when they passed. But then he added he saw just one more airplane coming after them and it wasn't making any noise at all until it passed overhead when there was a big, big boom, and all of the windows fell out. Although he didn't know one airplane from another, when the German police asked him to describe what the airplane looked like, he replied they all had big black crosses on their sides." The weight of the world suddenly dropped from my shoulders and I told the liaison officer if that kid were here, I'd kiss him.

When everything finally got sorted out, it seems a flight of four German F-104's had departed Mindeg Air Base, a German field lying approximately forty-five miles northeast of Bitburg, on a training sortie unknown to Rhine Control and had remained at very low altitude just above the Mosel River and beneath the Rhine's radar coverage. Apparently they had taken off single ship at fifteen second spacing inter-

(USAF File Photograph)

Figure 36—Lockheed F-104C Starfighter

vals with the leader accelerating to a high, subsonic airspeed and turning left down the Mosel River. The numbers two and three aircraft had successfully overtaken the leader and were joined in formation, but evidently the number four man was lagging and had inadvertently let his "Zipper[61]" slip though the mach.

With the walls of the canyon on both sides of the Mosel River acting as a funnel for number four's mach wave, its effects were magnified even more than its already considerable overpressure, resulting in the extensive damage reported. Needless to say, the commute from Bitburg back to Ramstein in my fire-breathing Z-28 was totally anti-climactic, as my "flickering low-level light" for speed had been totally extinguished, at least for the time being.

---

[61] Zipper: Nickname for the F-104 Starfighter.

Down To The Last Drop

- 1972 -

Prologue

The following story illustrates the incredible complexity of the aerial combat arena which surrounds a major strike force incursion into enemy territory. Its diverse cast of players, individual brilliance, bone-headed stupidity, and "dog luck" make up what Clausewitz called "The Fog of War." A more mundane but equally accurate characterization is seen on the rear bumpers of some Texas, pickup trucks, "Shit Happens." This is an account of Buick Flight, a flight of four F-4s from Udorn RTAFB comprising the ingress CAP for a Linebacker raid against targets in the vicinity of Hanoi on the morning of 6 October 1972. I was the leader of that flight, Buick 01.

Story

The primary target of the Alpha Strike on the morning of 6 October 1972 was the steel works at Thai-Nguyen, located about 40 miles north-north-west of Hanoi. The integrated strike package was typical of the "Eight hundred Pound Gorilla" approach used in both the Rolling Thunder and Linebacker bombing campaigns. The frag had the package ingressing and egressing from the west side, with participants coming from many of the major fighter bases in Thailand and South Vietnam. Typically this meant there would be F-4 MiG cappers and RF-4C recce out of Udorn, F-4 chaffers and bombers out of Ubon, F-105 bombers and F-4 MiG cappers out of Korat, EB-66 jammers, EC-121 radar control platforms, dozens of KC-135 tankers, and HH-54 Jolly Green rescue choppers with A-1E "Sandy" escorts, etc.. The sheer magnitude of this armada was never more apparent than at the mass rendezvous for pre-strike refueling. As far as the eye could see, there would be cell after cell of tankers, each with several sets of fighters on their wings, and one on the boom.

On this particular mission, I was leading Buick Flight, the Ingress CAP. Now the Ingress CAP was the flight of F-4s on the point, flying directly ahead of the strike package (the bombers and their accompanying escorts). It was a prized mission because of the increased probability of MiG reaction. I felt particularly good about our chances on this day because I had a great bunch of guys in my flight. Every man was on, at least, his second combat tour, the birds were loaded for bear, all carrying 3 tanks, 4 AIM-7Es, 4 AIM-9Js, and three of the four birds had an internal gun. I was flying an F-4D, hence no gun. However, I felt it was worth it because this was one of the few birds equipped with a "Combat Tree" in the rear cockpit. The "Tree" was a classified piece of equipment which could interrogate the MiG's IFF transponder, thus giving you a positive ID for BVR missile shots.

As was our practice, we took five aircraft to the tanker so as to have an airborne spare in the event one of the four primary aircraft air-aborted. On this day, if the spare was not needed, he was to accompany the flight to the vicinity of the Gorilla's Head at the Laos/North Vietnam border, where he would climb to high altitude and set up orbit to act as a radio relay if necessary. Our rendezvous with the White 55 tanker was uneventful, and after confirming with the strike package leader that they would be on time, we began our ingress along the designated route with 3 full bags of gas, feeding centerline.

The wing's policy concerning the jettisoning of external tanks stated, if you didn't need to get rid of them, bring them home as they cost money and were sometimes in short supply. The F-4 carried a 600 gallon tank on the centerline and two 370 gallon tanks on the outboard wing pylons. You always strived to feed out the centerline tank first because of the drag and maneuvering limitations it imposed. Also, unlike the 370 gallon outboard tanks which could be jettisoned cleanly under almost all

(USAF File Photograph)

Figure 37—Flight of F-4 Phantoms air-refueling from KC-135 tanker

flight conditions, the 600 gallon "bathtub" on the center line had a nasty habit of rolling along the bottom of the aircraft and striking the stabilator as it departed. The recommended jettison parameters for the centerline tank were straight and level 1G flight at 300 knots, but we were still getting aircraft strikes using these criteria. Through trial and error, we found that if it was jettisoned during a steady 4G pull-up from level flight (with the ball centered), it always came off cleanly.[62]

Our route of flight took us from the tanker drop-off point, past the Gorilla's Head, over the southwestern tip of Thud Ridge, to our designated CAP orbit which was about 30 miles north of the Phuc Yen Airfield. The radios were strangely silent until we reached our designated orbit point (2149N, 10556E) and did a "ninety right" to take a look at Phuc Yen with the "Tree." During that turn, the UHF command frequency and guard channel sprang to life when Red Crown, Disco 3, and Tea Ball all "stepped on each other" as they announced to me that MiGs were airborne out of Phuc Yen and headed our way. As we rolled out of the turn we blew the centerline tanks on my call and went to "min-burner" to kill the telltale trails from our eight J-79 engines.[63]

Almost immediately 1/Lt. Jack "Karst" Smallwood, got a single sweep paint on a MiG-21 before the bandits killed their IFF transponder (they too had figured out how a Combat Tree worked). Jack held the MiGs 60 degrees left for 60 miles. In a continuing barrage of radio transmissions over both UHF and guard channels, Red Crown, Disco 3, and Tea Ball issued updates confirming we were on a head-on collision course with the MiGs. I was most interested in what Tea Ball had to

---

[62] As an aside, the centerline tanks provided a "flying billboard" upon which the crew chiefs and bomb loaders spray-painted informative little messages to the peace loving North Vietnamese citizens upon whose heads these tanks rained on a daily basis. I was always struck by the originality and creativity of those authors who daily scribed these "pearls of wisdom", as there never seemed to be a repeat. However the theme itself was repetitious in that the vast majority dealt quite explicitly with the heritage and social habits of the ever popular Jane Fonda.

[63] I have nothing but praise for the J-79. It was tough as a boot, was immune to throttle abuse, and would eat 23mm sized projectiles and still bring you home. The less than perfect thing about a J-79 was it created a tremendous smoke trail at power settings below afterburner range. The result being the F-4 could be seen at incredible distances because of the black lines in the sky that pointed directly to it. I once read the debriefing report of a MiG-21 pilot who commented that he had been briefed that the F-4 smoked badly, but the first time he actually saw one in flight he thought it was on fire. When the Air Force procured the J-79, General Electric offered them a relatively inexpensive option that would have made it "smokeless." However, in an unbelievably wrongheaded decision, it was deemed that such an attribute was not an operational requirement. It was not until years later that the "smokeless option" was exercised, working exactly as advertised.

say, since his information was derived directly from the radio transmissions between the MiG flight leader and his control agency. Just as Tea Ball was transmitting to me, somewhere in the war zone a SAR, for a Wolf FAC who had been shot down, kicked off with the SAR forces transmitting on Guard for the downed aircrew to "come up voice." As the range decreased to 7 miles at a combined closing velocity of about 1,200 knots, Tea Ball came through loud and clear with an announcement that the MiG's altitude was unknown, but the leader had us in sight and was attacking.

Red Crown called our flight paths merged just as the Master Caution Light illuminated when the left generator dropped off the line. I had no sooner reset the generator when the RHAW scope lit up with a classic E-SAM Lo & Hi activity, flashing Launch Light and tone. Calling "pods on", Buick flight "took it down" in full burner with a two-ring strobe at 11 o-clock. I was almost dead certain this was a rouse designed to divert our attention while the attacking MiG-21s lined us up for an unobserved Atoll shot, but ignoring it entirely was simply not a viable option.[64]

---

[64] Unlike the sophisticated SAMs of today, the SA-2 was an early and simplistic missile, easily defeated (if seen in time). So, the first order of business was to visually acquire the missile. To do this, you needed to put the strobe on the RHAW scope in the vicinity of the 10 or 2 o-clock position so the pilot could look for the missile there, while the GIB looked to the sides and aft for missiles from the adjacent sites (the back shooters). The SA-2 kicked up a lot of smoke and dust as it left the pad which provided a good cue to locating it. The reason for "taking it down" was twofold: First it gave you the energy to maneuver, and secondly if the missile was in flight, you wanted to get below it so as to commit it nose-low, thus forcing it to pull against "God's G" when it came time to "set the hook." Once you picked up the missile visually, you could look at its smoke trail and flight path to determine if it was guiding. If it had a smooth smoke trail, it was not receiving command guidance signals and was simply on a ballistic path. Also if you were the target, when you changed your flight path the missile would adjust its own path to continue a "lead-collision" course. "Setting the hook" was a matter of timing. As it approached your aircraft, about the time that it appeared to be about the size of a pencil held at arm's length, or at the point you could begin to distinguish features on the missile, it was time to do a nice hard 6G pull-up. Since the missile traveled at very high speeds and had little-bitty canards for directional control, it simply could not match your rate of turn and would be "spit out" beneath your flight path. In some instances it would come close enough that its proximity fuse would fire, but since its frag pattern resembled a cone whose apex originated at the missile, you would usually only feel the shock wave from the blast, which always felt to me like a car running over a speed bump at 75 miles per hour. Once it passed under you, it was gone and time to worry about the next one. If there were multiple SA-2s in flight against you and individually "setting the hook" on them was not a viable option, you could create tremendous lead-collision prediction problems for them by doing a continuing series of 4G barrel-rolls.

Seeing nothing by the time we descended through 9,500 feet, we "took it up" in a 500+ KCAS left climbing turn. I called Buick 3 to "split the plane" and continued the turn in an attempt to pick up the MiGs. After approximately 360 degrees of turn Red Crown and Disco "stepped on each other" on the UHF just as Guard transmissions announced the outset of a SAR for an F-4 which had been shot down somewhere in the area. Disco 3 retransmitted his message saying the MiGs had "blown through" the merge and were now 360 degrees at 18 miles and headed for the strike package. I rolled Buick out on a northerly heading, unloaded the aircraft in 4th stage afterburner to pick up 1.2 mach, and the race was on. Tea Ball announced that the MiGs were going to try for the trailing elements of the F-105 strike flight which would be crossing our flight paths from left to right enroute to their roll-in point for bomb release on the Thai Nuyen Steel Works. Since the MiGs had to come left to a westerly heading to "lag" the Thud flight, it gave us an opening to intercept them before they reached firing position for the Atoll shots.

At this time, there were numerous transmissions on the command channel. I became vaguely aware another control agency was vectoring Chevy Flight (F-4 MiG CAP near Yen Bai) to intercept a different set of MiGs and they seemed to be in the same general vicinity as the ones we were chasing. Tea Ball transmitted that the MiGs were at 26,000 feet (we were at 24,000 which gave us a look-up angle for radar acquisition). Just as Disco 3 advised the MiGs were still 7 miles away, Buick 2 called, "MiG at one o'clock glinting in the sun, quarter of a mile, slicing left." As hard as I looked I simply could not pick him up. Seconds later Buick 2 transmitted, "Slicing left at 10 o'clock." at which point I punched the UHF transmit button and said, "Buick 2, take the lead."

At this time the Buick 3 element had not seen the MiG and was flying low on our left side about 3,000 feet out. When I passed the lead to Buick 2, he was flying line-a-breast on my right side, about 500 feet out. As he broke hard left and began a roll over the top of me, I rolled sharply left and stomped hard bottom rudder to stay on the inside of his turn in a left fighting-wing position. I then called for Buick to jettison the now empty, outboard tanks. The sudden change of flight path of my element put us on a collision course with Buick 3's element. However Buick 3 was led by Captain Geoff Egge, a great, experienced fighter pilot, who apparently pulled up and did an unloaded right-hand roll over the top of us as he and Buick 4 blew their tanks.

Under normal circumstances his maneuver would have rolled his element out in perfect supporting position, but on this day, Chevy 01 (with Chevy 02 in left fighting wing) apparently passed squarely between our flight paths in pursuit of a different set of MiGs heading east. As Buick 3 completed his roll, he visually acquired and joined the Chevy 01 element as they raced toward Phantom Ridge in full afterburner.

(USAF File Photograph)

Figure 38—MiG-21 Fishbed C

From my left fighting wing position I finally picked up the silver MiG-21, who by now was in an unloaded 25 degree dive in full afterburner, with Buick 2 looking straight up his tail pipe from approximately 3,000 feet back. Expecting at any moment to see multiple AIM-9s ripple from Buick 2's missile rails, I asked for and got 5 mile bore sight from Smallwood, put the pipper on the MiG and hit the radar auto-acquisition button. The radar locked-up immediately with the range analog bar on my pipper in the 4 to 5 o-clock position (4,000–5,000 feet). However before the 4 second missile speed-gate settling time had expired, it broke lock.

Swearing to myself, I told Jack to lock him up, which he did immediately. Once again the radar broke lock after about 3 seconds. There was now no doubt that the MiG was flat-ass opening the gap between us and was rapidly moving beyond the AIM-9 employment envelope, although we were in 4th stage afterburner, unloaded and going supersonic down hill in F-4s.

I could not understand why Buick 2 was not shooting and assumed something had to be wrong with his weapons system. In hopes of either killing the MiG, or at least making him turn so we could arc him, I told Buick 2 that I was going to fire. Hearing this, Buick 3 thought I had said Buick 1 was on fire and asked, "Is that Buick 1 on fire?"

My plan was to try a bore sight illumination AIM-7 shot. It was a last ditch shot with very low P_k because it was not initiated with a "full system lock-on", and required the pilot to hold the 35 mil depressed pipper squarely on the target throughout the entire flight of the missile. I put my pipper on him, squeezed the trigger, and a moment later a single Sparrow blew vertically from the left-aft missile cavity, its rocket motor ignited, and it streaked directly toward the fleeting

MiG-21. I thought it was going to score, but it passed just to the MiG's right, the proximity fuse did not detonate and the MiG did not turn.

I was about to fire a second missile when Buick 2 transmitted, "Buick 2 wants to shoot." "Shoot 2." was my immediate reply, at which time he ripple-fired 4 Sparrows. The first blew up 800 feet in front of us as the minimum-safe, separation fuse timed out. The second one came off, took a good lead pursuit cut at the MiG, appeared to guide perfectly, but in the end flew harmlessly past the bandit when its proximity fuse did not detonate. The third missile did a "carbon copy" imitation of the first, and the fourth and final AIM-7E2 simply fell into "The City on the River" when its rocket motor did not ignite.

Disgusted and disheartened because the MiG was now clearly out of range and walking away, I became painfully aware we were directly over downtown Hanoi, and squarely in the heart of the AAA envelope. "That 85mm is really close." Smallwood said from the rear cockpit, just as Buck 2 transmitted something similar. I replied, "Roger that. Take it around to the left, Buick 1's got the lead. Let's bugout, bugout." Coming out of afterburner to mil power, we began a 4G left climbing turn that traded our supersonic speed for altitude. It was not wise to fly much above 20,000 feet within the confines of the SAM rings since maneuverability was limited in the thinner air, while at those altitudes the SAMs really began to hum. Not seeing the element I asked for their position to which Buick 3 replied he was off my left wing at one mile.

Still not seeing them I said, "Buick, fuel check", Buick 1 is Bingo." "Buick 2 is Bingo, Buick 3 is Bingo minus 3, Buick 4 is Bingo minus 3." came the replies. Almost immediately Buick 3 asked, "Buick 1, are you proceeding east along Phantom Ridge?" "Negative." I replied, "Buick 1 is north of Bullseye heading west." "We're not with you Buick 1" came the reply. I told Buick 3 to turn west immediately and climb, and then attempted to contact Disco to get the emergency tanker started north. When I got no reply Buick 5, our relay, came on the air and repeated my request and received acknowledgment from Disco 3. I had briefed that should we become separated we would assume a "loose duce" formation and proceed until we could get back together.

While Buick 2 and I were enroute to the "H in the River" near Hanoi, we passed through a tremendous gaggle of F-4s, wing tanks, Thuds, and confusion. The flight above us had jettisoned their tanks, which were now falling though our altitude. Several F-4s began to parallel our southwesterly course and I could no longer distinguish which one was Buick 2 so I started calling all heading changes. As it turned out, the F-4 I ended up flying with did a "split-s" away, so it was not Buick 2. I directed Buick Flight to climb as soon as the last SAM ring was passed, and we individually began climbs to 36,000 feet.

At this time Buick 5, flown by my friend and fellow flight commander, Major Bill Harris turned toward us from his high orbit point at the Gorilla's Head and interrogated our Mode III, Code 6100 squawk on his APX-76. He immediately picked up both elements, with the Buick 03 element in 10-15 mile trail, and visually watched all four aircraft pass under him. Hearing this, I was heartened and took my element over to the emergency tanker frequency where Buick 3 and 4 were already up. At this point Disco 3 took charge of the rendezvous and started giving what sounded like good vectors for rendezvous with the Red 17 tanker. It also sounded good to Buick 5 who set course for Channel 70 (Udorn).

With Disco 3 telling me that Buick 2, 3, and 4 were within a 10 mile cone directly behind me, I got a visual on the Red 17 tanker who was in a left-hand orbit, and slid onto the boom for a quick 2,000 pounds of fuel. I directed the tanker to hold his left orbit and told Jack to pick up the rest of the flight visually as they approached. Disco 3's vectors continued and he called the remainder of Buick flight in trail with the tanker at 2 miles. Neither Jack nor I could see them.

Both the tanker and I gave UHF hold-downs for a DF steer but the element's equipment could not pick it up. Buick 2 called numerous tankers in sight, which turned out to be the normal Red Tanker Cell scheduled for post-strike refueling. I told Buick 2 to get immediately on a boom and take fuel, which he did. I had Buick 3 "hold down" and I tried to DF him with no luck. I had the tanker dump fuel to provide a highly visible fuel cloud in the sky. Buick 3 squawked emergency for positive ID and told Disco emphatically there simply was no tanker there.

(USAF File Photograph)

Figure 39—Lockheed RC-121 (Disco)

The situation was now becoming dire as Disco 3 issued a new vector to the tanker 14 miles from their previous instruction. I asked Buick 3 for his fuel and he replied he had 1,000 pounds. At this point I told Disco 3 he had to get the element on the tanker immediately. Buick 3 asked for vectors and got no reply, nor could I. Disco 3 simply quit talking for what seemed an eternity. When he did come back up, he gave Buick 3 and 4 a vector of 112 degrees for 23 miles, which was 23 miles behind them! My heart sank, as I couldn't believe what I was hearing. Going up Guard channel I contacted King 03 (The C-130 command and control bird) to get the SAR package headed toward our position. I then switched to the Air America common frequency, where I got immediate response from three Air America choppers who turned north to help us.

Four damn good men now sat in the cockpits of Buick 03 and 04, and stared squarely at the possibility they would soon "punch out" to an uncertain fate in the Barrel Roll combat sector of Laos. It was either try for the tanker, if Disco finally did have their act together, or establish an "L/D Max" glide at 250 KCAS after flaming-out, then hope to glide across the border into Thailand before ejecting.

As the Red 17 tanker turned toward the element, Captain Geoff Egge, a superb fighter pilot on this 3rd combat tour, made a tough, heroic, and correct decision from the front cockpit of Buick 3 as the rest of us simply watched and listened, "Say your fuel Buick 4." "Buick 4's got 400 pounds." "Buick 3's got 200, I can't make it." "Buick 4, you try for the tank, Buick 3 will go for the border."

Buick 4, flown by Captain Bob Whitfield, a great fighter pilot on his 2nd tour, came immediately on the air, "Red 17 this is Buick 4 heading 112 degrees, don't miss me babe! Say your altitude." "Red 17 is at flight level 240." came the reply.

From the right wing of the Red 17 tanker Jack Smallwood and I strained our eyes to pick up Buick 4 whom we knew would be coming down hill from high altitude. Just as we both spotted him, Captain Whitfield in Buick 4 saw the

(USAF File Photograph)

Figure 40—KC-135 Boomer's view of F-4E in refueling position

tanker directly ahead, closer than expected. "Tallyho, turn the tanker and push it up[65]" was his immediate transmission. I watched the KC-135 begin to roll slowly

---

[65] The KC-135 normally cruised at 300 KCAS until it was time for the fighters to get "on the boom", at which time they accelerated to 325 KCAS. A "point parallel rendezvous" was required when the fighter and tanker were approaching each other head-on. The instant for the fighter to transmit to the tanker to "turn the tanker and push it up" occurred when the fighter's radar indicated an antenna train angle of 26 degrees to the tanker and a separation distance of 21 nautical miles.

left into a standard 30 degree bank turn when Whit's voice cracked, "No goddam it, turn!", at which point the pilot of Red 17 literally stood the tanker on its left wing, making the fastest turn I have ever seen by a tanker. As the tanker rolled out, Buick 4, now shorn of all tanks, missiles and armament pylons was coming down hill at idle power with its speed brake fully extended and skidding alternately left and right in a desperate attempt to slow down to the 325 KCAS tanker speed. Knowing Whit had only seconds of fuel remaining, I held my breath in hopes he would be able to dissipate his speed before reaching the refueling position. However within moments I realized he would not, as he agonizingly overshot, finally stopping almost directly under the nose of the KC-135.

With Whit now looking straight up at the belly of the tanker to hold formation, he began to slide aft at an increasing rate that I knew would carry him beyond the boom envelope if he didn't add some power. At this point though advice from the "cheap seats" was not what he needed, and I simply said to myself, "Power Whit." Recognizing the need for power too late, Buick 4 passed rapidly aft though the boom envelope, where I was certain flame-out would occur within seconds.

At this moment, the boomer of Red 17, a man whom I had never met, lay on his stomach in the cramped refueling compartment of the KC-135 and observed the F-4E 20 feet beneath him sliding rapidly away. In a single swift motion he lowered the boom slightly as he lined it up horizontally, then extending it to the full outer limit of the "red extension", rammed it home into the open air refueling receptacle of Buick 04. As the over-center locking ring of the receptacle's cleaves slammed shut, the fifteen ton F-4E stopped dead in its tracks. Bob Whitfield later told me at the instant he felt the jolt, he looked into the cockpit to see the fuel counter click over to zero, then immediately begin to spin-up as the Red 17 boomer pumped fuel at maximum pressure. Upon Buick 4's transmission, "Buick 1, I'm taking fuel." I departed the tanker to organize the SAR for Buick 3.

As it turned out, Buick 3 managed to make it just across the border in the vicinity of Vientiane where they "punched out" and were picked up by an Air America chopper and returned to Udorn. The aftermath was not a thing of beauty. There were the second guessers, the blame assignors, the finger pointers, the ass kissers, and the CYA crowd. It is damn easy to sit around a conference table with a mug of coffee in your hand and tell eight guys what you would have done had you been in their shoes. It is an entirely different matter to be there when it is all happening.

Do I wish that the radio discipline had been better? Or that the radar on my plane had not continued to break lock? Or that the missiles had worked? Or that Disco had not blown the tanker rendezvous? Or that I had been smart enough to do something else, anything else, that might have avoided the loss of an aircraft? You bet I do. The facts are however that a whole host of damn good, highly trained professional warriors, with their asses on the line, made and acted on decisions in which they believed so strongly they were willing to bet their lives on them.

In my reflections upon thousands of flying hours and experiences such as this, I have come to realize the greatest satisfactions for a fighter pilot are not derived from events, but instead stem from the daily association with the likes of Egge, Whitfield, Smallwood, and the unknown boomer of Red 17, whom I put in for the Distinguished Flying Cross. In my eyes they will always be America's best, and the epitome of the old fighter pilot tribute to men of such stature:

"So here's a nickel on the grass to you, my friend, and your spirit, enthusiasm, sacrifice and courage—but most of all to your friendship. Your's is a dying breed and when you are gone, the world will be a lesser place."

Letters, Ramblings, and Opinions

Flight Discipline

- 1982 -

Prologue

In 1982, I was the Deputy Commander for Operations of the 1st Tactical Fighter Wing at Langley AFB, VA. When a series of "pilot error" aircraft accidents occurred within Tactical Air Command as a result of a breakdown in flight discipline, I wrote the following letter to the pilots of the wing's three F-15 squadrons for which I was responsible. It was published in the January 1982 issue of *Right Stuff*, the wing's quarterly standardization and evaluation newsletter.

REPLY TO
ATTN OF: DO

SUBJECT: Flight Discipline

TO: Al 1st TFW Pilots

1. In light of recent events within the command, it would be totally appropriate and most convenient for me to issue a "I view with alarm letter." Let there be no misunderstanding on this score. I <u>do</u> view these events and their implied genesis with wide-eyed dismay. In the 1st TFW, blatant disregard for established flying regulations will not be tolerated. The queue of motivated and disciplined pilots who would "sell their soul" to be in the 1st Wing is far too long to put up with such free-style antics.

2. Discipline is the key trait of a professional fighter pilot. It's what separates us from all others. Discipline is what makes a bunch of game young men, with almost their whole life ahead of them, fly into Route Package Six for $35 a day...while their civilian counterparts collected mega-bucks for flying into the fringes of Laos. Discipline is what enabled Claire Chennault's pilots, flying out-classed P-40's that couldn't carry a Zero's shoes out onto the field, to attrit their Japanese adversaries at a rate of over twelve to one. Discipline was the lynchpin in Bubi Hartmann's incredible 352 victories...while never losing a wingman...and never being hit by an airborne fired projectile. Discipline insures predictability of performance under stress...and the business of aerial combat is rife with stress.

3. Don't look at discipline as just a bunch of do's, don'ts and regulations that inhibit your performance. Look at them as a challenge and revel in the fact that you have the guts and drive to live by them. Air discipline axioms come from good stock. They were bought and paid for by the blood, sweat and lives of a lot of good men who preceded us. It is therefore totally appropriate that we all become extremely irate when some "yo-yo" takes it upon himself to risk defama-tion and criticism of our legacy.

4. Discipline. It's our keystone. Without it we're just another bunch of pilots.

Philip W. Handley
Colonel, USAF

Cars and Jets

- 1995-

The following article published in the January/February 1995 Edition of *356 Registry*, a magazine for owners of classic Model 356 Porsches, included the following introduction by James Graham, a United States Federal Judge:

Contemplating the 30th anniversary of the purchase of my '64 coupe, I decided to try to locate the original owner to see if he had any materials I might include in a scrapbook. A letter to the Military Locator Service produced a response from a recently retired Air Force Colonel who was delighted to learn that I still had the car. Colonel Handley promised to write a brief history of his ownership of the car. When I received it, I thought it was so interesting and so well written that it should be shared with other 356 Porsche lovers.

Background Statement
On My Former 1964 Porsche 356C

For as long as I can remember I have loved fast cars and airplanes. The fact that I accumulated over 7,000 flying hours as a career fighter pilot and owned sports cars such as A.C. Bristol, Alfa Romeo, Triumph, Lotus, Iso Griffo, Ferrari, and Porsche would seem to support this contention. Since I am now too old to fly fighters and can no longer afford sports cars, I find I am left with merely reflecting on the virtues of the "best of the best" in both categories.

In the fighter category it would be very easy to pick the spectacular F-15 Eagle as it clearly remains to this day the best fighter ever produced. On the purely nostalgic side there is the magnificent F-86 Sabre. It was truly one of the most beautiful jets of all time, built during a period when their color was polished aluminum vs. the painted magnesium alloy of today. However in the end, my thoughts always come back to the veritable F-4 Phantom II. Fondly nicknamed "The McDonnell Rhinoceros" by those who flew her, it could not do a single thing as well as the F-15. However it was a big, strong, mean-faced, fighting machine with a "don't mess with me" look about it, which I along with the hundreds of other men who flew her in combat, could never forget.

Similarly in the sports-car category the 1958 A.C. Bristol was my first and would be analogous to the F-86 on the nostalgia side of the ledger. My Lotus Super 7, a thinly disguised Formula Jr. with fenders and lights, was clearly a blast to drive. Strong parallels could be drawn between my beautiful red Ferrari 246 Dino and the F-15 as it was fast, handled well, and was outright gorgeous. However like the F-4, there is no car I respected and enjoyed more than my 1964 Porsche 356C. It was not particularly fast, had heavy steering, handled only moderately well, and was regarded by many as "funny looking." Whether driving to work, on the track, on vacation or to the store it was simply a joy to drive, anywhere and everywhere. Built like a tank, it simply didn't rattle, or break, or give you anything but the performance Porsche built their reputation on. The following is a brief synopsis of my all too short ownership of this classic automobile.

In the fall of 1963 I was a 28 year old USAF First Lieutenant. My wife Solvejg and I were living just outside Evreux, France. At the time I had a Lotus Super 7 as my work car, with the family machine being a 1951 Volkswagen, complete with split rear window and "machts nichts sticks" turn signals. Since we knew we would be returning to the States in the coming spring, we wanted to take advantage of the great European currency exchange rate existing in those days with $1 US = 4 DM, to buy a much needed replacement for the VW. At that time the Jaguar E-Type had just hit the market and was the rage among sports car aficionados. To make it even more tempting for overseas servicemen there were some absolutely fantastic bargains ($3,450) provided the car was purchased and delivered through a particular dealership in Athens, Greece.

Accordingly we had tentatively decided on an E-Type coupe and placed a $500 down payment with the Athens dealer to get the order started. However as beautiful as the original E-Jag was, I could not help reflecting upon the hundreds of horror stories I had heard about the trials and tribulations of Jaguar maintenance and reliability:

Question: Why do the English drink warm beer? Answer: Because Lucas makes their refrigerators.

So on one Sunday afternoon as I was browsing through my copy of Road & Track Magazine, I came across a Porsche ad showing a partial cut-away of the 1964 Porsche 356C. It started me thinking of all the Porsche owners I knew, I had never heard one of them utter a single negative comment about their car. Since I was only a few hours away from Stuttgart where I could immediately pick up the exact replica of the car I was now ogling in this magazine, I had to ask myself why on earth would I want to go through all the hassle of importing a documented maintenance nightmare all the way from Athens? In the end it simply would not pass the common sense test. I eventually passed my Jag order to a friend, who was very glad to get it and did take delivery on the car, while I took the train to Stuttgart where I paid just under $3,250 for my ruby red 356C.

From the moment I drove it away from the factory I knew there was something really special about this car. Perhaps the endless love affair of all those Porsche owners, with their automobiles, was not just so much idle talk. It felt so solid, the shifter was perfect, the brakes were fantastic, and the geometry of the clutch and brake pedals had been designed by someone who understood "heel and toe" operation. Everything about the car was simply right and it was a pure joy to drive.

Almost immediately upon returning from the factory with the car I had to depart on an extended TDY (temporary duty) to India. Since I really didn't have time to give Solvejg a through "checkout", I simply told her it drove like a super VW and if she handled it just as she had our old '51 model she would do just fine. Upon my return from TDY I found she was doing exactly what I had recommended. Since she had constantly driven the VW "flat out" just to stay up with traffic, she was using the same technique in the Porsche. This came to light during a "white knuckle" ride from our home to the base during which she was doing over 80 miles per hour within the city limits of Evreux.

As the time approached for us to rotate back to Lockbourne AFB, Ohio, in the States, I drove the car over to Bramerhaven, Germany where it was put on a military chartered boat returning cars to the United States. Unfortunately my father became critically ill just a few days before we were scheduled to depart, so a fellow officer picked it up for me at the port in New York City and drove it to his home in Gary, India where I subsequently picked it up following my father's funeral in May 1964.

Because Solvejg had learned to drive while in France, she, along with many of the other returning wives, had only a US Forces Overseas drivers license issued by the base. Since these had no validity in the States, all of these gals were required to take a driving test to get an Ohio driver's license. Accordingly there ensued much discussion among them about the perils of the dreaded parallel parking test. As the day approached for her driving test, which was to be in Circleville, Ohio, I suggested I, "The Old Pro", should go early with her to Circleville and give her some hands-on, parallel-parking instruction and practice before the check ride.

Despite use of my best instructor pilot techniques, things did not go particularly well. She finally allowed the reason she was not getting it right was a direct result of too much instruction and not enough patience forthcoming from the right seat and were I outside the car instead of seated next to her, she would do much better. Always eager to please, I immediately complied by stepping outside to the curb where I would observe in silence, at which point she simply drove away, leaving me standing like a fool on the streets of a strange town.

Fortunately there was a restaurant nearby where I had a Coke while I cooled my heels. Sure enough, soon after walking back outside, the ruby red Porsche approached and came to a stop. I entered without a word and nothing further was said as she proceeded to her rendezvous with parallel-parking destiny. As it turned out all of her buddies, who had given her so many tips on the fine art of parallel parking, flunked, mainly because they were driving cars the size of Chevy Impalas. In contrast Solvejg found the poles so far apart at the test site she deftly backed the 356 into the seemingly enormous space without effort. The evaluator was suitably amused and I don't think she has parallel parked a single time since.

While at Lockbourne AFB during the winter of 1964 we learned I would be reassigned to Williams AFB, Arizona in the coming year. Knowing this, we took the opportunity to take a leisurely vacation out to Arizona to scope out the situation. Our son, who was then three years old, had a great time playing on the folded-down back seats and got into all kinds of mischief. We were tooling across the barren stretches of New Mexico at about 80 mph when I saw the rapidly approaching blue lights of a state trooper in my mirror. I was certain I would get nailed for speeding, but instead he wasn't steamed about my speed at all, but about littering of all things.

It seems my son had learned he could pull Kleenex tissue, one by one, from an open box he had found on the back seat and release them to fly out from the little swing-out windows. The trooper said he had been following our trail for ten miles. Fortunately he let us go with only a warning. My son fondly remembers the incident to this day.

In certainly one of the most wrong-headed decisions I ever made about an automobile, I decided, because of the Arizona heat, I needed to sell my "non rag top Porsche with a black interior" so I could buy a white Alfa Romeo Spider Veloche. So one day in the fall of 1965 shortly after I had placed an ad in Road & Track, I received a call from a young Ohio lawyer who came with his wife to see the car, and in almost no time it was gone.

Over the ensuing twenty-nine years I had wondered on numerous occasions what had become of it. So in February 1994 when I received a letter from a Federal Judge in Columbus, Ohio inquiring if I might be the same Phil Handley who used to live at 4946 Sutherland Drive in Columbus, I knew the mystery had come to an end. I was delighted to learn, not only was the car alive and well, but during its early days with the Judge he had driven it competitively on the SCCA circuits with considerable success. Upon subsequently receiving a picture of the car I couldn't believe how truly beautiful it still was.

(James Graham)

Figure 41—1964 Porsche 356C and McDonnell Douglas F-4C

Although I will never forgive myself for letting it get away, when looking at that picture I cannot help but smile and take genuine solace in the fact that such a wonderful piece of machinery has been truly appreciated and lovingly maintained all this time. I sincerely hope the next thirty years are as kind to her as those just passed.

The Rescue of Basher 52

- 1995 -

The following Letter to the Editor was published in the Midland Reporter Telegram, in Midland, Texas on the Fourth of July, 1995.

Like most Americans I was thrilled by the news on the morning of June 8th that Captain O'Grady, whose F-16 had been shot down by an SA-6 missile over Bosnian Serb held territory some six days earlier, had been located and rescued by a successful search and rescue mission (SAR). However in the ensuing week I became increasingly annoyed by the endless procession of news correspondents, analysts, and politicians who seemed to operate under the theory, "Anything worth doing is worth overdoing." Their collective efforts resulted in the gross over embellishment of an event perfectly capable of standing on its own considerable merits. However, of greater concern were the flawed conclusions and false impressions that may have been created as a result of their zeal to outdo one another.

Let there be no misunderstanding here that I feel nothing short of genuine admiration for Captain O'Grady and the SAR forces that extracted him. As a career fighter pilot who flew the line for twenty-six years, I know the mettle of such men far too well to harbor any convictions to the contrary. From the moment Captain O'Grady spoke to the assembled crowd at Aviano Air Base, Italy, throughout the numerous "dog and pony shows" he was forced to endure, he conducted himself with an air of dignity and humility which should make every American proud. Indeed, his was the lone and persistent voice which continually shunned the "hero label" and assigned credit where due. Additionally, he attempted to point out his survival and rescue were not unique in the annals of SAR, but simply the latest in a long and proud series of such actions by dedicated fighting men who acted in the finest traditions of our armed services.

I believe three basic false impressions may have been created. The first would be that Captain O'Grady is unique among his fighter pilot peers, and his actions under stress were somehow above and beyond those which might be reasonably expected from any one of the other two-dozen fighter pilots in his squadron. As a former wing commander whose responsibility was to train fledging fighter pilots such as Captain O'Grady, I can tell you unequivocally that any such impression is dead wrong. Although I have never personally met Captain O'Grady, I have met, trained, and flown combat with thousands just like him. The real story the press missed is that Captain O'Grady is not an anomaly, but in fact totally representative of his peer group, and we as Americans should revel in the fact there are indeed entire fighter wings populated with pilots and weapons system officers of such ilk.

The second impression I feel may have been created was that Captain O'Grady's survival for six days was unusual with the SAR effort bringing him out being one of the most daring ever undertaken. One must wonder just where the press was languishing during the long months of the Rolling Thunder and Linebacker air campaigns of the Vietnam War. It is a matter of record that SARs of the "Basher 52 magnitude" took place on a continuing basis and seldom got more than scant mention in the Stars and Stripes newspaper, let alone national media coverage.

As an example I site the rescue of Captain Roger Locker on 2 June 1972. Just as Captain O'Grady, Locker was assigned to the Triple Nickel (555th Tactical Fighter Squadron). After his F-4D was shot down by MiG-19 cannon fire just outside Hanoi on 10 May 1972, he evaded capture by a large and dedicated force of North Vietnamese regulars at the very door step of Hanoi, and survived for a total of twenty-three days. He was unable to make contact with potential rescuers until the

(Author)

Figure 42—Sikorsky HH-53 "Super Jolly Green Giant" Helicopter

morning of the twenty-second day, when weak, dissipated and near death from lack of protein, he observed a flight of four F-4s egressing at high speed down a valley close to where he was hiding. Although he only had time to send a fleeting emergency "beeper" signal from his survival radio, it was sufficient for the WSO (weapons system officer) in the lead aircraft to hear it and mark the location on his map.

That afternoon a flight of four F-4s from the Triple Nickel intentionally overflew the location and made voice contact. The next morning a dedicated strike package created a huge diversion by attacking military targets in Locker's vicinity. During the height of the raid, with the whole world seeming to blow up around Locker, a single HH-53 (Jolly Green Giant) accompanied by propeller driven A-1D (Sandies) flew low and slow right into "the jaws of hell" to make the pick up.

During the extraction and the egress from North Vietnam, despite the continuous bombing and strafing runs by the Sandies and other fighters, the Jolly Green was riddled with automatic weapons fire, yet it still managed to return Locker to the ramp of his home base at Udorn Air Base, Thailand. Such acts of gallantry among SAR forces were the norm, not the exception, and were precisely the reason Jolly Green Giant crewmembers found it difficult to ever pay for their own drinks at a fighter pilot bar.

The final impression I would like to address is the notion there was some sort of dramatic decision process to determine whether or not a SAR effort would be mounted once the precise location of Basher 52 had been established. There may well have been some hand-wringing going on in certain diplomatic circles, but I would wager you that such was not the case where "the rubber meets the road" at the military operational level. Just as US Marines don't abandon their dead or wounded, and the US Army Rangers in Somalia fought to their death to protect their own despite a serious lack of support from Washington, American fighter pilots don't run off and leave their wingmen. If one of their own is shot down, still alive, and not yet in enemy captivity, they will either come to get him, or die trying.

During the Vietnam War I have seen entire strike packages consisting of hundreds of aircraft, diverted to support the SAR for a fellow pilot who was down in enemy territory. More often than not this resulted in the downing of more aircraft, which created the need for even more SARs, yet that is precisely what was done. Among fighter pilots, the calm, sure knowledge that such an irrevocable bond does exist is priceless. Along with individual faith and personal grit, it is a sacred trust that has often sustained hope in the face of terribly long odds.

In summary, the rescue of Basher 52 should be celebrated not only because a fine young man was returned to friends and family, but because neither his actions, nor those of his rescuers were an abnormality. They were in fact wholly representative of the caliber of performance routinely expected from dedicated Americans who daily "put it on the line" to keep their fellow citizens alive and free. Indeed they are far more than heroes, they are a national treasure.

Nixon the Movie

- 1995 -

Prologue

After watching an American Broadcasting System (ABC) Sunday television program, *Face the Nation,* during which Oliver Stone's latest movie *Nixon* was the subject of discussion, I became so appalled by the tenor of the arguments supporting Stone's work I wrote the following essay. An abbreviated version of it was published two weeks later in the 7 January 1995 edition of *The Midland Reporter Telegram*, the daily paper in Midland, Texas. Approximately one year later I sent a copy of the complete article to The Richard Nixon Library & Birthplace in Yorba Linda, California. On 1 April 1996 I received the following letter:

April 1, 1996

Dear Col. Handley,

On behalf of the Richard Nixon Library & Birthplace I would like to thank you for your letter of January 18th and your article "Of Movies, Myths, and Men of Courage", describing the President Nixon you served.

Last week the archives section of the Nixon Library received a copy of both your letter and article with the request that they be placed in the collections here. I have just finished reading your remarkable piece and can clearly understand why. Your account is, indeed, as powerfully written as it is historically important.

Even though you have requested no reply or thanks, I simply could not catalog and add your article to the collection without expressing deep appreciation for the service you have given our country and the service you have now rendered President Nixon. Thank you again and again.

> With best wishes,
> <Signed>
> Susan Naulty
> Archivist

Movies, Myths, and Men of Courage

Several years ago a move named *Top Gun* was a smash hit because of its supposedly authentic glimpse into the world of jet-fighter aviation. I personally found it thoroughly entertaining in that the producer had wrapped some really magnificent aerial photography around a harmless, fictional story line. I didn't really mind that the screen writer's scenario bore no resemblance whatsoever to actual aerial combat, let alone the lifestyles of the men who flew the jets. It was good, innocuous entertainment which didn't hurt anyone, encouraged fantasy, and provided an impeccable recruiting tool for U.S. Naval Aviation.

In stark contrast we now have the movie *Nixon*, the latest offering by Oliver Stone, Hollywood's first "investigative director", who also brought us those other gems of painstaking research such as *Platoon*, *JFK*, and *Natural Born Killers*. We are not talking now about fictional characters the likes of Maverick, or Goose, or Iceman in the *Top Gun* movie, but about the lives and deeds of the thirty-seventh President of the United States, his family, and those within his immediate inner circle, many of whom are alive today. As one might expect, the movie is one more expression of Stone's loathing for America and his obsession that everything is rooted in some sort of top- secret, governmental conspiracy.

His depiction of Nixon as a boozing, pill-popping, foul-mouthed paranoid flys in the face of truth, recorded history, and the testimony of those who were actually there. Every serious review of this movie has acknowledged these gross distortions. Yet, there is an insidious tendency among the pseudo-intelligentsia to "wink at such lies" and pass them off with offhanded observations such as, "After all, it's only entertainment." or "It's Stone's creative genius as Hollywood's greatest story teller." or one of my personal favorites, "Although there are obvious inaccuracies, one must look at the entire enigmatic character of Nixon." All of this is of course pure rubbish from diehard "Nixon haters" who simply can't resist one last chance to vilify their favorite Watergate conspirator.

As contemptible as Stone's latest work is, the real tragedy could be that many viewers with little or no knowledge of Richard Nixon might regard this movie as a serious work deserving of their confidence. Never mind that those living individuals who were actually there, i.e. Kissinger, Haig, Colson, Liddy, Nixon's daughters, et. al., have personally debunked it as shameless, character assassination with total disregard for the canons of history. But what do they know? After all, they were all probably part of the ongoing conspiracy.

So, since Monsieur Stone feels compelled as "Hollywood's premier story teller" to provide his comprehensive insight into Nixon's character, I'll now exercise the same right. However my observations bear a significant difference in that the story I will tell you is true and in my opinion provides more insight into the personal grit and sense of responsibility of our former Commander in Chief than all of the twisted fairy tales Hollywood directors of Stone's ilk can contrive.

The air war in Southeast Asia was waged above three distinct areas, South Vietnam, North Vietnam, and the bordering countries of Laos and Cambodia. Any serious observer of the war knew about the extensive air campaigns occurring beyond the borders of Vietnam, but the principal combatants of the war found it politically inconvenient to admit anything was going on in these third-world counties. Nevertheless, because of their strategic location and intricate networks of roads, passes, fords, and tunnels, they comprised the major infiltration routes into South Vietnam.

Aptly named the Ho Chi Minh Trail, they were the conduit through which thousands of tons of supplies from North Vietnam made their way south on a daily basis. Predictably, considerable effort was expended by the tactical fighter units stationed in South Vietnam, Thailand, and afloat on carriers in The Gulf of Tonkin to interdict these supply routes, especially those in Laos.

(Russ Everts)

Figure 43—Mu Gia Pass choke point with numerous bomb craters visible

Fighter missions flown into the Steel Tiger and Barrel Roll combat-operations sectors of Laos were not generally as tough as those directed at the heartland of North Vietnam. However such sorties came with a serious drawback. Since neither side was willing to admit its combatants were present in Laos or Cambodia, there was little or no compunction on the part of the North Vietnamese to abide by the tenants of the Geneva Convention pertaining to the treatment of prisoners of war (POW) taken in these countries. The bottom line was, if you were a fighter pilot in Southeast Asia, the absolute worst choice of places to be shot down was Laos. In South Vietnam there was a good chance you might be rescued and returned to your home base. In North Vietnam you were seldom killed outright, but interned to endure months, and years of unbelievable torture at the hands of your captors.

However in Laos, your options were usually limited to immediate murder or murder after torture and mutilation. In rare instances those taken prisoner were transported back to The Hanoi Hilton or some similar POW camp. They could then look forward to the same daily regiment of torture and abuse afforded their buddies who had been fortunate enough to be shot down within the political borders of North Vietnam, but at least they would be alive with some hope they might one day be repatriated.

(Russ Everts)

Figure 44—"The Roadrunner" VR landmark on PDJ of the Barrel Roll combat operations sector of Laos

The following account concerns a personal friend who made his way from Laos to the hell-hole prisons of North Vietnam, and how his fate, as well as all of those other POW's of similar Laotian lineage, was ultimately determined by the moral courage of their Command in Chief, Richard M. Nixon.

In early February of 1971, a 25th Tactical Fighter Squadron F-4D was shot down by anti-aircraft artillery (AAA) in Laos near "The Dog's Head" at Ban Karai Pass. The aircraft was flown by my squadron commander, Lt. Col. Bob Standerwick, with a personal friend, Major Norb Gotner in the backseat as the WSO. As was our practice, a search and rescue (SAR) effort was immediately mounted, but the weather was totally uncooperative. Although radio contact was quickly established with both crew members, the thick cloud cover prevented any potential pickup. Nevertheless flights of fighters were kept overhead around the clock to do what we could. It was during one of these sorties on the first day after the shoot down that my squadron commander's last words over his survival radio were heard as he was hit by automatic weapons fire.

Major Gotner, a big guy and as strong as a mule, continued to evade capture for two more days and used his survival radio in disciplined, battery-conserving intervals to communicate with the SAR forces orbiting overhead. Just when it looked as if the weather would give us the break so desperately needed, a final, out-of-breath radio transmission from my friend broke the hearts of those who heard it. Speaking in a low but firm voice he said, "There's a truck load of troops at the bottom of the hill, they are coming up now and they know where I am. I want to thank all of you gallant guys for everything you've done to get me out."

Our hearts sank as we were far too familiar with the fate of those who had faced similar circumstances.

It was only after the peace accords were initialed on 24 January 1973 in Paris by Henry Kissinger and Le Dac Tho, his North Vietnamese counterpart, when I finally learned my friend had indeed survived. Six months later when we were both attending Air Command and Staff College in Montgomery, Alabama, I sat with him at his kitchen table where he told me the details of what happened after his final radio transmission. It turned out he had been incredibly lucky after the intervention of some NVA college boys from Hanoi, one of whom spoke prefect English. This chance encounter prevented his immediate murder by Pathet Lao troops. Norb told me that after an extremely heated argument between the "English speaking" NVA college boy and the Pathet Lao troops, the young fellow turned to him and said, "Let's turn around and walk slowly away, and don't look back."

He said it was the scariest walk he ever took as he expected at any moment to be shot in the back. He was subsequently transported by foot and truck back north along the Ho Chi Minh Trail to Hanoi, where he was interned with a handful of fellow POW's who had also survived in Laos. Although he almost died from malnutrition and torture during his imprisonment, personal grit, moral support by his fellow POW's, and the grace of God kept him alive.

Norb told me not all of the guards were totally hostile, and one in particular took it upon himself to keep him and his fellow POW's informed of the progress of the seemingly endless peace talks between the U.S. and North Vietnam delegations in Paris. Things seemed to be looking better as 1972 was drawing to a close, and when Henry Kissinger announced to an anxious America on 26 October 1972 that "peace is at hand", the friendly guard relayed the information telling them it was a certainty they would all be going home soon. However several days later, the same guard, with genuine sorrow told the POW's from Laos they would not be leaving with the others since their presence could not be acknowledged by his country. Norb said that in all his life he had never felt such utter despair.

At the time of Kissinger's "peace is at hand" announcement, he had sincerely felt the final accord was only four to five days away. But as the rest of October and November of 1972 drew to a close, Kissinger and his negotiating team had tried in vain to work out the final "sticking points' of the agreement, among which was the release of the Laotian captured POW's. In typical style, the Le Dac Tho led team became increasingly intransigent in their position, and so yet another impasse seemed certain unless the U.S. was willing to compromise on the Laotian POW situation.

However a certain man named Nixon was equally firm in his position that we would get all of the POW's back and told Kissinger to warn the North Vietnamese unless they capitulated, he was prepared to bring the full force of American air power down on Hanoi and Haiphong. Having heard idle threats such as this from previous U.S. Presidents, the North Vietnamese were unimpressed. They should have been, for on 14 December 1972 when President Nixon ordered Admiral Thomas Moorer, Chairman of the Joint Chiefs of Staff, to resume air attacks north of the 20th parallel, he added the following comments:

"I don't want any more of this crap about the fact that we couldn't hit this target or that one. This is your chance to use military power to win this war and if you don't I'll hold you responsible."

And so on 18 December 1972, and succeeding ten days, waves of B-52's by night and tactical fighters by day appeared relentlessly over and about North Vietnam's two largest cities and began the process of methodically reducing their industrial base to rubble, a task which they could have performed at any time during the course of the war had they been permitted to do so.

The official name of the campaign was Linebacker II, but most Americans simply remember it as "The Christmas Bombing Campaign of 1972." The morale of the POW's who had been praying for just such raids for years, soared and they openly cheered as the 500, 1,000, and 2,000 pound bombs rained down. In contrast, the strut and swagger suddenly disappeared from those arrogant guards who had for so many years been their tormentors. With the North Vietnamese negotiators now clamoring to negotiate a settlement, Nixon called a halt to the bombing on 30 December 1972, and the final peace accords were signed in Paris at 12:30 PM on 27 January 1973. All of the POW's, including the man with whom I sat at his kitchen table, had returned "home with honor" by 28 March 1973.

An organization was founded during the Vietnam War called The Red River Valley Fighter Pilots Association, commonly known as the River Rats. It still exists today. The initial and overriding goal of the organization was to seek accountability of the POW's and MIA's and to hold a "real reunion" once they were all returned. Each year as the war dragged on, the River Rats held numerous "practice reunions" at fighter bases around the world while awaiting the real thing. When it was finally held in Las Vegas in late 1973 it exceeded all expectations. President Nixon received an invitation as a "special guest of honor", but was unable to attend and sent Al Haig as his personal representative. Throughout the course of the reunion, the mere mention by any speaker of President Nixon's name prompted heartfelt, sustained, and richly deserved standing ovations from the assembled crowd, many of whom literally owed their lives to their President.

Whatever other good or bad attributes might be laid at the feet of our thirty-seventh President, it is an undeniable fact he was a man who understood the bond of loyalty between America's fighting forces and their Commander in Chief. For when the "chips were down" he acted without hesitation on the courage of his convictions, and with total disregard for the negative political fallout certain to come his way. It is not surprising this seemingly critical character trait in a President of the United States did not find its way into Stone's latest "masterpiece." But on the other hand…what a pity that it didn't.

Philip W. Handley
Colonel, USAF (Ret.)

Postscript

In my search for further details surrounding the SAR effort to recover Lt. Col. Standerwick and Major Gotner, I contacted my old friend, Colonel Russ "Tits" Everts, who as Wolf 06, an 8th Tactical Fighter Wing Fast FAC, who was the first aircraft on the scene following the shoot down. The painting of a Wolf FAC F-4D in full afterburner which hangs in Colonel Everts' den appropriately captures the moment Wolf 06 dove into Mu Gia Pass over the infamous "Dog's Head" landmark, where immediately to the north Standerwick and Gotner had just been shot down. The following is a direct quotation of Colonel Everts' recollections of that day:

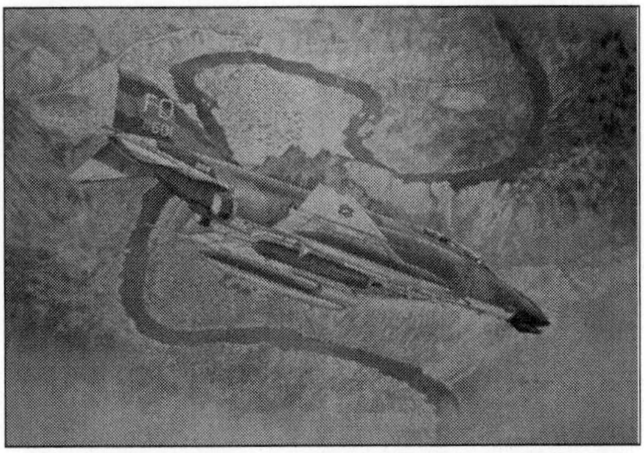

(Russ Everts)

Figure 45—Wolf FAC entering Ban Karai Pass at "The Dog's Head" VR landmark

"I was Wolf 06. On the day L/C Standerwick went down, Hank Baker (25th TFS backseat pilot) was in my pit. The weather was lousy and we were doing some visual recce, sort of, wherever we could find a clearing. We knew, from the frag, that he was scheduled to put down a string somewhere around the Dog's Head and made sure we were out of the way. Right about his scheduled time, we heard beepers and not long after that both he and Gotner came up on their survival radios. They were not real close together, location wise.

I got below the weather about 25 miles away from the Dog's Head and VR'd my way to the general area. We got pretty close to where Lt. Col. Standerwick was, but had to pull up and out. The clouds were right down on the karst tops and we were flying into a box canyon; no place to be. As I recall, one of the two of them said they heard us (an F-4), so we were in the general area. Seems like I started the SAR and got the system moving. This all occurred during my second period, as I recall, so I went to the tanker and returned. The weather was too bad to do anything but listen and provide encouragement and hope for a break in the clouds. That never happened in the next hour or so.

After my third period, Wolf 01 (Mike Hall—he might have been W 02 then, as he was the Ops Officer for awhile before taking command) came out and I handed off the

SAR effort to him. He later told me what you wrote, that Lt. Col. Standerwick was shot while having the radio keyed. He heard the whole thing. That happened fairly quickly, during Mike's first or second period. Pretty ugly, and Mike was really down that he could do nothing to help him, as any of us would have been. I am sure Mike can hear his words to this day…

I recall working on Norb's SAR on and off for the next few days, until he was captured. Did you ever hear his story of that? He was nabbed initially by the Pathet Lao, who were about ready to shoot him, when some NVA regulars showed up and interceded. So the story goes, they were arguing over who was going to get him, when this young Vietnamese kid walks up to Norb, gives him a banana and becomes the interpreter for him. He tells Norb to walk down a road a bit while they decide who gets him and told him to root for the NVA, as they would take him to Hanoi, whereas the Pathet Lao would most likely execute him on the spot. The NVA won and off he went to Hanoi. He almost died in his initial captivity, but made it. I believe his story in Hanoi is well chronicled in the book "Honor Bound" by Rochester and Kiley (the best book on the POW experience that I have read, and I've read most of them)."

Remembering D-Day, June 6, 1944

- 1998 -

The following Letter to the Editor was published in the Midland Reporter Telegram and Dallas Morning News in the summer of 1998.

When I saw the movie *Saving Private Ryan*, it moved me to tears. Since I was born in 1935, I was only a kid during World War II, but not so young I didn't realize what was going on. Growing up during that era forever left me with an abiding admiration for a generation of Americans who not only endured the Great Depression, but also unflinchingly stepped forward to do their duty when our country called.

As a young United States Air Force officer I was stationed in France only a few hours driving time from the beaches at Normandy. Early on a June morning in 1961, I drove to the site where seventeen years earlier the Allied Forces of Operation Overlord had landed. As the sun rose over Omaha Beach, the hair on the back of my neck literally stood on end as I gazed in awe at the utterly devastating field-of-fire commanded from a crumbling German bunker. Some nineteen years later, I would experience this same profound sensation as I stood atop the hill, Little Round Top, at the Gettysburg Battlefield in Pennsylvania.

Later in 1962, while flying along the Normandy coast at low altitude, I was presenting what I thought to be a noteworthy historical tour to my navigator, a major who looked "pretty old" to me. Flying west from the British and Canadian beaches of Sword, Juno and Gold, I pointed out a 100 foot cliff named Pointe du Hoc that lay between the American beaches of Omaha and Utah. After describing the remarkable D-Day assault up its near vertical face by U.S. Army Rangers, I said, "Can you imagine how tough that must have been?" My navigator replied, "Yes, I can", then simply added, "On June 6, 1944 I was nineteen years old. I was a private in the 2nd Ranger Battalion, and I went over the top." Realizing this man with whom I now flew was one of only ninety Rangers who survived the hand-over-hand climb up the shear rock face, my historical rhetoric suddenly seemed pitifully inadequate, while my navigator no longer seemed old, but somehow about two feet taller.

Only the men who were on those beaches over a half-century ago are truly qualified to comment on the authenticity of the movie. Those with whom I've spoken say it is pretty damn close. It is a film without joy, bluntly depicting the documented horrors of a single nine-day period of combat as it really happened. If nothing else, perhaps it will help to dissuade the utterly silly notion that women should be placed in combat.

I was openly touched by this movie not only because of the profound sadness of the situations portrayed, but also because of a nostalgic remembrance of a time when duty, honor and country came first. When dodging the draft was a disgrace, character was a cherished virtue, and individuals took personal responsibility for their actions.

If you have never thanked a WWII veteran for what they did, now might be a good time. There are still a lot of them among us, but they are a dying breed, and when they're gone America will be a lesser place. We shall not likely see their likes again.

Philip W. Handley
Colonel, USAF (Ret.)

Missiles, Guns and BFM

- 2005 -

Since my earliest days as an Air Force pilot I have heard the old refrain, "Missiles will make dog-fighting with guns a thing of the past." Indeed such high-minded thinking drove the ill-advised decision which saw the great F-4 Phantom II produced without a gun, a mistake initially corrected by hanging external gun pods on the armament pylons and finally, <u>finally</u> getting it right when the M-61 gatling gun was mounted in the chin of the F-4E.

History shows none of the highly vaunted air-to-air missiles performed up to expectations throughout the duration of the Vietnam War. However, in recent years they have become dramatically more capable, and indeed would appear to finally be approaching the long dreamed-of "I wish you were dead weapon." So once again there is strong advocacy in certain circles for the notion that mounting guns on a fighter are unnecessary and a waste of weight better used for missiles or fuel. Maybe some day that will be true, but in my opinion…"not quite yet."

With all of its stealth, maneuverability, and missile sophistication, the F-22 Raptor still carries an internal gatling gun. I've been told by fighter pilots who are still in the game that a "set piece" engagement against a flight of F-22s is a frustrating experience because you can't paint them on your radar and won't acquire them visually until long after each member of your fight has systematically been informed, "You're dead." Even if you are flying a "nose-pointer" like the F-16 and get into a turning fight with the F-22, you will soon validate the old axiom "speed may be life but rate kills"[66], when the Raptor's vectored thrust brings the jet's business end into sharp focus in your mirrors.

So, even if you are privileged to fly a jet the ilk of the F-22, it is a fair bet in training exercises and certainly within a "Clausewitzian fog of war" environment, you will eventually "find yourself in a phone booth" looking across a turning circle at a capable fighter flown by a pilot who is dedicated to gunning your brains out. At this point it's like "riding a hog", as there is no way to get off. You had better be

---

[66] In this instance, "rate" refers "rate of turn" or the ability of a fighter to "point its nose." Even if one fighter is far faster than an opponent, it is of little consequence if the slower fighter has the ability to bring its forward firing ordnance into launch parameters at close range or within the weapons delivery envelope.

able to max perform your jet if you expect to prevail and it would certainly be nice to have a weapon, such as a gatling gun, whose effectiveness does not depend on "magic", but instead on your own ability to bring it to bear on your opponent.

My contention is that regardless the sophistication of your jet and its weaponry, BFM remains a key factor in air-to-air combat training. Guns drive BFM training. BFM teaches you to fly your jet to its limits, inspires self-confidence, improves every aspect of your piloting abilities including instrument and formation flying, makes you a safer pilot, makes you more combat effective, and finally, it instills "the spirit of attack borne in a brave heart" of which the great German Ace, Adolph Galland spoke so eloquently many years ago.

Burning Your Radial-G Green Stamp

- 2005 -

The best "how to" book I ever read on golf was Harvey Pinnick's *Little Red Book*. It is to the point, non-pretentious, and full of common-sense techniques which actually work.

In my opinion if it has a counterpart the field of fighter aviation, it has to be *No Guts No Glory* by Major "Boots" Blesse, which wasn't really a book at all. It was in fact a series of tactics bulletins he wrote when he was commanding officer of the 3596th Combat Crew Training Squadron at Nellis AFB, Nevada after the close of the Korean War. Although written for the F-86 era, nearly all of the axioms, maneuvers and techniques he advo-

(USAF File Photograph)
Figure 46—North American F-86F Sabre

cated are timeless and continue to work as well in today's fighters as they did in the Sabre. Although I never had the privilege of meeting the double ace "Boots" Blesse before he retired in 1975 as a Major General, I have served with many who did. To a man, they unanimously agree he "set the gold standard" for following generations.

For those lucky few who are privileged to fly today's great jets, I would offer the following description of a simple maneuver which I employed hundreds and hundreds of times with very good results. So, paraphrasing Tom Selleck's great line in the closing scene from the movie *Quigley Down Under*: "This ain't Dodge City and you ain't Wyatt Earp." I now say, "This ain't Korea and you ain't Boots Blesse."...so here goes.

The maneuver, which I always called "burning your radial-G green stamp" simply involves forcing the bandit to bury his nose on the first pass and to meet you head-on with his nose down and yours up, with zero turning room. You will then be in an enviable position to exploit the God given radial-G which will accrue to you at the top of the maneuvering egg to gain a significant advantage.

Think about all the times you have been designated the "duck" for a student's offensive BFM training, where your assigned role is to break into the stud's stern attack then hold a 4G turn as he performs the gamut of stock maneuvers to maintain nose-tail separation. Have you not often though to yourself, "If this were for real I'd pull into this guy with max G and point my nose at him?" Well since there are no "ducks" in real combat, that's precisely what you had better expect a real bandit to do. Never underestimate the ability of a low wing loaded fighter to turn around and meet you at a much shorter range than you think possible. When this happens, your best laid plans go on hold and your initial advantage vanishes as the old adage "speed is life but rate kills" comes squarely into play.

Let's assume you have arrived undetected at a stern position on a bandit and as you are pressing in he suddenly breaks into your attack. Unless you are absolutely certain you can maintain nose-tail separation with one of the stock lag maneuvers (lag pursuit roll, high yo-yo, barrel roll attack, etc.), dive immediately to lag position at his six o-clock low to force him to turn as far as possible *and to enter a dive* before he can get his nose pointed at you. Your goal at this point is to time your pull-up into him so as to initially pass him head-on, close aboard, at corner velocity, *with your nose up and his down.*

If you can arrive at this position, you'll be able to exploit the radial-G advantage you will enjoy at the top of the maneuvering egg. When drawn out on paper with precise geometry and mathematical calculations, everything cancels out on the second pass and no advantage is shown. By the same token it won't work in a simulator where cheating is possible because simulators are bolted to the floor and at best simulate bone-crushing Gs by squeezing your G-suit or turning out the lights. But there is an old saying, "Paper horsepower doesn't climb hills."

This maneuver works for the following reasons:

- It is infinitely easier to pull maximum G while hunkered down and looking at your opponent through the front windscreen than attempting to do the same while twisted around to maintain visual contact with an adversary in your rear quadrant.

- Unless the bandit followed you down as you dove for his six o-clock position, he will almost always fail to control his airspeed as he recognizes too late he has to dive to deny you turning room. This will result in his airspeed being well above corner velocity which exacerbates his problem.

- In contrast, because you have a plan and are paying attention to your airspeed, and thanks to the great thrust-to-weight ratios of today's jets, you can easily maintain corner velocity with your left hand throughout the initial maneuvering of the engagement.

- Your turn rate as you pull down over the top will be dramatically greater than that of the bandit at the bottom of the maneuvering egg, who will probably be above corner velocity, fighting radial-G, and looking over his shoulder in an attempt to maintain visual contact.

As you come over the top the first time, watch the bandit closely to see if he does anything other than pull straight back into you. If he turns in either direction during the pull, immediately lag to the outside to prolong his turn as he strains to maintain a visual on you.

If the bandit does continue to pull up in a straight path, simply lag to one side or the other to force him to turn in an attempt to stay in your plane-of-motion, *then flatten your turn to minimize your dive angle and lag further to the outside of his turn*. You'll have room to do it and you'll chip away at the angle-off each time you come around.

Carefully control your corner velocity at the bottom of the egg and repeat these steps on each subsequent pass, then pick your time, get into his plane of motion and take either a high P_k snap-shot or tracking, gun kill. This will usually occur before the third time around.

Control your overtake and track while firing.

Fate is the Hunter

Prologue

I am not a superstitious man by nature. I am a Christian by faith, but not one that wears his religion on his sleeve. However I do believe I have probably had more meaningful conversations with The All Mighty than most. On four occasions during the fourteen year period 1972-1986 I was directly involved in separate, mysterious events concerning premonitions of death which simply fly-in-the face of logic and conventional thinking. I, for one, am convinced these events were not sheer coincidence, but were in fact "supernatural or paranormal" in nature and fall into a body of knowledge we as humans find difficult to accept or comprehend.

"Bullet"

- 1972 -

I was the D-Flight Commander of the 58th Tactical Fighter Squadron when we deployed from Eglin AFB, Florida to Udorn RTAFB, Thailand in the spring of 1972 to support Operation Linebacker I. After we had been flying air-to-air combat missions for about two months, one of the pilots in my flight, Captain Bob Whitfield, told me he feared that something was simply not right with his designated WSO[67] and good friend, Captain Don "Bullet" Boulet. He said that following each mission, he had noted that Bullet's hands were shaking so badly he had to steady his writing hand in order to complete the flight log and when he discussed this with Bullet, he simply would not admit anything was amiss.

(Don Boulet)
Figure 47—1/Lt Don "Bullet" Boulet

I found all of this very strange since Bullet had earlier completed a combat tour with the 366th Tactical Fighter Wing at DaNang, where he flew as a Stormy Fast FAC, certainly not a mission for the faint-hearted. His combat record was flawless as supported by the fact he had been awarded multiple Air Medals, Distinguished Flying Crosses, and the Purple Heart. Within the squadron his reputation as a professional WSO was impeccable.

---

[67] Among the WSOs (Weapon systems officers) who flew in the back seats of the F-4s during this era, there were both pilots and navigators. The theory behind putting rated pilots in the back seat was they would gain valuable experience from the more experienced pilot in the front cockpit and better prepare themselves for upgrade to the front seat. Although a noble idea, the arrangement produced mixed results as many of the "pilot backseaters" were less than impressed by the skills of those from whom they were supposedly learning. This unfortunate circumstance was created when the available pool of experienced fighter pilots available for second and third combat tours was exhausted and senior pilots with little or no fighter experience were assigned as F-4 aircraft commanders. Indeed, in more that a few instances the flying skills of the pilot backseater far exceeded that of his aircraft commander which caused consternation and resentment in general. On the other hand, those who were paired with capable aircraft commanders did form a strong and beneficial bond. There was absolutely no friction or resentment by Bullet regarding his current aircraft commander, as he had himself been a back seat pilot on a previous tour and was a totally capable and experienced fighter pilot.

The next day I asked Bullet to come over to my hooch after work and initially got absolutely nowhere in my attempts to understand the post-mission behavior his aircraft commander had described. However after gentle probing and a few drinks, he finally told me, as his flight commander and friend, what was going on.

He told me that as his one-year tour at DaNang was nearing completion, he awoke one morning with an absolutely foreboding feeling he was going to be shot down on that morning's mission. Wondering to himself why on earth he would have such a premonition, he said he simply couldn't shake it during breakfast or the mission brief. He said that as they began to taxi from the revetment and he returned the salute of the crew chief, he knew in his heart he was seeing him or for that matter anyone or anything at DaNang for the last time. Despite these convictions, he said nothing about it to anyone and the mission departed as scheduled.[68]

By mid-morning, the script played out as he had envisioned it when he and his front seat pilot ejected from a burning and out-of-control F-4 which had been fatally hit by AAA. Injured from the violent ejection, he concealed himself as best he could in the dense vines and undergrowth along one of the routes in Laos which led toward the Ashau Valley in South Vietnam, some 40 miles to the east. Also occupying the area where he went down were approximately 40,000 NVA troops. Only through the heroic efforts of the men involved in a dedicated SAR, and in particular those of a U.S. Army Dustoff Huey crew, were he and his front seat pilot rescued. At the end of the day, he could not believe he had survived what he knew in his heart was surely going to happen.

Since he had only a few weeks left on his tour at DaNang, he told no one about his premonitions, although they persisted as strongly as on that morning he had first experienced them. Knowing he would shortly be reassigned to the 58th TFS at Eglin AFB, he made the tough decision to simply "gut out" the few remaining missions, although he remained convinced he would not be lucky a second time.

---

[68] In my preparation for this chapter, I contacted Captain Boulet who graciously sent me a letter which provided far more detail of his premonition than he revealed to me during our conversation in 1972. His expansive letter also provides absolutely invaluable glimpses into the Fast FAC and SAR missions. Don's letter is so well written and insightful that I asked and received his permission to include it as a postscript at the end of this chapter. I would urge anyone seeking a true sense of the danger, heroics and gallantry that typically surround the Fast FAC and SAR missions to read his letter carefully, as it comes from a courageous officer who was there and lived to tell the story.

He flew the missions which were uneventful, returned to Eglin, and quietly applied for honorable discharge to the civilian life he richly deserved.

Since the crews chosen for the current Linebacker I deployment were based on the most experienced available, his name appeared on the list. Still confiding in no one, he deployed with the squadron and had stoically flown every assigned mission without a moment's hesitation. It was obvious to me such courage was driven by a fear greater than death, that his action might somehow be perceived as letting his squadron mates down. Looking me squarely in the eye he said, "Major Handley, on every mission we fly, I would give a thousand-to-one odds that I will be killed." So there it was.

I told him he had no reason whatsoever to continue to fly under such conditions; he had damn well done his part many times over; there were GIBs back at Eglin who would cut each other's throats to get over here; that I would explain the situation to the Wing DO back at Eglin and see to it he would be swapped out with a replacement WSO on the upcoming R&R (Rest & Recreation) flight, and finally that I sincerely admired the courage he had eloquently displayed throughout this ordeal.

The switch out I had proposed occurred on the next R&R rotation and everything appeared to have worked to everyone's total satisfaction. However when I returned to Eglin on a subsequent R&R several weeks later, I was stunned when the DO informed me that the Wing Commander viewed the situation in a totally different light, and had preferred charges against Bullet under provisions of Article 99 relating to "cowardness in the face of the enemy." I couldn't believe it and told him I needed to explain the situation directly to the wing commander. He said it was too late because the paperwork had already been submitted and the wing commander's mind was made up. Despite this I did meet with the wing commander and explained in detail the injustice of his actions, which resulted in the worst Officers Effectiveness Report (OER) that I ever received.

I returned to Udorn totally disheartened and gathered all of the pilots and WSOs to tell them what had happened. They were, to a man, predictably outraged. Among the assembled group was a WSO whom we had nicknamed "The Tree" because of his gigantic frame. It so happened "The Tree" was an English major who could flat-out write. So over the course of the next two hours in a non air-conditioned, day room, we all gave input while "The Tree" composed an extraordinarily succinct letter accurately expressing our collective outrage. It was then typed and signed, complete with smudges and sweat marks by every pilot and

WSO in the deployed squadron, and mailed directly to Secretary of the Air Force Robert C. Seamans, Jr.

In approximately the amount of time it took for our letter to reach the Secretary's desk, the charges against Bullet were dropped. He was honorably discharged from the Air Force shortly thereafter and awarded an additional "end of tour medal" for his service, a fitting award which he richly deserved. Ironically, "The Tree" died in an F-4E crash shortly thereafter.

Post Script

Captain Don "Bullet" Boulet, the subject of this story, graciously provided the following detailed account of events on the day he was shot down. Here, in his own words is "the rest of the story."

The Loss of Stormy 03—2 December 1970
Don "Bullet" Boulet

When I began flying the Stormy missions, I loved it. There was no flying anywhere else, I am sure, that matched the thrill of 600 or more knots on the deck, while maintaining every unnatural attitude imaginable, under near-constant heavy G's for 20 minutes at a time, trying to stay between the clouds and the rocks, and then trying to actually 'see' something on the blur of the ground as you go by it. And I especially enjoyed the flights when I was paired with Dave Rickert. I trusted everything about Dave, who, by that time, I believe, already had his 500 mission patch.

I was with Dave when he took his very first hit over Cambodia on a Stormy mission. I was making the straight-in back at DaNang, after the mission, when the first evidence of the hit occurred to us, as I called for flaps down. As the flaps lowered, the aircraft rolled inverted on me, which I'm sure was sort of an exciting view to the fishermen in the small boats below us in the bay. Dave, of course, immediately took aircraft control, cleaned it up, lit the burners and rolled it upright while doing a go around and then brought it back in for an uneventful, no-flap landing. The crew chief found a tiny bullet hole just in front of the vertical stabilizer and almost directly in the middle of the top spine of the fuselage. I later saw some pictures showing it had cut some wire bundles, which apparently affected the aileron-flap interconnect. And as we turned out the lights and went to sleep that night, I remember Dave was still talking about it. It was almost like he couldn't believe, after 500 missions without a hitch, that he could take a hit. He was planning to meet his wife and little daughter, and I was to meet my wife, in Bangkok when we were to take leave and travel there together at the end of the next month.

I think I flew Cambodia missions for about a month, or maybe a little more, before Stormy, in a long political lobby, finally wrested a part of Steel Tiger from the grasp of the Wolf FACs over in Ubon. We began flying the southern portion just as the monsoon was beginning to lift.

It was quite a bit different from the flat terrain and low AAA threat in Cambodia. And also made for some more exciting flying. And about a week or two later we had some really close calls. By then I was flying fairly regularly with the same AC. And I liked Robby's seeming self-confidence and easy-going ways. One morning we went down south by the northern Cambodian border to let down at dawn, and headed back north VR'ing the main n/s route of the Trail. A few miles up the road, and as we crested a hill, barely above the vegetation, suddenly tracers were screaming by just over the cockpit, over both wings and under both wings. Robby later told me they were also passing right under the nose. There was literally no place to go but up, so he probably overstressed the aircraft, pointed it at the midheaven, and we zoomed to altitude to catch our breaths and try to calm our shaking nerves for a few minutes.

We went a little farther north and let down again out in the hills and made our way toward the route we were going to continue to recce. And just as we got there, the same thing happened again. This time, we went to the tanker, and neither one of us could figure out how in the hell we had escaped those cones of AAA we were immersed in, not once but twice. The rest of the mission, through several more VR periods, was fairly uneventful, as I recall. But we probably could have seen a few giant, purple dragons on the road below and not thought a thing about it, considering what we had just been through.

When the same thing happened on the next ride, two days later, we were pretty sure they were using spotters and radios to try to take us down. There would be no other way for a gunner to have his weapons pointed directly at the EXACT hill we were about to crest at the speeds we were going and jinking all over the sky as we were, so at the very moment we crested the ridge, the rounds would be in the air waiting for us. But they definitely had us plotted and pegged.

When I got back, I told everyone I could, to be extremely careful over there now because I had a feeling someone was going to be shot down very soon. Some remembered me saying it later. At the time, I didn't know it would be us.

A couple days later, I awoke with a strange feeling I just couldn't shake. I didn't have a clue about what it meant, only that I felt strange, like a heavy and ominous fog surrounded me. Robby and I met at the little Stormy office well before dawn, where we grabbed a weather and an intel brief, then got a van and went to the chow hall where we sat in a darkened corner, pretty much alone in the place, except for the cooks, and ate our breakfast in virtual and uncharacteristic pre-mission silence. I learned later I wasn't the only one 'feeling strange' that morning. Robby told me he 'knew' something was up, too. He also told me later this was his birthday. It was Dec 2nd. But this explains why we didn't engage in the normal chatter that day. Neither one of us felt like initiating a conversation due to these inner thoughts we were experiencing. As I recall, we didn't even bother to joke or complain about the formaldehyde taste in the eggs that day.

We then went out to the aircraft, did a preflight, strapped in and started engines. In Stormy, the backseaters made nearly all radio calls, so after checks, I called for taxi clearance, and we eased out of the revetment into a left turn. And as I turned my head to the right returning the crew chief's salute, I knew with certainty we would not be returning this aircraft to this crew chief in 4 hours. This 'knowing', which is the only thing I can call it, came to me as a visual image of the tail of our bird that appeared superimposed over my normal vision of the crew chief at attention, with the tail number clearly showing. In that instant, I knew something I wasn't supposed to know, and something this crew chief likely had no inkling of.

Nothing like this had ever happened to me before, except perhaps, the several times in childhood I would tell my mom that PeeWee and Skeeter, my cousins from across the state, were coming today. And they did.

I put it immediately into the back of my mind and went on with the mission, doing my basic checks as we taxied out to the far end of the runway. But something else unique happened that morning. Dawn was breaking over the bay as we passed the tower and the little shack serving as the squadron building of the A1E Spads. And my attention was drawn out of the cockpit long enough to notice they were changing alert crews at the time. Never before had I witnessed them during shift change, nor had I ever heard them doing parrot checks before. And little did I have time to think about the fact, except later in retrospect, that these fresh crews would have some work to do in a few hours. My mind was on the mission.

As an aside, one of the things I loved about Stormy was all of the stick time that I got. Generally, I was able to do all of the flying after takeoff, except for the actual recce down low, and it usually entailed 3 to 4 aerial refuelings, plus the recovery and landing, on missions that would sometimes last almost five hours. And my refueling skills later paid off as I was paired with a green AC who had been a T-38 instructor but simply could not hang in position to refuel. And since we usually flew long, night, Stinger escort missions which required several refuelings, this became quite a problem.

It was very embarrassing to him, I'm sure. And especially so when there were other flights waiting to get topped off. I went to the scheduling officer and tried to get us some daytime refueling missions so he could become proficient in daylight and hopefully better able to handle the night ones, but they were difficult to come by at the time. Eventually he got a little better at it, but I worried what would happen to him when I left for the states and he had a navigator for a backseater who perhaps could not do the refueling for him in dicey conditions. I never found out how he fared when I left but I hoped no news was good news.

At any rate, Robby and I were probably the first to take off that morning at DaNang. And we soon arrived in Steel Tiger where we let down and did our first VR period without even getting shot at. On the second period we got hosed over pretty good, but they were not as close as previous mornings, so we were probably feeling a bit more confident. And during that period, we ended the VR and headed for the tanker just as we were about even with the intersection of the road leading east past the Golf Course and on to the Ashau Valley in S. Vietnam. As we climbed out we were able to see that the road was clear of clouds for the first time this year, and made plans to give it a look, from here on down to the border, after refueling.

Once back down on the deck, we were jinking eastward on down the road, which I think was called 92 Echo, but I wouldn't swear on it at this late date. It was, however, perfectly dry and usable, which is the main thing we wanted to report to intel. About halfway to the border, we surprised a bunch of workmen and soldiers on the road, who only had time to stand there and watch us fly over. But I saw they were rebuilding a bridge over a stream, and Robby thought he saw something else (he never told me what) and wanted to get some photos of it. We continued on to the border and turned around.

Personally, I had some misgivings about the tactic of revisiting the same road from the same direction we had just disappeared toward a few minutes earlier, but I didn't say anything since we had not been shot at, to our knowledge. I think maybe we both were thinking it was perhaps too soon after the monsoon rains for them to have set up their AAA sites in that area and maybe they had been concentrating them on the main n/s routes first. If that's what we were thinking, we were soon to find out we were certainly wrong.

Robby got the camera switches set up and we were flying rather large sine waves back and forth across the road toward the target area at roughly 90 degrees of bank and at approximately 500 knots. Suddenly, I heard him make a kind of "oh-oh" sound. Backseaters really don't like to hear AC's do that. I realized a split second later what he meant as I saw the bridge go by off the left wing while we were in a tight left bank on the north side of the road. Thus, of course, the camera was pointing away from the target.

At this point Robby apparently made a snap decision I would never have agreed with had I known beforehand what it was. He immediately pointed the nose at the sky and we zoomed to about flight level 200. I thought we were maybe heading for the tanker and would come back later to take a picture. But no, that's not what Robby had in mind.

We floated over the top and he pointed the nose straight down at the bridge again. I could hardly believe what was going on at this point and to this day I have no idea what possessed his thinking at this juncture. But he was obviously dead set on getting that picture of a bamboo bridge, come hell or high water.

On the near vertical dive, I noticed he didn't seem to be pulling out as smoothly or as quickly as I would deem normal. So I had my hand resting lightly on the stick, as I usually did in dicey situations. Later Robby told me the aircraft seemed to be a bit mushy from side to side and the stick felt harder than usual. I told him it was a good thing he didn't tell me that at the time, because I might have ended up as a greasy spot on that bridge.

As we finally leveled out, heading west, we were nearly tangled in the bamboo of that bridge. I mean JUST above the dirt! And immediately Robby said we had a fire light on the left engine. And a split second later, we had a fire light on the right engine.

These are the kinds of things no one wants to hear when all alone on the deck, over enemy territory, in a 10 mile wide valley which was obviously, actively occupied, and with no place to hide. But we both knew instantly, I think, we were going to have to get out.

Robby retarded the throttles to see if it had any effect on the fire lights but it didn't, so he pushed the throttles back up to use any thrust they might have left in them to help us get as far away from the area as possible. The left engine went to zero and the right one only went to about 92% power as I recall. Meanwhile, my head had already swiveled 360 degrees to find the best ejection area and I told him to break to the right (north) as there was a tree-covered, rocky plateau of sorts about two miles distant and it was still shrouded in low overcast.

We gradually turned north in the climb as Robby struggled with aircraft control and I went out on the radio with the Mayday and position. We had plenty of airspeed of course, and that little bit of power from the right engine helped us keep most of it for a time. But the radios were screwy by then and I had to use the intercom override button to talk to Robby. I did get an immediate response from Nail 51, though. This was his area and he was looking for us already and asked me for our location again. So, as we headed north for as long as this beast would fly, I spent my time talking to Nail and getting in position for an immediate ejection. I estimate we made it about 8 miles north of the bridge before Nail 51 said he was in trail and had us in sight. He yelled for us to "get out of that thing" as the whole ass end was on fire. Robby heard this and yelled something to me. But the intercom was cutting out badly so I asked him to repeat it after I engaged the intercom override. He yelled, "Wait a minute! Wait a minute!"

I found out later he was afraid I was going to eject us both and he told me he was "all elbows and assholes" trying to cross control the thing with full rudder and aileron. But the next thing I heard, almost immediately afterward was, "Get Out! Get Out!" I pulled the handle as the aircraft snap rolled to the right.

The ride out of the aircraft was smoother than I expected, then all hell broke loose. I immediately felt as if the entire Green Bay Packer line hit me at once head on. A split second later, I began to cartwheel and gyrate across the sky at 400 knots as I heard all of the ejection seat sequences taking place, with charges firing and belts flapping, though I realized I was blind from the G forces. I then heard and felt the seat separate but this only added to the violent cartwheel-in-every-attitude effect where my arms and legs were simply uncontrollable. I realized my helmet had been ripped off my head. I believe the drogue chute on my seat did not deploy, and this led to all the other problems. In the mid 90's I chanced to meet a former personal equipment specialist on the F4 and he told me this was because I ejected in a 90 degree right bank which somehow affected it.

Suddenly, after a seeming eternity in the shaking jaws of a mad monster, there was the extremely violent opening shock, then everything came to a stop. What greeted my vision when it returned a second later, was a sight I can still see when I close my eyes today. It was accompanied by full sound as well. My head was hanging down on my chest as a natural consequence of the slam to what seemed like near zero airspeed, and directly between my two combat boots was a "picture" of the flaming aircraft just below me, heading straight down. The sound of it was deafening.

In one second, it seems, reduced in size to a dot, it disappeared into the cloud bank below. One second the visual and the sound was there, and the next second it no longer existed. I didn't hear it hit or explode. It was like it disappeared into hyperspace, leaving me floating in the sky above Laos with nothing for accompaniment but the strange bird sounds of a Tarzan movie being played from the jungle below me. This peaceful sound was so out of place under the circumstances it felt like the ultimate oxymoron.

Even more so, when I looked up to check my chute and gasped at what I saw flapping in the breeze. I estimate I only had about 8 or 10 shroud lines still intact on the chute. The rest had been cut or snapped in two and were flapping around the canopy. And the canopy itself had four or five huge holes in it. Thankfully, there was a shroud line on all four corners, so the chute hadn't collapsed. I wondered how fast I was falling but there was no real way to tell until I got closer to the clouds about 2000 feet below me. I estimate we were about 3000 agl when we ejected.

After this quick inspection, I was already pulling out one of my two radios to tell Nail 51 I had gotten out and was looking for Alpha but didn't see him. Nail told me he had watched us eject from his deep in-trail position and asked if I was about to enter the clouds. And as he told me this, I looked down and to my left and saw Robby's chute just about to enter the clouds. But I also looked to the left at eye level, as I suddenly heard an aircraft engine, and was aghast to see Nail 51, an OV10, in a steep left bank which he would need to see Robby's chute. He was directly at my altitude and heading straight for me. I yelled back on the radio, "NO! I'm right in front of you!" This gave him just the moment he needed to look up and swerve slightly to miss turning me into a bug splat on an OV10's canopy. I was very happy I had taken my radio out first thing. I was also happy Robby had gotten out okay and that Nail had a fix on our position before we went into the clouds.

There was only one other thing I knew I had to do before I went into the clouds to meet an uncertain fate. I had to tear the little black Stormy patch off my left shoulder. It was sewn on. All of my other flight suits which had velcro on the patch were dirty that morning, so I had worn this one which I usually wore only on base. As I ripped at the patch with my teeth and flung it into the wind, I cursed myself for neglecting to put velcro behind this one.

Descending through a cloud layer which, as far as I knew might have been ground fog, at higher than normal chute speed, in a rocky-jungled territory, with no helmet to protect my head and face, is what worried me next. So rather than try to protect my armpits with my hands, I had to try to protect my face and eyes. But I also wanted to be able to see, in case I popped out of the overcast before I hit the ground. So I peeked through my fingers while holding my arms in tightly, knees and feet together, and head as upright as possible. It's a good thing I did, too, because the next sight greeting me was about the umpteenth miracle in a whole string of them that day, which, by all rights, should have been my last.

From the time I slipped beneath the cloud layer to the time I hit the ground was probably no more than 2.5 seconds. And in that instant of time, I was able to see I was coming down in a small valley, next to a creek. There were a few patches of small trees in the valley but it was mostly composed of high grasses and vines. The slopes of the ridges began about 50 feet either side of the creek and they were heavily forested. I could also see the tops of the ridge lines were right at the bottom of the clouds. They were rocky with a few small trees on them.

The sight that caused my next gasp was a small, bare sapling, long dead and stripped of limbs and leaves, sticking up about 25 feet from the ground like a vertical lance set in concrete. The point of this lance was heading directly toward my navel. I reached up and grabbed the left riser to swing my body to the right with all my might, and the point of the lance passed swiftly just a few inches from my left shoulder, immediately before impact. Since I only weighed 137 pounds at the time, my actual impact was not too hard.

My chute hung up on another tall sapling next to the 'lance', and try as I might, I could not pull it down. I knew it looked like a giant, flaming orange, neon sign from the ridgelines, so I also knew I'd have to do some traveling to get well away from it. I immediately began to sort through my seat kit for items I might need, while radioing to Nail that Bravo was on the ground and would have to move. He told me the SAR was already underway and the Spads and Jollys would be airborne shortly.

A few minutes later I could hear Nail talking to Alpha, so I knew Robby had made it down as well. But I couldn't hear his transmissions as he was in another valley. And from this, I put together a scene of the landscape in my mind. To the east, maybe a mile or less, was the main river which ran to the south, and it was probably the same stream which emptied into the big valley where they were building the bridge. And emptying into this main river from both east and west were many small, valley streams like the one I was near. Robby was in one to the south of me.

Unfortunately, as we all found out, when a map says the territory on the map is unverified and unreliable, it means exactly that. And consequently, no one above the overcast had a clue as to exactly where we were.

I then stowed my radio, grabbed the survival gear bag out of the kit after cutting it loose from the lines, and plunged into the deepest jungle I could find. After struggling through this for about 15-20 feet, heading uphill, I was aghast to find I had broken through to a wide and seemingly recently used trail. I decided to go along the slope instead of up but ran into the same thing, another trail. There were trails no matter where I went. Later I was told by intel we were in the midst of about 40,000 NVA troops.

After about 45 minutes of this, I finally realized I was more apt to be found trying to slug my way through this undergrowth than if I would just find a good hiding place and camouflage it the best I could. Then, if the overcast didn't break and I wasn't out by nightfall, I could try to move farther. That's what I did. I ended up a few hundred yards from my chute, which I could see down in the valley below, and tucked myself beneath some vines and grass right next to a little spring gurgling out of the rock.

From here on, it was all pretty much a blur of waiting. Nail announced he was turning the SAR over to Spad lead, but by then I had already been talking to Wolf 06 a fast FAC out of Ubon, who later became one of my good friends at the 58th TFS. We met for the first time later in parachute training and orientation at Eglin and when he found out that I was Stormy 03 Bravo, he offered his handshake and said "I was Wolf 06." That was Mac Poll. Mac was a real hero.

Back in the jungle I spent some time going through my survival items and deciding I was not going to need shark repellent and a few other things so I lightened the load in my bag and buried the stuff. I also spent a lot of time vectoring different types of aircraft over my position by sound, so they'd know generally where we were if the clouds broke enough to get in with the Jollys. There must have been 30 or more aircraft up there holding at various altitudes on up to the fighters who had been diverted to the SAR and the tanker which had been reserved. I couldn't see any of them but I got to know them by their sounds. Eventually, Wolf 06 had to RTB and Nail 51 was replaced by another Nail who kept us company, checking in every few minutes. But it basically was a waiting game. As time wore on we were told that the weather might not break that day so we should start thinking about spending the night down there.

Unknown to us, a group of 4 volunteers, who were to become the real heros of that day, took off in their little, unarmed, US Army issue, Huey with the red cross on the front and headed "out west" where the aircraft commander had heard, when he stopped by the command post after his rescue mission of the day, that a couple of jet jockeys were down. He had no idea where we were. They thought we might be in the Ashau Valley. He ran over to the pool hall and got a couple of enlisted volunteers, and then by the hooches to get his co-pilot. They all took off in their recently refueled chopper, with a tree penetrator no one had ever used before, and one Browning Automatic Rifle. They were going to go "pick these guys up." Simple as that.

What they didn't know, however, was that we were a wee bit west of the Ashau Valley. And when they got near the border, they were told this by GCI. The pilot feigned radio breakup and plunged right on across the fence, anyway. They switched over to SAR frequencies and invited themselves to the party.

Several hours, it seems, were taken up in their treetop level search. I learned later how they did it. They found the main river as it emptied into the clear valley and would follow it up to the first tributary, turn to the west or east and follow that tributary until it got so shallow they were in the clouds again. Then they'd pop up through the clouds and go back to that same entrance point on the main river and head up it again to the next tributary, repeating the same pattern for each possible valley.

And one of their problems was an AAA site right near the entrance point in the big valley. They had to evade it every time they went back in. At one point they got hit, were losing oil pressure and had some tail rotor damage. But that didn't stop them. They knew they were the only ones who knew where we WEREN'T so went back to Quang Tri and got a fresh Huey and plunged right back into the thick of things.

This time, when they came back, they had three or four Cobra gunships for escorts. And we could hear them firing several times. We also heard the BAR open up on what one of the crew members later told us was a search party. About this time, I also heard a pack of dogs off in the distance.

We went down about 0930 in the morning by our recollection and some time around 1330, I saw one of the Cobras come around the bend in my valley and hover above my chute. He swung it around in a 360 degree turn, as several more Cobras and the Huey appeared around the bend, while I parted the vines around me and stood up waving, telling them on the radio where to look. They saw me immediately, and came over to hover as closely as possible to the slope below me while they tried to figure out how to work the tree penetrator. One of the Cobra pilots asked me if there were any Gomers around, "cuz I'd sure like to put something in for you." Meanwhile I took two steps out of my hole in the vines and was tripped by strings from the survival vest hung up in the vines, fell head over heels and rolled down the slope to where I ended up right below the chopper.

When I was about to get on the tree penetrator they jerked it, hitting me in the forehead, nearly knocking me out. I saw stars but wasn't in a complaining mood. Eventually they hauled me in and I pointed to where I thought Robby was. He was already telling them his location from the sounds they were making, and we skirted over to his location to pick him up.

The ride back to Quang Tri would probably rival any Stormy ride I ever had. Once we were out of Laos and past the Ashau Valley, they put it down so low that the skids were almost in the dirt, while Robby and I joked with them about pushing up the throttle. They were maxed out at a little over a hundred knots.

Out both sides of the chopper, in a wide V formation was the strangest assortment of choppers and reciprocators I'd ever seen. It looked like a Mad Max air assault. There must have been 30 aircraft in the whole gaggle, and others such as OV10's, O2's, and O1's, plus a few jets, making close passes over the formation and then fly off.

At Quang Tri we were given quick medical exams, and one of the crewmen brought us a couple of hot beers, fresh from the PX. Someone told us Jolly was there to pick us up and as we exited the little room, serving as a medical facility, a little, old, heavily-wrinkled, Vietnamese man with tears in his eyes grabbed my right sleeve and told me in broken English, translated for us by someone, "Thank you for what you are doing for us."

That was the only time I remember being thanked by a civilian for just doing my job. But I never forgot the tears on that man's face. He had obviously suffered greatly during this war.

Robby had a few scratches after landing in the trees, but he was able to start flying again in a couple of days. I, however, was DNIF for most of the rest of December, because I could not move my head at all without excruciating pain. I had Doc Rooks x-ray my sternum a couple of times because it felt like it was cracked down the middle when I'd breathe deeply or cough. However, since the x-rays looked fine, we chalked it up to ligaments in the chest being pulled away from the bone during the violent cart wheeling. And it was almost healed by the time Dave and I went to meet our wives in Bangkok later that month.

About two weeks after the SAR, before we left for Bangkok, the wing gave what was termed by one of the Officer's Club employees, the 'biggest party in DaNang's history" for the four incredibly, brave men who picked us up that day. They all got Silver Stars.

Later that night, after far too much champagne and I think maybe way too much tequila, Woody, the aircraft commander of the Dustoff Huey, was up in my room with Dave and I and a few close friends, where we had some of my strong, Cajun coffee, exchanged patches, and generally chatted while we wound down. He told us he had received a call from an Army general just after the incident, and thought, "Oh no, here it comes." It seems he and all Army pilots had signed affidavits saying they would never take their aircraft outside the territory of South Vietnam. The general, sounding gruff, asked him if it was true he had directly disobeyed this standing order. Woody answered, "Yes sir."

The general, after a long pause for effect, replied, "Shit Hot[69], soldier!"

---

[69] "Shit Hot" (or more politely stated as "Sierra Hotel") is a long standing term widely used in the fighter community to indicate strong approval or congratulations. The term itself would appear to have its two words reversed, as "Hot Shit" would seem to be more logical than "Shit Hot." If you ever wondered how it got started, the explaniation offered by Les Prichard, a fighter pilot of the Vietnam era, would seem to hold the answer:

"I was assigned a BOQ room upon arrival at Bitburg in 1960 next to a Captain Charles G. "Moose" Healey, an F-100 pilot in the 22nd TFS and one of the "all-time" characters. There are many, many stories of his antics, in the air and on the ground. He could drink more beer faster than anyone I've ever known in 50 years of pub-crawling. Anything that pleased Moose (results of dice games at the O-club bar, etc.) would be proclaimed as "Hot Shit" in a booming voice. We teased him that after about three years in Germany, he didn't know one word of German. He went to the Oases Bar in Bitburg and a bar girl, Mona, aka "The Big M" taught him how to say "Hot Shit" in German, "Scheiss Heiss." The Berlin Crisis brought the George AFB F-104's TDY to USAFE/Bitburg and the 104 guys (Dick Lougee, Tim Torson, Bob Kelly, Snake Pitts, et. al.)sitting at the Bitburg bar wondered what this big guy at the other end of the bar was bellowing. They asked young German bartender, Bernie Schultz (15 years later moved to Las Vegas and ran the Nellis stag bar for years) what he was saying? Bernie explained ("scheiss" was shit and "heiss" was hot) so they decided that Moose was saying "Shit Hot" and took that back to George AFB where the 8th TFW was regenerated in 1965 with F-4s and the term propagated from there to Ubon, then to SEA, and eventually throughout the fighter pilot world."

But when Woody left my room that night, bound for his own temporary quarters, I later found out that apparently my Cajun coffee had not been enough. Early the next morning he was found sleeping in a mud puddle, in the rain, at the foot of the stairs to our BOQ. And I would wager he had quite a headache.

He will remain the finest kind of hero to me.

"Karst"

- 1973 -

The 58th Tactical Fighter Squadron stationed at Eglin AFB, Florida was notified in the late spring of 1973 they would once again be deployed to Udron RTAFB in Thailand, although they had just returned from there some five months earlier. I was personally disappointed I would not be going with the squadron since I had been selected several months earlier to attend Air Command and Staff College at Maxwell AFB, Alabama during the period of the deployment.

(Author)

Figure 48—1/Lt. Jack "Karst" Smallwood on ramp at Udorn Royal Thai Air Base, Thailand.

On the fine Saturday morning in June 1973, my wife and I drove out to Eglin to "see the guys off" as they departed on a C-130 for the first leg of their trip back to Udorn. After intentionally saying my goodbyes to the other members of the squadron first, I saved my final fond farewell for my personal friend and GIB, Captain Jack "Karst" Smallwood.

As we stood on the tarmac immediately behind the C-130 where I had singled Jack out, I was joking around with him and making small talk when his eyes suddenly welled-up with tears as he stepped forward and hugged me. When he stepped back he said, "Phil, I'll never see you again." Stunned, I replied, "What are you talking about, Jack? After all we've been through together, this will be a piece of cake. Hell, the war is almost over." Before I could say anything further he put both his hands on my shoulders and while looking squarely at me said, "I love you Phil." Without another word he turned and never looking back, walked up the aft cargo ramp and disappeared into the waiting C-130.

I was shaken to the core. First of all, such talk was totally uncharacteristic of Jack. Second, men of my generation, at that time, were certainly not in the habit of telling another man they loved him, as such affections were reserved for sweethearts and family. When I told my wife what had happened, she could not understand it any better than I.

The incident was still on my mind when we departed the following week for a family vacation to Holland where we would stay with my in-laws. After we had been there for several days, we were walking along the scenic crowded dock at Volendam on a Saturday morning when suddenly a small car resembling a Mini Cooper came roaring out of nowhere heading for me. I managed to jump out of its path at the last instant before it continued speeding down the dock and disappeared. The other tourists present were also alarmed as they shouted "idiot' in various languages.

Later that evening, at my in-law's house, the telephone rang and my wife's father told me it was a call from the Air Force back in the states. When I answered I found the call was indeed from the 33rd TFW command post at Eglin. The voice on the other end was that of a friend who had been assigned as a command-post, duty officer. He hesitantly began by saying how much he dreaded telling me something that would spoil my vacation, but knew I would want to know Jack Smallwood had been shot down in Cambodia. When I asked about a SAR, he said none had been mounted as the FAC on the scene had reported the F-4 took a direct AAA hit going down the chute on a high-angle dive bomb pass. He further reported the aircraft went straight in, impacting at 12 o'clock to the target, with no chutes and no beepers. My heart sank.

When I later researched details of the crash, I was stunned to learn that when the time differences between Cambodia and Holland were taken into account, the time of the crash coincided precisely with the speeding car incident on the dock at Volendam. To my knowledge, Jack and his front seat pilot were the last U.S. Air Force officers to die in the Vietnam War when their F-4E Phantom was shot down in Cambodia on June 16, 1973

"Aggie"

- 1981 -

While assigned as a staff officer in the personnel division at Tactical Air Command (TAC) Headquarters at Langley AFB, Virginia, I sometimes got the opportunity to make staff visits to the field and "sandbag" a flight or two. When the opportunity arose for a visit to Nellis AFB in Las Vegas, I jumped at the chance and called a couple of old buddies who were assigned there to line up some flights.

They were Captain Bob "Aggie" Ellis, a fine young officer who had been under my charge when I was a flight commander at Eglin AFB and during the 58th TFS deployment to Udorn RTAFB for the Linebacker I operation. He was among the initial handpicked cadre selected to fly the F-15, and subsequently won the coveted Risner Award Trophy presented to the outstanding graduate of all the Fighter Weapons Instructor Course (FWIC) conducted annually at Nellis.

The other was Major Russ "Tits" Everts, an outstanding weapons officer, former Wolf FAC at Ubon RTAFB, and a flight commander I had personally picked when I commanded the 22nd TFS at Bitburg. We had flown numerous training and combat missions together.

After arriving at Nellis on a Sunday afternoon, I was invited over to Everts' house for a get together that evening with many old friends. When Bob Ellis arrived at the party and we began to talk, I could not explain the strange feeling of apprehension I suddenly felt and simply couldn't shake. After Bob left the party, the feeling abated as I continued to visit with the others who remained.

I had essentially forgotten about it until it all came back when I reported to the flight briefing for the mission Bob and I would fly. The sortie would involve a flight of four F-15s accompanied by two F-16s, opposed by a flight of four F-5 Aggressors. It was truly a dream mission which I had eagerly anticipated. Bob conducted a totally thorough and professional flight briefing as I knew he would. Nevertheless, as we strapped into the F-15B, I had butterflies in my stomach which I had never before felt in an aircraft. I was as nervous as a cat throughout the entire scenario which went off without a hitch, and after the debriefing found myself wondering what on earth was causing me to have such strange apprehensions.

That afternoon I flew in Russ Everts' back seat on another mission, which was easily more challenging than that of the morning's flight, and felt nothing but the same sense of exhilaration to which I had become accustomed during my past 6,000 hours of flight. On my flight back to Langley I pondered the emotions I had felt over the past three days but simply could not find a rational explanation.

The following Monday morning, as I sat at my desk in the basement of the Personnel Building at Langley, I heard some chatter outside my door concerning an aircraft loss at Nellis. The apprehension I had felt one week earlier instantly returned, hitting me like a sledge hammer. Knowing my boss, Colonel J. B. Davis, the TAC Deputy Commander for Personnel, would know the details of any such occurrence, I picked up the phone and dialed his office on the second floor. When he answered, I asked if he had heard anything about a loss at Nellis. He replied with the answer I absolutely knew would be coming. "Bad news, Phil. It was Bob Ellis. Apparently there was a mid-air collision between Bob's F-15 and one of the Aggressor F-5Es. It looks real bad."

As details of the accident trickled in, I learned Bob was flying in the same tail number F-15B he and I had flown precisely one week earlier. The takeoff time, 4 v 6 mission scenario and assigned practice area were identical to the previous week's mission. The only significant difference was the occupant of the rear cockpit of Bob's F-15B was not me, but instead a young captain who was a ground controlled intercept (GCI) controller flying an orientation ride. The feelings of anxiety I had experienced one week earlier no longer seemed so mysterious and were replaced by the deep sense of sadness that follows in the wake of the loss of a friend.

Subsequent findings by the accident investigation board concluded there had been no violations of ROE (rules of engagement) and the tragic mid-air collision occurred when on the initial merge, the Aggressor pilot mistook one of the trailing F-16s as the lead F-15 and initiated an attack bringing him through the F-15's altitude block. In all probability both Ellis' F-15 and the Aggressor F-5E were "belly-up" to each other at the time of the collision and never saw it coming.

As strange as my premonitions might have seemed, they paled in comparison to events which occurred during the accident investigation that immediately followed the crash. The story concerning the involvement of a psychic who was instrumental in the search for two of the three men killed has circulated for years within the fighter pilot community. As the story was passed along it became greatly embellished, in all likelihood totally without mal-intent, but simply through misunderstanding and lack of details. I had personally heard and passed on an embellished version as related to me by trustworthy and honorable officers who would not distort the truth as they knew it.

The fact is this is a story needing no embellishment. Since I knew my friend and fellow officer, Colonel T.C. Skancky was the investigating officer widely quoted in the story, I called him to verify the accuracy of what I had heard.

Here now in his own words, Colonel T. C. Skanchy sets the record straight, in detail, about what actually happened in the aftermath of that tragic accident in 1981.

Roba Kia
Colonel T.C. Skanchy, USAF (Ret.)

Sally Baronowski, our command section secretary, stuck her head in my door and said Colonel Pete Hayes urgently needed to talk to me. I had formerly worked for Pete, but now as Vice Commander of Red Flag, I was no longer in his chain of command.

Pete didn't mince words on the phone, "T.C., we've just had a bad accident up at Mormon Mesa, and we want you to take charge." Startled, I tried to get the details, but Hayes said he wouldn't talk about it on the phone. He told me to get an interim accident board together and get moving.

Sally stuck her head in the doorway again. This time her complexion was quite flushed. She said, "Sir, there is a man on the phone who identifies himself as Roba Kia. He wants to talk to you now. He says it is very important." Startled, I picked up the phone and said, "How can I help you Mr. Roba Kia?" The stranger's voice replied, "Didn't you get my letter? Why didn't you do something about it?" "What letter, I asked, what are you talking about?" "The accident, he said, I sent you a letter warning you this accident would happen." "Who are you?" I demanded, "You sent me a letter?" He said, "I am Roba Kia the psychic, I'll be calling you back." Hanging up the phone, I couldn't believe what I was hearing.

The mid-air had occurred at around 23,000 feet, scattering wreckage over several hundred square miles. From rescue helicopters, it appeared nobody survived. The F-15 was piloted by Major Bob Ellis. He was an outstanding, experienced fighter pilot who had just been awarded the coveted Robby Risner award, given for advancing fighter tactics, the previous Sunday. In Bob's back seat was a young captain who was a ground-controlled, intercept (GCI) controller flying an orientation ride. I had known Bob Ellis for many years. I was his commander at both Luke and Nellis Air Force Bases. Flying the F-5E was a highly experienced Aggressor pilot I also knew and respected.

I quickly put together an interim accident board consisting of Majors Buzz Buzze and Phil Hoffman, both able F-15 pilots whom I trusted implicitly. I also asked for a medical expert, specifying Lt. Col. (Dr.) Earl Yuntis. "Doc" Yuntis was an Air Force flight surgeon pilots trusted. Most flight surgeons were looked on by pilots as arch enemies because they would or could ground pilots on a whim or some absurd technicality. Not Yuntis, he'd move heaven and earth to keep a pilot healthy and flying.

Within three hours after the accident, my team was well in motion, writing up an accident message to go out to higher headquarters, and collecting evidence. Gathering useful material included taking statements from witnesses, impounding tape recordings from ground stations, and getting the participating aircraft video tapes.

An F-16 flown by an outstanding fighter pilot Major Joe Bob Phillips, had been able to video tape the accident a second after the violent impact and explosion. Modern fighters have a video system that tapes what the pilot is seeing on the aircraft's radar and on the head's up display (HUD). The tape system is activated by the pilot.

Joe Bob was part of Ellis's flight fighting against the Aggressors who simulated Soviet style tactics. Joe Bob was several thousand feet below and a couple of miles behind Ellis's F-15.

Just as the accident happened, Phillips reacted by pulling his aircraft's nose up towards the fireball. The video system was already activated. Captured on the tape was the tremendous explosion with Joe Bob's commentary. Pieces of flaming wreckage were documented on tape flying off in various directions. Also documented on the tape were Phillip's F-16's heading, airspeed, attitude, and altitude, providing valuable clues about the accident.

The afternoon of the tragedy, I hopped into a Nellis helicopter and flew up to the accident scene at Mormon Mesa, about 50 miles northeast of Las Vegas. Hundreds of pieces of wreckage were visible from the air, as we flew to the site. The on scene commander reported to me that search parties had been unable to find any of the three men's remains. I thought that Joe Bob's video tape would provide some indication as to where the remains could be.

Getting back to my office at Red Flag, I had a message from Roba Kia to call him at his residence. That telephone number will be forever burned into my mind. Talking to a real psychic was an experience very different than the "1-900" phone-in psychics. In each of many conversations I had with him, he seemed to know exactly what I was doing without me telling him. He said, "I know you are having trouble finding the remains. Tell them to look under wreckage for one of them. One is still in the cockpit, and the other may still be alive." His words were haunting, depressing, and spurred me to faster action.

I went over the Phillips tape with a Red Flag photographic analyst again and again looking for clues. We noticed that a large piece of flaming F-15 wreckage was thrown 90 degrees away from the heading the F-15 was traveling at the instant of the impact. Could this be the cockpit portion containing the bodies of the two men? I thought this could be true, so I arranged for my team to fly in a helicopter up to the site at first light the next morning. Before going home, I stopped by the Ellis house to pay my respects to the grieving Ellis family, his wife Marge and two children.

Early the next morning, we flew up to Mormon Mesa. Our plan was to search a suspect area. This sector was where I thought the flaming wreckage seen flying away from the main wreckage had fallen. First, we reconnoitered the area of interest from the air, plotting on our maps pieces of metal we observed. Landing, we commenced a search on foot, dividing into teams of two. We all walked miles finding small pieces of metal that turned out to be hundreds of pieces of radar confusing chaff, dropped by fighters in the realistic exercises held at Nellis. We did not find any aircraft wreckage. The suspect wreckage we were looking for proved to be a large ball of burning fuel violently torn out of the disintegrating F-15.

At the crash site, a hundred airman were at work gathering up the fragmented pieces of wreckage and searching for human remains. Roba Kia told me to look under wreckage for one of the deceased. I diplomatically told the on site commander to have his men search carefully under wreckage for human remains. The F-5 pilot's body was soon found, but the other bodies were still missing as we helicoptered back to Nellis late that afternoon.

Arriving back at my office, I found several messages from Roba Kia and the letter he claimed to have mailed to me the day before the accident. Before I contacted the psychic, I had a number of details to act on. An old friend of mine, Lt. Col. Bill Crossman, commanded an Air Force Reserve helicopter search and rescue outfit that was part of a Red Flag exercise in progress at Nellis. Besides the helicopters, the unit had personnel trained by Army Special Forces who could search for downed airman in enemy territory and get them out on foot if necessary. I asked Bill to dispatch a search team to the area to conduct a foot search through the rugged terrain.

I also arranged for a Boise, Idaho Air National RF-4C reconnaissance aircraft to overfly the area and take pictures with infrared cameras to help in the search. The infrared should have been able to detect wreckage and the bodies. The pictures taken by the RF-4C the next day were of no help.

I then alerted my accident team and the helicopter crew to join me in searching the main wreckage tract the following morning. I changed into my dress blues, and with my wife, Karen, went to the base chapel for the evening memorial services for the three men.

I called Roba Kia. Without me bringing up the subject, he expressed satisfaction that we had recovered the remains of one of the pilots. I wondered how he knew this sensitive information because I hadn't released the information to outside sources. He just knew. He told me all of the remains of the F-5E pilot had not been recovered, and described in graphic detail what was still missing and where it could be found. I told him, we'd finish the job, and added I had received his letter.

The envelope contained a typed letter and a hand written diagram depicting how the aircraft would collide with his written description of the accident. He also had a paragraph pleading for me to help him prevent future accidents. I could not prove one way or the other if he had actually mailed the letter the day before the accident as he claimed. The psychic had dated his diagram the day prior to the accident. I asked Roba Kia how he knew I would be handling the investigation, and he claimed it came to him in a vision.

I gave the diagram to the accident board president who had relieved me of the investigation as is the procedure in the Air Force. After the inquiry, the document was returned to me. I kept the original accurate diagram in my papers which were lost by a moving company returning my personal affects from Daytona Beach, Florida to Springfield, Virginia.

The conversation with Roba Kia shifted to finding the other two victims. He told me that the F-15 pilot was still in the cockpit of the aircraft and the other man, who had lived for awhile, was in kind of a "rocking chair" laying on its right side. Neither of his statements seemed too probable. I asked Roba Kia if I could meet with him at his house the next afternoon after returning from the crash site.

It was on a Thursday, the third day after the crash that my team and I flew in the helicopter to Mormon Mesa. This time, we had plotted on a map the pattern of

F-15's located wreckage and noticed a pattern that led over a cliff and into a deep gully. After several hours of hiking down the gully in the direction of the debris, we were surprised to find a large portion of the F-15's cockpit. Inside were the remains of Bob Ellis, still strapped in his ejection seat.

Flying back to Nellis, I reported to my boss, General Kelly who told me to continue the effort of locating the third victim. Although the Air Force would move heaven and earth to find accident victims, the still to be located body had taken on an even greater urgency. Not released to the press or known outside a small circle of people, the young GCI captain was a black man. There had been no mention in newspapers, TV, or on the radio about the race of this man. General Kelly felt that it would look very bad to find two of the three remains, Caucasians, and not the black officer. I agreed with him. He told me to find this man, whatever it took.

I also told Kelly about my ROE violation investigation. Although not finished, I told him, I felt there would be no smoking gun. All participants in the air-to-air engagement had been professional and flew according to the ROEs.

It was soon time to drive to Roba Kia's house. He lived in Henderson, Nevada, out towards Hoover Dam. I had a street map and soon found his residence. The psychic and his wife lived in a large mobile home. Roba Kia met me at his door, introduced his wife who departed immediately, and invited me to sit down. I spread out the detailed maps I had brought.

Roba Kia was a kindly looking Caucasian gentleman of about 55 years of age. He had white hair and stood about 5 feet 8 inches tall with a medium build. He looked like any body's grandfather except for his eyes. They were a penetrating blue, almost turquoise color that seemed to take in everything. As I talked to him, he would look deep into my eyes as if he was penetrating my brain and reading my thoughts.

He said he already knew we had recovered the F-15 pilot and the portion of the F-5 pilot he had mentioned the day before. He gave me various messages for the families of the deceased Roba Kia said he had received from the dead through séances at the crash site.

He then told me news that rocked me. He said the evening before, he had been with the "black man" who's remains are in a "rocking chair on its right side." I was startled. I said, "Mr. Roba Kia, how did you know that this man was black?" He said, "Oh, I've known since I first visited him." Roba Kia went on to say, "This man is fun loving and likes music. He has changed into white pants, a tropical shirt, and wears a wide brimmed hat that he likes to throw up in the air and catch." Furthermore the psychic said, "He runs up and down the cliff where his earthly remains are, laughs and sings." It was as if I had been kicked in the stomach. I was speechless to hear this kind of talk. Roba Kia then indicated that this man had lived for a short span of time after the moment of the impact. The psychic said we could have saved the young captain if we had gotten to him sooner. This proved not to be the case, thank God.

I presented the search plan to Roba Kia for the next day (Friday) using my maps. I was highly interested to hear where on the map Roba Kia thought we could find the missing body. The psychic had no idea. He said that he could not relate to what he saw in his séances or visions to what the map showed.

I asked the psychic if he would be interested in a séance while we searched the next day. I thought that if he was not faking, we could be at a given location at a given time and be able to correlate the place with the psychic. Roba Kia was not interested. He said he would drive up to Mormon Mesa in his 1975 Chevrolet and look over the terrain. He felt he could tell us where to look by looking over the bigger picture of a non-séance view.

True to his word, as we helicoptered up to Mormon Mesa following the Southern Pacific railroad tracks that cut through the area, there was Roba Kia in his Chevrolet kicking up a cloud of dust.

The road to the crash site was an unimproved Southern Pacific maintenance road. Roba Kia should have been in a jeep. Not long after we overflew him, his Chevrolet became stuck. After some hours, a track maintenance crew came along and helped Roba Kia turn around and head back towards Henderson. The psychic was unable to get up to the crash site.

Our efforts also proved futile. We needed to search the rougher terrain in the area to the east, but I didn't push our luck. The Nellis helicopter crew was not very experienced, and I did not want to pressure them into flying beyond their capabilities—especially me being a passenger in the helicopter.

Getting back to Nellis that Friday afternoon I called Roba Kia. I wanted to see if he could help us out with a séance. He said he thought he could.

I arranged for the two Nellis UH-1 helicopters and a Department of Energy (DOE) UH-1 to fly a grid search on that Sunday. The DOE helicopter was painted red, white, and blue. The two Air Force helicopters were painted olive drab. The helicopters were only good for about an hour of search time, so only one helicopter would be airborne at a time. The other two would sit at the staging area on Mormon Mesa, awaiting the appointed time to takeoff and search the specified area.

My plan was to talk to Roba Kia on the phone while he had his séance out to where the final victim lay. I had a very carefully timed plan for grid searches. If he could really project himself out to the site, I would know exactly where he was by having only one helicopter flying a specified area at a stipulated time.

I drove over to Henderson to again meet with Roba Kia. I saw his beat up Chevrolet and hoped he didn't plan on suing me or the Air Force for the damage. The car appeared to have had a lot more wear and tear on it than a few days earlier.

I explained the methodical search plan set up for Sunday and asked if he agreed. He said that the plan was great, and he'd be able to work with me in a séance. Still highly skeptical, I asked the psychic what color he thought the helicopters would be. He said, "Brown, or dark green like army trucks." I thought it was just fine that he didn't know about the red, white, and blue DOE helicopter.

I asked, "Roba Kia, how come you go to all of the time and effort to do this? I can't pay you nor can the Air Force." He replied, "I have done this for a thousand years, and if I refuse to help people, God will take my gift away." He went on to tell me that his daughter was also a psychic and that his wife did not have the power. He also said that he knew who he was in previous lives, and we are all reincarnated.

Roba Kia then turned to me and said, "You know, you have psychic powers. I can tell by looking into your eyes. All you need is a little practice." Pulling out some written material and drawings out of a drawer, he showed me some mystical psychic symbols, and how a séance worked. I felt very uncomfortable and wanted to get out of there.

Telling the psychic I needed to get back to Nellis, I gathered up my maps and started to leave. He stopped me and said he had some "personal messages from the dead for their families." I listened to him, then he said, "Tell the woman with the big black dog to be careful, the dog will bite her hand three times." Well, the Ellis family had an Irish Setter, and I thought perhaps that message was for Marge Ellis.

That evening, I was late getting home due to paper work, making final arrangements for the helicopters, and stopping by the Nellis Officer's Club for a well earned beer. Arriving home, Karen said that Roba Kia needed to talk to me. She said, "When he called, he said, "I know you are sewing. I am sorry to disturb you, but I need to talk to your husband." Well, Karen went on, I sew about once in a year and somehow he knew I was sewing." Well, that is Roba Kia.

The next day, Saturday, came and went. No further progress was made in finding the body although several search parties including the Reserve rescue team was combing the hills.

I spent the day out at Nellis AFB pouring over transcripts and depositions on the accident. I still owed General Kelly my report on how I thought the accident had occurred. The official report wouldn't be available to the general for several more weeks.

That night, Karen and I went to a farewell dinner for our old friend, Colonel Jerry Cobb, who was transferring to Alaska to be the wing commander at Elmendorf, AFB. While at the dinner, I got a message to call my daughter, Jill, at home.

I phoned Jill, who knew nothing about this psychic. She was in a little shock and said this "strange man" with a haunting voice called. Roba Kia told her he knew Jill was our daughter, and I was to call him back. I told her it was okay since I knew the man.

I called Roba Kia. He had some more of his insight about the accident, the victims, and wanted to confirm the plan was still on the following day. It was. The helicopter search was to begin at 10:00 a.m. the next morning.

Sunday morning, I was very troubled about the psychic powers Roba Kia seemed to have. Trying to keep busy, I decided to clip our little black Cockapoo, Angus. This dog had an awful disposition, especially when he was clipped. He hated the process and had real malevolence towards me while I was clipping him. Out on the back deck, I was cutting his hair with clippers and scissors, not paying close attention to the dog or what I was doing. My mind was far away, thinking about Mormon Mesa.

Suddenly, I nicked that little Tasmanian Devil. Before I could move out of harms way, he bit me hard three times. My right hand was bandaged for some days after the incident. Roba Kia was right about the dog and the bites. He was wrong about the Ellis dog. It was Skanchy's dog.

At around 9:30 a.m., I called the Nellis Command Post and confirmed that the helicopters were at the base site and ready to go. I then called Roba Kia and said we would start the session at 10:00 a.m.

Exactly on time, Roba Kia went into that strange state in the séance. He spoke with a deep voice exactly the way psychics or people hypnotized are portrayed on television and in the movies.

He told me he was standing on a cliff beside the "rocking chair" with the deceased soul still strapped in. I told Roba Kia the day before, he was describing the man in his ejection seat but Roba Kia chose to refer to the seat as a "rocking chair."

The first helicopter had been airborne for sometime, flying over the grid that I thought was the most likely location of the dead man. Roba Kia couldn't hear or see a helicopter. I asked the psychic to tell me where the sun was from him, hoping that would help pinpoint his location. He said he couldn't see the sun because he was in a box canyon with a black, water stained cliff at the end. I asked Roba Kia to describe the surroundings. He said the ejection seat was half way down the black cliff, laying on its right side. At the base of the cliff were trees, shrubbery, two or three springs, and farther down the canyon, towards the entrance, were several old mines with tailings piled around. I thought this a highly unlikely description. Nothing in the accident area looked like that to me.

By this time, the second helicopter had flown its search pattern and had departed. Roba Kia still hadn't heard or seen a helicopter. I thought this effort would be a failure, and my confidence was fading.

I was wondering if the people I was working with would think I was going off the deep edge. I carried on the eerie conversation with Roba Kia. The third helicopter was now carrying out the prearranged search. This UH-1 was the DOE red, white, and blue helicopter. Following where the helicopter should have been searching on the map, I kept asking Roba Kia if he had seen or heard the helicopter. There was only about ten minutes remaining in the search.

Suddenly the psychic said, "I can hear a helicopter coming. Now I can see it. Tell the helicopter to stop, it is right over the top of me." I told him, I didn't have direct contact with the helicopter. Rapidly drawing a big red circle on my map I asked him, "Roba Kia, what color is the helicopter?" He said, "It is red, white;"— he hesitated then said, "Red white, and blue." That was good enough for me. I told the psychic I thought we had located the site. I did not mention to Roba Kia the next steps I was to take. I didn't want the psychic to be in the way. The circle on the map was to the east of where we had been looking. It was on Mormon Mountain.

I noticed that the local TV weatherman was forecasting a heavy spring snowstorm moving into the Las Vegas area the following (Monday) evening. I called the Air Force weather people, and they confirmed they expected heavy snow on the ground by Tuesday up on Mormon Mesa.

I needed to move fast so I called Bill Crossman. I told Crossman I needed his three search and rescue helicopters for a special mission the next morning and to forget about the Red Flag participation. Bill called me back. He said the mission was on and asked where to have the crews for the briefing? I replied in the briefing trailer behind the Red Flag building at 7:00 a.m. the following morning.

I then called the Base Commander and asked for an aircraft fuel truck full of jet fuel. I arranged for several trusted Red Flag staff to lead the truck to the right location. I wanted the truck to be positioned on a flat clearing where the Southern Pacific service road came off a hard surfaced highway. This would provide a landing and refueling spot for the helicopters. The truck was to leave at 5:00 a.m. the next morning.

Sunday evening seemed to drag by. My adrenaline was pumping, and I wanted to get this thing over with. Laying awake at about 11:00 p.m., I heard three distinct knocks coming from what I thought was our front door. I laid there and listened. Three more knocks. I said, "Karen are you awake." "Yes", she replied. "Do you hear those knocks?" I asked. She answered she did.

I went down stairs and opened the front door. Nobody was there. I looked around outside. Nobody was there, so I climbed back into bed. Once again, three knocks. Shaken, I sat at the top of the steps to try to catch the knocking phantom in action. Three more knocks. This time, it sounded like the knocks were coming from my daughter's bedroom to my right.

Grabbing a flashlight, I quietly walked into the room and turned the light towards where the noise seemed to be coming from. It was Paige's gerbil banging the water bottle. Clang, clang, clang, a pause and clang, clang, clang. Roba Kia wasn't trying to get a message to me after all.

The next morning, I was at Red Flag an hour or so early to confirm the fuel truck was on its way and to work out the briefing. I ran into my boss, Colonel Jim Woods. Jim said, "T.C., you can't take any Red Flag assets", meaning I couldn't use the helicopters. This was one time I would defy a direct order. It was probably our last chance to find the poor, deceased soul.

With my trusted help, Major Phil Hoffman and Doctor Yunas, I briefed the three helicopter crews. These guys were real pros, and if we had a chance of succeeding, the reservists could help us pull it off.

I briefed the crews what the mission was, what we were going to look for, and how I knew what to look for. I told them about the psychic, the body in the ejection seat, the blind canyon, the cliff, the mines, and the springs. Bill Crossman then took over the briefing, providing the details: Takeoff time, search patterns, refueling at the truck, and safety details.

Sally Baronowski came back to the briefing trailer and said, "That man wants to talk to you again, and now." I said I would follow her to the office. Walking back with her, Sally told me she was humoring Roba Kia when he called. Roba Kia said, "Get a pencil and take this message now." Sally told me she didn't have a pencil or pen in her hand because she'd remember his message for me. When Roba Kia began to dictate the message, all of a sudden he shouted into the phone, "I said get a pencil, now." Sally said it was like he was looking over her shoulder. I told her I thought Roba Kia was.

He had given Sally a cryptic message about smoke and a dove which made no sense to me so I called him. Roba Kia said he knew we were going on a search mission and he'd be there. He said, "Look for the dove and the smoke. That is how I will lead you to the body." What did that mean I mused to myself?

Taking Phil and "Doc" with me in the helicopter I believed would find the body, off we went. Unfortunately, I was in a great deal of pain from internal injuries received in a plane crash years earlier. I knew this was going to be a tough day.

The weather was already turning sour. We wouldn't have too many hours to search. We overflew the fuel truck at the refueling spot and turned up the Southern Pacific railroad tracks and then up to Mormon Mountain, the eastern defining point of Mormon Mesa.

The helicopters set up their search patterns on the western face of the mountain. Crossman was taking the highest grid, we were in the third helicopter searching the lowest grid on the mountain. After about thirty minutes, the pilot of the middle helicopter radioed, "We've gotta delta oscar." That was code for having located a "dead one." Our helicopter moved up to the location. There on the side of a dark, stained cliff was the ejection seat, about half way down.

On a reasonably level spot at the base of the cliff, our helicopter hovered a foot above the ground allowing us to get out with a little equipment and a body bag. We climbed up the side of the cliff to the ejection seat, and I cut the body out of straps with a knife. We then carried the body down to where the helicopter could hover and pick us up. Dr. Yunis thought it was doubtful the captain had survived the collision with the F-5E. If he did, he died as his body crashed down the cliff.

The ground search team dispatched by Crossman were attracted by the helicopters and made their way down the steep cliffs. There is a good chance that if the helicopter search had not been launched, this team would have eventually found the body as they searched on foot. The ground team was picked up by one of the helicopters and were flown back to Nellis with us.

I kept wondering about Roba Kia's signs—the white dove and the smoke. I was in so much physical pain that I couldn't concentrate on the signs but was still very intrigued. I found it was a great emotional release flying back to Nellis. The search was carried out so fast the helicopters did not require refueling from the awaiting truck.

My report concluded that the accident was most likely caused by the F-5E pilot seeing the trailing F-16 and not Ellis's F-15. Thinking that the F-16 was the leading attacker, the Aggressor inadvertently descended through the F-15's altitude, colliding with the Eagle when both aircraft were belly up to each other. I did not believe there was any willful violation of ROEs. It was a simple miscalculation on the part of the Aggressor with tragic results.

I then called Roba Kia. He said he knew all about the search and recovery. He said he was there and asked me if I spotted the signs. I told him no. I then asked if I could drive over to see the gray haired man the next morning. He agreed to the meeting.

I composed a nice, heart-felt letter of appreciation from the Air Force to Roba Kia signed by me. Sally typed up the letter and I drove over to see the psychic. I shook hands with Roba Kia very gingerly because of my injured right hand. I showed where the "big" black dog had bitten me three times as he foresaw. Except, it was me with the dog bites, not Marge Ellis. He smiled about that. I told Roba Kia about the pervious day's mission and how appreciative the Air Force and our country was for his efforts. I stated that he was a fine American and gave a lot because the Air Force couldn't pay Roba Kia for his efforts and I sure couldn't. I then presented the psychic with the framed letter of appreciation.

I asked Roba Kia how he made a living when he wasn't helping preventing accidents, solving murders, and finding lost children. He smiled and said, "I am a consultant and tell people what numbers to place bets on." Well, he was a gambling consultant, a good profession for psychics in Las Vegas.

He then turned very serious and said he wanted me to be a "conduit to the aviation world" for prevention of future accidents. I told the psychic I didn't know if I could do this. It would take a lot of grit to do so, trying to talk people out of flying because a psychic saw dangers in their future. It would drain all a person's emotions, and I would have been branded a crack pot for sure.

Closing his eyes and looking very perplexed, Roba Kia said that the Thunderbirds had something wrong with the "tail" of one of their aircraft. The psychic said, "If something wasn't done, six aircraft would crash, killing all six pilots." I was astounded. What was he talking about? Nothing like that could possibly happen in a thousand years.

Going out the door of his trailer house, I shook his hand again, and told Roba Kia I would get back to him about becoming his "conduit to the aviation world." The truth was, I wanted to get a lot of distance between myself and Roba Kia. The mid-air had taken a lot out of me, and part of the stress was working with him.

Some months later, I was attending the University of Southern California's Accident Investigation School then taught at Norton AFB, San Bernardino, California. After school one evening, I was enjoying a beer at the Officers' Club. I struck up a conversation with a pilot I had never met before. Within minutes he was telling me a wild story about a psychic aiding an aircraft accident investigation at Nellis. His story was greatly embellished and exaggerated. I told him, I was the guy, and the way it really happened. This was the first of many times I heard the Roba Kia story. Each time, the story was far different from the truth.

A year later, Karen, the girls, and I were at the Army War College, Carlisle Pennsylvania. That spring of 1982, six Thunderbird pilots were killed when their T-38s crashed. They were bottoming out of a loop while practicing at Indian Springs Auxiliary, 30 miles northwest of Nellis AFB. A foreign object had made its way into the slab actuator of the Thunderbird leader's T-38. The actuator could not function properly, making it impossible to pull hard enough to keep from hitting the ground. It was too late for the wingmen to make individual recoveries when they realized that something was amiss.

Dear God, I knew those men! What a shock. How tragic. I gasped, I choked, and tears streamed down my face when I heard the dreadful news. I had been warned a year earlier but didn't do anything. What could I have done? Roba Kia did all he could do. Sometimes we have all of the forewarning in the world, and yet are unable to do anything about impending disasters. Still, I wonder. That accident still haunts me. I will live with this horror until my dying day.

T.C. Skanchy
Colonel, USAF (Ret.)

And that's the way it really happened almost a quarter century ago.
Hands

"Hatfield"

- 1986 -

As a young captain I was assigned to Williams AFB, Arizona in 1964. We lived in Tempe, Arizona on Riviera Drive, where a cotton field lay just behind our back yard and you could see the Superstitions Mountains out past Apache Junction as if you were looking through a pane of glass. There was absolutely no smog in those days in "The Valley of the Sun" and it came as close as I had ever seen to paradise.

My commute to Williams AFB, some 22 miles down two-lane blacktop roads was shear joy. Driving an Alfa Romeo 1600 Veloche Spider with the top down at the crack of dawn down along the near deserted two-lane roads that led to Williams AFB, I could often keep pace with the T-37s flying their 100-knot final approach to Runway 12 Right as I sped along the final mile of Williams Field Road toward the front gate.

It was here that my wife and I bought our very first new house. It was a tract home of Spanish design and an absolute dream compared to the spartan accommodations to which we had become accustomed since we were married some three years earlier. Living in an identical home just around the corner was the Hatfield family with whom we became dear friends. Don was an airline captain flying out of Sky Harbor Airport in Phoenix. He was a veteran of the Korean War, where he carried a BAR (Browning Automatic Rifle) as a combat infantryman and earned the Silver Star for killing thirteen Chinese soldiers with a trenching tool when they jumped into the listening post bunker he manned.

He was a tough, pure warrior, ill-suited for the regiment of military obedience, but indeed a man you would chose to have on your side in a tough and desperate fight. He was the only Army veteran I personally knew who was honorably discharged as a PFC with the Silver Star. Following the Korean War he married a beautiful Hawaiian gal named Leilani who was the former Miss Maui. They had two kids near the age of our own and our families shared many mutual interests. It was a friendship that endured throughout the years.

After I had retired from the Air Force in 1984, I was working for a company named Perceptronics, Inc., one of the principal sub-contractors responsible for development of the computer-based, distributed simulation, virtual battlefield now widely used by our services for realistic, combat training. It was called SIM-NET in those days, shorthand for simulator network.

As I sat in my office in Woodland Hills, California on a Monday morning in July of 1986, I had a sudden urge to call my old friend Don Hatfield, who had less than a year earlier lost his wife Leilani, after her long battle with kidney failure. I rationalized there was no reason to call until after work, but simply couldn't concentrate on anything because of the urge that wouldn't go away.

I dialed Don's number in Tempe, Arizona where he still lived in the house he had occupied since we were neighbors. When he answered, his voice seemed so thin and weak I hardly recognized it. He said the doctor had put him on some medication to lower his blood pressure and he felt, not only was it making him weak, but everything in him that could hurt, did. I offered what encouragement I could and told him I'd drive over the upcoming weekend so we could have a drink together and visit. He said he would really look forward to that, and then "out of the blue" said something totally out of character for this tough, battle-hardened, old Korean War vet, "I love you Phil."

A chill ran through me as I instantly recognized the words as identical to those spoken by Jack Smallwood to me on the ramp at Eglin some twelve years earlier. Before hanging up I searched for some words of comfort and assured him we'd get together the following Saturday. After hanging up the telephone, I was left with the same disquieting feeling I had experienced prior to the deaths of Jack Smallwood and Bob Ellis.

The following day I learned of Don's death. When members of his family had been unable to contact him because of a constant busy signal on his telephone they drove to Don's house where they found him lying on the floor next to the wall mounted telephone in the kitchen. His time of death was estimated to coincide with the call I had made to him the previous day. He had apparently dropped the receiver before replacing it in its cradle and fell to the floor, where he struck his head on the step-down ledge from the kitchen to the sun room.

The following Saturday I was a pallbearer and offered the eulogy at Don's graveside funeral at Forest Lawn Cemetery outside Los Angles. He was laid to rest with full military honors, beside his beloved wife Leilani, the former Miss Maui.

Dedication

I do realize an author's "dedications" and "acknowledgements" are normally one paragraph affairs found at the front of the book. In my case, there is only person to whom I would bestow these honors. I have chosen to write this final chapter toward that end because the old standard line, "Without the help and support of my wife this book would not have been possible." simply doesn't hack it. So if you're looking for a chapter on aerial combat, read no further for this relates directly to the lady without whose support and dedication, this little book, or ninety percent of anything worthwhile I ever accomplished would be possible.

I first laid eyes on my future wife in France at the Evreux Air Base Officers Club bar in the summer of 1960. Steve Larson and I were having a drink after work when both of us saw her at about the same time. Before I could react, Steve had crossed the room, introduced himself and was dancing with my future wife. After he returned to the bar he said he had learned her name was Solvejg, she was eighteen years old, and came from Holland. I asked him if she "spoke good English" to which he replied, "As good as you and me and with no accent at all." When the band struck up the next tune, I was at her table asking for a dance.

As we began to dance, I introduced myself and remarked I understood she was from Holland, which she acknowledged, and in return asked me where I came from in the States? After telling her I was from Texas I decided to display my wit and charm by smiling as I looked down at her dainty feet saying, "Well since you're from Holland, where are your wooden shoes?" She didn't hesitate for one second before glancing at my waist and replying with a wry smile, "Well since you're from Texas, where are your six-shooters?" In less than those first, twenty-five words we exchanged, I concluded not only was this gal drop-dead gorgeous, but smart, tough, witty, and not about to take crap from anyone. That first opinion has been totally validated for over forty-five years. I fell instantly in love.

We were married one year later in the base chapel with Solvejg wearing a beautiful, wedding dress she had created from cloth I had purchased while TDY to

Tripoli, Libya. My fellow officers held crossed swords, forming a path across the parking lot from the base chapel to the officers club where our wedding reception was held on the afternoon of 1 September 1961. Due to my extremely limited financial resources, we had contracted for a modest reception costing $200 at the officers club. We were stunned by the fabulous spread which awaited us when we arrived. Apparently, the club had confused our party with one that had been

(Author)

Figure 49—Squadron Dinner Party
Bitburg AB, Germany, 1977

arranged by a colonel's wife. This error caused the club officer a "near tears" reaction when I told him it was purely "his mistake."

As wonderful as the reception was, the guests suddenly began to disappear after the first hour. My squadron commander, Lt. Col. Bud Farris approached me saying, "You and your bride need to leave right now, and don't answer the phone or respond to anyone tonight." We left immediately and only hours later the entire squadron was recalled for immediate deployment after the Russians closed the three air-corridors to Berlin.

In the remaining three years we were at Evreux, I averaged nine months of every year TDY during which time Solvejg gave birth to our son. Excluding the rent we paid for our house on the economy, she operated our household on a budget of $50 per month and still managed to buy me a Rolex Datejust wristwatch for my birthday in 1963, which I have worn ever since

When my service obligation was up in 1965, the time was ripe for Air Force pilots like me to become commercial airline pilots. I explored the opportunity and after interviews could have signed on with any of the major airlines. It was a lucrative opportunity since the WWII glut of pilots was reaching retirement age and those who signed on during this period would achieve seniority very quickly. When Solvejg and I discussed the choice, she said, "Well Phil, the airlines and all that money sound great, but I know this. Ever since we met you have constantly talked about shooting down MiGs and being a fighter squadron commander. I don't think you'll ever do that flying an airliner, but it's up to you and I'll support you in either decision." That did it for me.

When I deployed on two occasions to Southeast Asia, she was totally resolute and had "a stiff upper lip" while many of the wives were blubbering over their fate. She wrote me a letter every day I was gone over those two tours, all the while raising our two kids and bolstering the morale of other wives in the squadron. Although not a superstitious man by nature, she had given me the little lace handkerchief she had carried when we were married for "good luck" and I carried it in the upper left pocket of my flight suit on all 275 combat missions I flew. When I realized on one of the last of those missions I had inadvertently left it in my quarters, I delayed my takeoff until it could be retrieved.

(Author)

Figure 50—Wives Cockpit Orientation Day Luke AFB, Arizona, 1984

Later in my career when I was the Wing Commander of the 405th Tactical Training Wing at Luke AFB, Arizona, I was surprised by a visit from a colonel from the security branch of Headquarters 12th Air Force. Behind closed doors in my office he told me it had been noted my wife was not a U.S. citizen, but in fact still held Dutch citizenship. He then suggested because of the sensitivity of my position and the security clearances I held, my wife's foreign citizenship posed an unacceptable security risk. He added, it was felt unless I took immediate steps to ensure she obtained U.S. citizenship, my own security clearance, as well as my job as wing commander, would be in jeopardy.

With carefully controlled anger, I related to my visitor a brief history of the supposed "security risk" with whom I had lived for the past twenty-one years. I concluded by saying, "You can tell whoever sent you here I have absolutely no intention of putting pressure on my wife to change her citizenship. She is the most loyal and trustworthy person I know, and when she decides to become a U.S. Citizen, the decision will be hers, not that of some pinhead bureaucrat. If it costs me my job and clearance, so be it. In short, you can tell them I said to stuff-it."

As the colonel rose to leave, he turned back extending his hand and said, "I've got to tell you Colonel, that's one of the gutsiest statements ever heard. I wish you good luck." I never heard another word about the subject and ten years later, on November 19, 1991 my bride decided the time was right and she became a U.S. citizen, all on her own.

So here's the final "nickel on the grass" to you, *My Fair Lady*. For hanging in there through thick and thin, twenty-six moves, endless TDYs, raising our two wonderful kids in a foreign land, and too many great dinner parties to count. Most of all, thank you for being my best friend for all these years. You were the glue that made it all happen. I'll not forget it.

Glossary of Terms

AAA Anti-Aircraft Artillery

AC Aircraft Commander

Across the fence entering enemy territory

AFSC Air Force Specialty Code; a four digit code identifying a job within the Air Force; an F-4 pilot would be an 1115F; the 1115 shows him to be a fighter pilot, while the F suffix shows the fighter is the F-4

AGL above ground level

Aggressor training personnel playing the role of an enemy combatant

Alpha refers to the pilot in a two-place fighter

Air America CIA operated fleet of aircraft that performed overt and covert operations in the theater

Alpha Strike primary morning raid of the day into North Vietnam

APX-76 an onboard electronic unit used to interrogate desecrate codes transmitted from another aircraft's IFF

Arc to cut across the turning circle to create a shorter path to the target

Assault takeoff a tactical maneuver for troop carrier aircraft that involves getting airborne on the takeoff roll as quickly as possible, then climbing at a steep angle

Attitude indicator a gyroscopic instrument that displays the aircraft's orientation in relationship to the earth's horizon

Atoll AA-2 heat-seeking air-to-air missile; USSR copy of US AIM-9B Sidewinder

Ban Karai Pass a major interdiction area for the Ho Chi Minh trail as it entered southern Laos north of the DMZ…it lay southeast of Mu Gia Pass and was just on the Laotian side of the border from North Vietnam

Bandit confirmed enemy aircraft

BAR Browning Automatic Rifle

Barrel Roll an aerobatics maneuver…also, the nickname for the combat sector of the northwest portion of Laos (the southwest portion was named "Steel Tiger")

BFM Basic Fighter Maneuvers

Bingo The fuel required to disengage and either return safely to home base, an alternate base, or the refueling anchor

Bogie an unidentified aircraft

Boom the telescoping pipe like conduit through which the refueling tanker passes fuel to the receivers

Boomer the refueling boom operator in a tanker

Bought the farm to perish

Bravo refers to the WSO in a two-place fighter

BrigGen abbreviation for a USAF Brigadier General

Bugout disengage and leave the area

Burning a Green Stamp slang term applied to the exchange of the old S&H Green stamps for merchandise

Bury my nose diving at an angle that puts the aircraft flight path below the horizon

BVR beyond visual range

CAP Combat Air Patrol; an aircraft patrol provided over an objective area, over the force protected, over the critical area of a combat zone, or over an air defense area, for purpose of intercepting and destroying hostile aircraft before they reach their target

Chaffer aircraft with a mission to drop radar-blocking chaff

Chopper nickname for helicopter

Clausewitz a widely studied and quoted German military strategist of the 17th Century

Clean term that refers to an aircraft configuration devoid of external stores and their associated mounting pylons and munitions racks

Cobra nickname of the Bell AH-1, two-man gunship

Cold mike to stop transmitting on the radio

Corner velocity the indicated airspeed at which an aircraft can perform its quickest and tightest turn…it is based on the minimum airspeed at which the aircraft is aerodynamically capable of pulling the maximum G allowed before danger of structural failure of the wing

Counter flow proceeding in the opposite direction of the other aircraft or element within your flight

Crossing the fence passing into the combat operations sector; a "fence check" is performed at this time to prepare the aircraft and its ordnance for combat

Curve of pursuit the flight path described by a fighter attacking a target from its rear hemisphere

CYA cover your ass

Dash-1 a reference book associated with a specific type aircraft describing its characteristics, limitations, normal and emergency operating procedures

DF direction finder

Differential thrust in the case of the C-130, the engines on one wing are operating at greater power than those on the opposite wing

Disco radio call sign for the EC-121 aircraft which provided airborne navigational assistance, border warnings, and MiG warnings

Discrete frequency radio channel used for private communication among members of your flight

DNIF duty not involving flying

Down the chute the initial portion of the curved, descending path described by a fighter attacking a target from above

Down the slide same as "Down the chute"

Duck the designated target for student basic fighter maneuvers (BFM) training…the "duck" often operates with closely defined and limited maneuvering options

Dustoff Huey a UH-1 helicopter used to evacuate wounded personnel from the battleground

E-SAM the radio frequency of a surface-to-air missile whose radar control guidance operated in the E-Band frequency range; example SA-2 Guideline

FAC Forward Air Controller.

Fighting wing a tactical formation that places the wingman in a 30 to 60 degree cone off the leader's tail and 200 to 500 feet out

Five mile boresight a radar mode that focuses the radar antenna's beam on a line coincident with the pilot's aiming index on the combining glass…the result is that if the pilot places the pipper on the target and presses the "Auto Aux" button on the inboard throttle, the radar will lock up the target being illuminated

Flew the hump slang term used to describe the airlift sorties flown over the Himalayan Mountains during WW-II

Flight level 200 approximately 20,000 feet altitude

FNG acronym for fucking new guy

Folland Gnat fighter a small, single engine fighter of British design

Forward slip the aircraft flys in a banked attitude without turning because of applied rudder opposite the direction of the bank

Frag slang for frag order—a fragmentary operations order, the daily supplement to standard operations orders governing the conduct of the air war; directs a specific mission

Gaggle slang term for a poorly defined or unstructured flight formation

GCI ground controlled intercept

Get on the gages to use the aircraft's instruments for orientation

GI government issue

GIB guy in back

Golf Course an established landmark on a particular VR route

Gomers slang term for Vietnamese enemy combatants

Gorilla's Head a well know landmark pattern that is formed by the river dividing Laos and North Vietnam

Guard the emergency UHF radio frequency (243.0 mz)

H in the River geometric pattern formed by the confluence of the Red and Black Rivers in the vicinity of Hanoi; an easily recognizable landmark for navigation

Hi-G deflection shot a gun shot taken at a high angle off when a tracking solution is not possible…in such case, the shot is made by shooting a stream of bullets in front of the target so that his flight path will take him through the path of the bullets

Hold down holding down the UHF transmit button so another aircraft can determine the direction to your aircraft

Hosed shot at by AAA

Huey nickname for the Bell UH-1 helicopter

ID identification

Initial point (IP) a geographic point, usually distinguishable visually or by radar, used as a starting point for a bomb or recce run to the target

In the grove on the proper flight path for landing and touchdown

IP instructor pilot

Intel intelligence

J-8 attitude indicator a gyroscopic aircraft instrument which displays the attitude of the aircraft in relationship to the earth's horizon

Jam the bogie's turn-rate into you is denying you the turning room you require to stay behind and within his turning radius, which could lead to loss of nose-tail separation and overshoot, at which point you could lose your role as the attacker and become the defender

Jammer refers to electronic interference to enemy signals and communications

Jink to violently change the aircraft's flight path to defeat aimed projectiles (like bullets)

Jolly Green nickname for the HH-53 rescue helicopter that flew the SAR (search and rescue) missions

Jollys multiple Jolly Green Giant HH-53 helicopters

Karst a jagged, angular outcrop of a limestone rock formation often found in Southeast Asia

KCAS Knots Calibrated Airspeed

King radio call sign of the KC-130 that coordinated activities of the SAR forces

KISS acronym for "keep it simple stupid"

L/D Max the airspeed at which the aircraft will glide the longest distance

Lag pursuit to place your projected flight path outside that of the bandit

Lead pursuit flight path pointed ahead of that of the bandit

Linebacker JCS-directed USAF strikes against targets in North Vietnam; Linebacker I began 9 May 1972 and ended 22 Oct 1972; Linebacker II ran from 18 to 29 Dec 1972

Loose Deuce US Navy 2-ship tactical formation

Maneuvering egg refers to the path traced by an aircraft when doing a constant G loop…because of the effects of radial G, the traced path will resemble the profile of a vertical standing egg with its large end at the bottom

Mayday term used during a radio transmission to indicate an aircraft in distress or other emergency situation

Merge the point at which the flight paths of opposing fighters converge

MSgt abbreviation for a USAF Master Sergeant

Mu Gia Pass a major interdiction area for the Ho Chi Minh trail as it entered southern Laos north of the DMZ.

Mil milliradian; one mil = 0.0573 degrees

Mil power maximum thrust available without use of afterburner

Mode III a code transmission band of the IFF (identification friend or foe)

Mutual support shared information and actions used to defeat an adversary

N/S north/south

Nickel on the grass a tribute and part of the refrain from an old fighter pilot ballad; "Throw a nickel on the grass, save a fighter pilot's ass."

Ninety (90) right a term referring to a 90 degree right turn for a tactical formation

NVA North Vietnamese Army

On the deck flying at an altitude just about the surface

On the numbers refers to landing on the large identification numbers that are painted near the ends of runways

On speed final approach speed as determined by the aircraft's configuration and gross weight

Overshoot loss of nose-tail separation during an attack resulting in a flight path that is outside that of the aircraft being attacked

Parrot check testing the operation of the aircraft's transponder (identification friend or foe)

Pealed-off the beginning of a fighter attack from above; see also "rolling-in

Phantom Ridge a mountain range approximately 20 miles east of Hanoi that was used for terrain masking and navigation within Route Package Six Alpha

Pipper a 2-mil diameter dot in the center of the optical sight reticle (gunsight)

P_k probability of kill

Plane of motion the arcing flight path that is perpendicular to the attitude of the target's wings

Pod slang for the electronic jamming device that was used in attempts to foil threat SAMs; the F-4 carried the ALQ-119 jamming pod

Pull lead maneuvering the nose of the aircraft ahead of that of the target before beginning to fire

Punch out to eject from the aircraft

Quarter-roll and zoom a high-G maneuver designed to maintain nose/tail separation which involves a simultaneous 90-degree turn away from the targets flight path accompanied by a sharp pull up (usually into the vertical)

Recce reconnaissance

Red Crown the voice call sign for the radar-equipped USS Long Beach stationed in the northern part of the Gulf of Tonkin

Red extension the refueling boom is painted in multiple colors to show extent of extension; the inter and outer limits are painted red

Red X a symbol used in the aircraft's maintenance log that indicates a condition that is unsafe for flight

RHAW refers to the Radar Homing And Warning equipment installed in the F-4 and other fighters

Re-cage refers to the manual erection of a gyroscopic artificial horizon instrument (attitude indicator) to the straight-and-level reference point

Reverse thrust occurs when the angle of attack of the propellers are rotated to produce thrust directed ahead of the aircraft...in the case of the C-130A, this is equivalent to 60% of the normal thrust achieved at full takeoff power

Ripple to fire successive missile in rapid order

Rolling-in an inverted diving maneuver used to begin an attack on a target below

Rolling Thunder nickname for JCS-directed USAF air strikes against targets in North Vietnam between 1965 and 1968

Route Pack 6 short for Route Package Six or Route Package VI

RTB return to base

Sabre official name for the North American F-86

SAFE Selected Area For Evasion

SAM Surface to Air Missile

SAR Search and Rescue

SCCA Sports Car Club of America

Scramble the term applied to the launch of air defense alert aircraft for an intercept mission

Scattered deck refers to a cloud layers covering less than 50% of the sky

Set the hook a high-G turn that creates a turn radius which cannot be matched by a pursuing aircraft or missile

SMSgt abbreviation for a USAF Senior Master Sergeant

Snap shot a high-angle gun shot (or deflection shot) taken when a tracking solution is not possible and flight path overshoot is imminent

Spad nickname for the prop-driven A-1 Douglas Skyraiders that escorted the Jolly Green on SAR missions

Sparrow the name for an AIM-7 missile

Split the plane maneuvering outside of the supporting wingman's or element's geometric plane of motion

Split-S an aerobatics maneuver that entails a half-loop from an inverted start

Squawk emergency to cause your IFF to transmit a distress signal that is monitored by all control agencies

SSgt abbreviation for a USAF Staff Sergeant

"Strafing him like a truck" slang referring to an easy gun attack against a helpless, stationary target

Stan/Eval shorthand for Standardization/Evaluation, a team comprised of highly qualified personnel that administer flight checks and examinations to individuals within fight crews

Stinger nickname for the AC-119 gunship

Sterno brand name for a canned heat petroleum jell used for cooking

Tallyho visually acquiring the target

TDY temporary duty (away from normal duty station)

The break the initial hard turn from to the downwind leg during a 360-degree overhead traffic pattern

The City on the River nickname for Hanoi

The Eight Hundred Pound Gorilla slang term for the integrated multi-aircraft strike packages that flew the Rolling Thunder and Linebacker campaigns

Thud slang for the F-105 Thunderchief

Thud Ridge nickname for mountain range that begins about 20 miles north-northwest of Hanoi and extends about 25 miles northwest...a well know land-mark used for navigation and terrain masking in Route Package VI-A

Topped off air refueling the aircraft's fuel tanks to full capacity

TFS tactical fighter squadron

Track to hold the aiming index (pipper) on the target while firing

Tree penetrator a heavy, metal, bullet shaped device with folding seats and straps suspended from a winched cable to lower the sling from a rescue helicopter through tree branches

Triple Immelmann the immelmann maneuver was invented by Max Immelmann during WW-I. It is performed by doing the first half of a loop with a roll to wings-level attitude at the top of the loop...a triple immelmann is three immel-mann maneuvers performed consecutively without pause

TSgt abbreviation for a USAF Technical Sergeant

Two-ring strobe refers to the length of the warning line that appears on a RHAW scope upon missile lock-on...the scope had 3 concentric rings; the longer the strobe, the stronger the signal

UHF ultra high frequency (radio signal)

Up-sun sun at your back in relationship to the target

Vector information on heading and distance to a destination or target

VNAF Vietnamese Air Force

VR visual reconnaissance

VR'ing performing visual reconnaissance

Vic formation a three ship formation that resembles an arrow head, with the leader at the tip and the wingmen spaced back on both sides

Visual eyeball contact with another aircraft

White Rocket nickname applied to the T-38 Talon because of its original white paint scheme

Willy nickname for Williams AFB, Arizona

Wind-milling airstart an airborne start of the engine during which the engine is spun up to starting RPM by the force of the ram air entering the engine's intake

Wx weather